T0178252

Lecture Notes in Computer Science 13146

Founding Editors

Gerhard Goos
Karlsruhe Institute of Technology, Karlsruhe, Germany
Juris Hartmanis
Cornell University, Ithaca, NY, USA

Editorial Board Members

Elisa Bertino
Purdue University, West Lafayette, IN, USA
Wen Gao
Peking University, Beijing, China
Bernhard Steffen
TU Dortmund University, Dortmund, Germany
Gerhard Woeginger
RWTH Aachen, Aachen, Germany
Moti Yung
Columbia University, New York, NY, USA

More information about this subseries at https://link.springer.com/bookseries/7410

Somanath Tripathy · Rudrapatna K. Shyamasundar ·
Rajiv Ranjan (Eds.)

Information Systems Security

17th International Conference, ICISS 2021
Patna, India, December 16–20, 2021
Proceedings

Editors
Somanath Tripathy (iD)
Indian Institute of Technology Patna
Patna, India

Rudrapatna K. Shyamasundar (iD)
Indian Institute of Technology Bombay
Mumbai, India

Rajiv Ranjan (iD)
Newcastle University
Newcastle upon Tyne, UK

ISSN 0302-9743   ISSN 1611-3349 (electronic)
Lecture Notes in Computer Science
ISBN 978-3-030-92570-3   ISBN 978-3-030-92571-0 (eBook)
https://doi.org/10.1007/978-3-030-92571-0

LNCS Sublibrary: SL4 – Security and Cryptology

© Springer Nature Switzerland AG 2021
This work is subject to copyright. All rights are reserved by the Publisher, whether the whole or part of the material is concerned, specifically the rights of translation, reprinting, reuse of illustrations, recitation, broadcasting, reproduction on microfilms or in any other physical way, and transmission or information storage and retrieval, electronic adaptation, computer software, or by similar or dissimilar methodology now known or hereafter developed.
The use of general descriptive names, registered names, trademarks, service marks, etc. in this publication does not imply, even in the absence of a specific statement, that such names are exempt from the relevant protective laws and regulations and therefore free for general use.
The publisher, the authors and the editors are safe to assume that the advice and information in this book are believed to be true and accurate at the date of publication. Neither the publisher nor the authors or the editors give a warranty, expressed or implied, with respect to the material contained herein or for any errors or omissions that may have been made. The publisher remains neutral with regard to jurisdictional claims in published maps and institutional affiliations.

This Springer imprint is published by the registered company Springer Nature Switzerland AG
The registered company address is: Gewerbestrasse 11, 6330 Cham, Switzerland

Preface

This book comprises the proceedings of the 17th International Conference on Information Systems Security (ICISS 2021), held at the Indian Institute of Technology (IIT) Patna from December 16 to 20, 2021, in a hybrid mode.

A total of 65 papers were submitted in response to the call for papers for this edition of ICISS. We received submissions from authors in several countries. All the submissions were subjected to a blind evaluation procedure by the Technical Program Committee, which was composed of 47 experts from academia and industry. Each paper was reviewed by at least three experts. The papers were evaluated and discussed online by members of the Technical Program Committee over a week. After careful consideration of the merits of the papers the conference accepted nine full papers, two short papers, and four work-in-progress papers. The net acceptance rate of the conference was approximately 22%. A wide range of topics in systems security and privacy are covered, both in theory and in practice, such as attack detection, malware identification, distributed system security, cryptology, and asset management through blockchains including applications of artificial intelligence and machine learning for security. In addition to the accepted papers, the conference program featured three keynote talks by three distinguished speakers working in the field of security. The keynote speakers, in alphabetical order by first name, were as follows:

- George Cybenko, Dorothy and Walter Gramm Professor of Engineering at Dartmouth College, USA.
- Milind Tambe, Gordon McKay Professor of Computer Science and Director of the Center for Research in Computation and Society (CRCS) at Harvard University, USA, and Director of AI for Social Good at Google Research India.
- Omer Rana, Professor of Performance Engineering at Cardiff University, UK.

Thanks to these experts who took their precious time to address the audience live during somewhat odd hours.

The success of ICISS 2021 would not have been possible without the contributions of the numerous volunteers who gave their time and energy to ensure the success of the conference and its associated events. We would like to express our gratitude to the Program Committee for their hard work and prompt submission of their evaluations of papers, and we thank the publicity chairs for attracting good submissions in this pandemic period. Our thanks go to the local organizing committee as well as the faculty, staff, and students at the Department of Computer Science and Engineering, Indian Institute of Technology Patna for all the efforts and support for the smooth running of the conference in the hybrid mode. Thanks also go to the Steering Committee for their invaluable support in these trying times of the COVID-19 pandemic. The Conference Management Toolkit from Microsoft was crucial in carrying out the arduous chores of examining submissions, reviewing papers, and alerting authors about the status of their papers. It is our pleasure to express our gratitude to Springer Nature for assisting us in disseminating the proceedings of the conference in the LNCS series as in the past. Special thanks go to Ronan Nugent and Anna Kramer for making the proceedings available online at the time of conference with very little leeway in terms of time.

Last but certainly not least, we would like to thank all the authors who submitted papers and the conference participants. We hope you find the proceedings of ICISS 2021 interesting, stimulating, and inspiring for future research.

December 2021   Somanath Tripathy
                                         Rudrapatna K. Shyamasundar
                                                    Rajiv Ranjan

Organization

General Chair

R. K. Shyamasundar   IIT Bombay, India

Technical Program Co-chairs

Rajiv Ranjan	Newcastle University, UK
Somanath Tripathy	IIT Patna, India

Publicity Chairs

Vishwas Patil	IIT Bombay, India
N. V. Narendra Kumar	IDRBT, India
Devki Nandan Jha	University of Oxford, UK

Local Organizing Committee

Jimson Mathew	IIT Patna, India
Preetam Kumar	IIT Patna, India
Samrat Mondal	IIT Patna, India
Mayank Agarwal	IIT Patna, India
Somanath Tripathy	IIT Patna, India

Steering Committee

Aditya Bagchi	ISI Kolkota, India
Venu Govindaraju	SUNY, USA
Sushil Jajodia	George Mason University, USA
Somesh Jha	University of Wisconsin, USA
Arun Kumar Majumdar	IIT Kharagpur, India
Chandan Mazumdar	Jadavpur University, India
Atul Prakash	University of Michigan, USA
D. Janakiram	IDRBT, India
Pierangela Samarati	University of Milan, Italy
R. K. Shyamasundar	IIT Bombay, India

Program Committee

Adwait Nadkarni	College of William and Mary, USA
Anirban Basu	Hitachi Ltd, Japan, and University of Sussex, UK
Anoop Singhal	NIST, USA

Atul Prakash	University of Michigan, USA
Bimal Roy	ISI Kolkata, India
Bodhisatw Mazumdar	IIT Indore, India
Bruhadeshwar Bezawada	IIT Jammu, India
Changyu Dong	Newcastle University, UK
Claudio Ardagna	University of Milan, Italy
Devki Nandan Jha	University of Oxford, UK
Donghoon Chang	IIIT Delhi, India
Eric Filiol	ENSIBS and CNAM, France
Haibing Lu	Santa Clara University, USA
Hayawardh Vijayakumar	Samsung Research, USA
Indrakshi Ray	Colorado State University, USA
Laszlo Szekeres	Google, USA
Lorenzo De Carli	Worcester Polytechnic Institute, USA
Luigi Logrippo	Université du Québec en Outaouais, Italy
Mahavir Prasad Jhanwar	Ashoka University, India
Mahesh Tripunitara	University of Waterloo, Canada
Manik Lal Das	DA-IICT, India
Mauro Conti	University of Padua, Italy
Michele Carminati	Polytechnic University of Milan, Italy
N. V. Narendra Kumar	IDRBT, India
Peng Liu	Pennsylvania State University, USA
Pierangela Samarati	University of Milan, Italy
Prem Prakash Jayaraman	Swinburne University of Technology, Australia
R. Sekar	Stony Brook University, USA
Rajat Subhra	IIT Kharagpur, India
Rajesh Pillai	DRDO, India
Ram Krishnan	University of Texas at San Antonio, USA
Rinku Dewri	University of Denver, USA
Sabrina De Capitani di Vimercati	University of Milan, Italy
Sanjay Rawat	Vrije University, The Netherlands
Saurabh Garg	University of Tasmania, Australia
Scott Stoller	Stony Brook University, USA
Silvio Ranise	Fondazione Bruno Kessler, Italy
Somitra Sanadhya	IIT Ropar, India
Stijn Volckaert	KU Leuven, Belgium
Souradyuti Paul	IIT Bhilai, India
Sourav Sengupta	NTU, Singapore
Subhamoy Maitra	ISI Kolkata, India
Sushil Jajodia	George Mason University, USA
Venkatakrishnan Venkat	University of Illinois at Chicago, USA
Vijay Atluri	Rutgers University, USA
Vinod Yegneswaran	SRI International, USA
Vishwas Patil	IIT Bombay, India

Abstract of Keynote Talks

Multiagent Reasoning for Social Impact: Results from Deployments for Public Health and Conservation

Milind Tambe

Gordon McKay Professor of Computer Science and Director of the Center for
Research in Computation and Society (CRCS), Harvard University, Director,
AI for Social Good at Google Research India

Abstract. With the maturing of AI and multiagent systems research, we have a
tremendous opportunity to direct these advances towards addressing complex
societal problems. I focus on the problems of public health and conservation, and
address one key cross-cutting challenge: how to effectively deploy our limited
intervention resources in these problem domains. I will present results from work
around the globe in using AI for public health, e.g., HIV prevention, Maternal
and Child care interventions, and COVID modeling, and AI for conservation,
e.g., wildlife conservation. Achieving social impact in these domains often
requires methodological advances. To that end, I will highlight key research
advances in multiagent reasoning and learning, in particular in, computational
game theory, restless bandits and influence maximization in social networks.In
pushing this research agenda, our ultimate goal is to facilitate local communities
and non-profits to directly benefit from advances in AI tools and techniques.

Data Privacy Re-visited During Covid19

Omer Rana

College Dean of International Professor of Performance Engineering,
Cardiff University, UK

Abstract. The COVID19 Pandemic has highlighted our dependence on online services (from government, e-commerce/retail, and entertainment), often hosted over external cloud computing infrastructure. The users of these services interact with a web interface rather than the larger distributed service provisioning chain that can involve an interlinked group of cloud providers. The data and identity of users are often provided to service provider who may share it (or have automatic sharing agreement) with backend services (such as advertising and analytics). We propose the development of compliance-aware cloud application engineering, which is able to improve transparency of personal data use – particularly with reference to the European GDPR regulation. Key compliance operations and the perceived implementation challenges for the realization of these operations in current cloud infrastructure are outlined. This talk will also explore how the convenience-vs-privacy challenges can be realised as users and service providers go on-line, and the economics behind delivering privacy services as part of cloud-based provision.

Modeling and Leveraging Attrition in Cyber Operations

George Cybenko and Roger Hallman

Thayer School of Engineering, Dartmouth College, Hanover NH 03755, USA
gvc@dartmouth.edu
roger.hallman@navy.mil

Abstract. Advanced adaptive cyber operations require some form of online learning in real time using feedback and reinforcement from ongoing interactions. It is well known that operating well in such an environment entails balancing exploitation of currently best-known strategies with exploration of actions that might improve performance. This is the case for example, when a variety of responses are possible to mitigate an ongoing attack. However, unlike offline simulations of reinforcement learning, online reinforcement learning can lead to attrition of assets when exploration results in bad actions. We will present modeling and analysis approaches for learning with attrition in such circumstances.

There is sustained interest in developing cyber and physical systems consisting of multiple coordinated components, each component being simple, inexpensive, and easy to replace. Consider for example the following kind of military vision:

"A military made up of small numbers of large, expensive, heavily manned, and hard- to-replace systems will not survive on future battlefields, where swarms of intelligent machines will deliver violence at a greater volume and higher velocity than ever before." ([Brose 2019])

Examples include cyber-bot networks, Internet of Things (IoT), swarms of unmanned autonomous vehicles (airborne, maritime and land based) as well as cloud computing infrastructures ([Campbell 2018], [Panfili et al. 2018], [Nguyen et al. 2017]). While many of the arguments for such systems are based on cost effectiveness and mission performance, we argue in this work that there are also compelling analytic arguments based on various advantages that machine learning, game theory and secure distributed computing offer for such systems. The goal is to explain those advantages in analytic terms.

The main question we address is "What provable, analytic advantages do swarm-type adaptive/learning systems have over monolithic systems?" Our particular interest is so-called Adaptive Cyber-Defense (ACD) in which cyber-defensive technologies adapt to changes in the attackers' techniques and/or behaviors, as well as to organic changes in the ambient operating environment ([Cybenko et al. 2014], [Jajodia et al. 2019], [Zhu et al. 2014]). Organic changes can be due to dynamic re-configurations of the information infrastructure, such as the addition or removal of compute nodes, sensors, applications and communications links.

The ACD's changes can be made by continuously monitoring the environment, learning its new characteristics, and implementing appropriate new control actions. The basis for making such adaptations in a stationary or slowly changing environment can be based on classical reinforcement learning and adaptive control ideas. However, if the operating environment changes because of adversary adaptations, existing mathematical and algorithmic principles for defensive adaptation do not directly apply with respect to convergence to optimal or near optimal solutions.

We study the problem of online learning using distributed Upper Confidence Bounds (UCB) algorithms [Auer 2002] in which cumulative regret (CR) is the performance criterion. CR is an appropriate performance metric because it captures the overall rate at which the systems' performance is improving, not just the asymptotic conditions under which optimality can be reached. The faster a system can approach some notion of optimality, the more it will outperform an adversary that is also changing but at a slower rate.

A key observation and technical contribution are the use of distributed systems to implement UCB-based learning. This entails the deliberate use of "suboptimal" actions to fully explore the values of the available actions. In other words, the system must sacrifice some of its capabilities to learn faster and perform better. However, because some agents within the distributed system are operating sub-optimally, they will be compromised and so some subset of information in the distributed learning system will lack integrity.

We have considered the problem of online learning, with cumulative regret minimization, for swarms of agents cooperating to achieve high assurance on missions' tasks. To achieve this, we have introduced the concept of "spatial" online learning by which action selection is guided by UCB-type criteria. Because we are dealing with multiple agents, multiple actions are possible by sampling the UCB modified Q-values. We have identified some regret minimizing challenges in so-called spatial learning and conjectured their solutions but without formal proof. Furthermore, we have performed principled simulations showing how learning and recovery rates can change the overall performance of a multiagent learning system.

Although we are keenly interested in convergence rates and algorithms for adversarial engagements in which all players are using online learning to improve play, the results here are solely for stationary environments in which adversaries do not adapt or learn during a single engagement. However, if we can adapt faster than our adversary, we can model them as short-term stationary which might be the best possible approach given no information about the adversary or their adaptation mechanisms.

We have identified some regret minimizing challenges in so-called spatial learning and conjectured their solutions but without formal proof. Furthermore, we have performed principled simulations showing how learning and recovery rates can change the overall performance of a multiagent learning system. While UCB-criteria have been used in offline parallel game play learning (Silver et al. [2016]) those uses are for parallel game playing, that is parallel independent engagement, not a single engagement in which adaptation/learning occurs as we have proposed here. A major opportunity for future work is cumulative regret minimizing, online reinforcement learning algorithms that make as few assumptions about the adversary's learning algorithms.

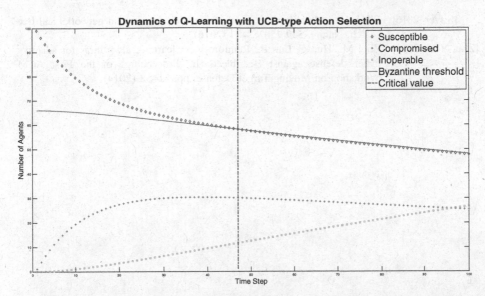

Fig. 1. This figure is typical of the kinds of simulation results from models of the tradeoffs between exploration and performance degradation due to attrition. Additional details and results can be found in [Cybenko 2021].

George Cybenko's research has been partially supported by ARO MURI Grant W911NF-13-1-042 and the US Air Force Research Laboratory. Roger A. Hallman is supported by the United States Department of Defense SMART Scholarship for Service Program funded by USD/R&E (The Under Secretary of Defense-Research and Engineering), National Defense Education Program (NDEP)/BA-1, Basic Research.

References

[Auer 2002] Auer, P.: Using confidence bounds for exploitation-exploration trade-offs. J. Mach. Learn. Res. **3**, 397–422 (2002)

[Brose2019] Brose, C.: The new revolution in military affairs: war's sci-fi future. Foreign Aff. **98**, 122 (2019)

[Campbell 2018] Campbell, A.M.: Enabling tactical autonomy for unmanned surface vehicles in defensive swarm engagements. PhD thesis, Massachusetts Institute of Technology (2018)

[Cybenko 2014] Cybenko, G., Jajodia, S., Wellman, M.P., Liu, P.: Adversarial and uncertain reasoning for adaptive cyber defense: building the scientific foundation. In: International Conference on Information Systems Security, pp. 1–8. Springer (2014)

[Cybenko 2021] George, C., Hallman, R.: Resilient distributed adaptive cyber-defense using blockchain. game theory and machine learning for cyber security, pp. 485–498 (2021)

[Silver 2016]   Silver, D.: Mastering the game of Go with deep neural networks and tree search. Nature, **529**(7587), 484 (2016)

[Zhu et al. 2014]   Zhu, M., Hu, Z., Liu, P.: Reinforcement learning algorithms for adaptive cyber defense against Heartbleed. In: Proceedings of the First ACM Workshop on Moving Target Defense, pp. 51–58 (2014)

Contents

Applied Cryptography

Attack Detection

Identifying Tactics of Advanced Persistent Threats with Limited Attack Traces

Khandakar Ashrafi Akbar[1]([✉]), Yigong Wang[1], Md Shihabul Islam[1], Anoop Singhal[2], Latifur Khan[1], and Bhavani Thuraisingham[1]

[1] The University of Texas at Dallas, 800 West Campbell Road, Richardson, TX 75080, USA
kxa190007@utdallas.edu
[2] National Institute of Standards and Technology, 100 Bureau Drive, Gaithersburg, MD 20899, USA

Abstract. The cyberworld being threatened by continuous imposters needs the development of intelligent methods for identifying threats while keeping in mind all the constraints that can be encountered. Advanced Persistent Threats (APT) have become an important national issue as they secretly steal information over a long period of time. Depending on the objective, adversaries use different tactics throughout the APT campaign to compromise the systems. Therefore, this kind of attack needs immediate attention as such attack tactics are hard to detect for being interleaved with benign activities. Moreover, existing solutions to detect APT attacks are computationally expensive, since keeping track of every system behavior is both costly and challenging. In addition, because of the data imbalance issue that appears due to few malicious events compared to the innumerable benign events in the system, the performance of the existing detection models is affected. In this work, we propose novel machine learning (ML) approaches to classify such attack tactics. More specifically, we convert APT traces into a graph, generate nodes, and eventually graph embeddings, and classify using ML. For ML, we use proposed advanced approaches to address class imbalance issues and compare our approaches with other baseline models and show the effectiveness of our approaches.

Keywords: Advanced persistent threat · Online metric learning · Data imbalance

1 Introduction

Advanced Persistent Threats (APT) are specifically well-known for their masquerading characteristics and damaging power. In the recent era of cyber warfare, it has become a powerful process to systematically damage or conduct espionage against competitors. Without proper knowledge of what is going on behind the scenes, e.g. in system-level interactions and operations, these threats can be disguised for a long time and can remain undetected even after they have completed

© Springer Nature Switzerland AG 2021
S. Tripathy et al. (Eds.): ICISS 2021, LNCS 13146, pp. 3–25, 2021.
https://doi.org/10.1007/978-3-030-92571-0_1

their target tasks. Due to the heavy use of computational systems, it is challenging to keep track of each and every system behavior. Moreover, identifying these types of threatening phenomena is also computationally expensive. Different stages of APTs have been defined [23] over the span of research in recent times. Different attack vectors are used at the beginning of the penetration of the system by the adversarial entities. These different stages can be achieved by using different tactics. Such tactics have corresponding techniques which execute the final task for the completion of the goals. For instance, writing malicious commands to the *bash_profile* and *.bashrc* system files is a technique that falls under the 'Persistence' tactic from the MITRE [1] framework. Figure 1a illustrates the overall system entity interaction for this technique that shows any process can use system calls 'read' and 'write' to access *bash_profile* and *.bashrc* system files and eventually write malicious commands to them.

With time, adversarial behavior evolves and so are their ways of compromising systems. Newly adopted tactics and techniques are continuously chased by security professionals to make intrusion detection frameworks and other security ensuring platforms more robust. Nevertheless, APTs are stealthy in nature and can easily avoid detection [23]. To detect such types of attacks, it is imperative to obtain low-level system traces to identify suspicious activities in a system. Take for example the Sykipot attack, in which the attackers targeted U.S. and U.K. organizations [34]. The attackers used the spear-phishing technique to send emails that contained malicious contents within. If such malicious content is clicked, a system can be harmed in ways that the malicious content establishes a foothold in the system which needs to be immediately tracked down after such email content has been received or executed. Therefore, these attack events based on different techniques, such as writing malicious commands in bash_profile or bashrc (system configuration files in Ubuntu), need to be inspected to classify or identify such phenomena as an attack tactic.

Adversaries use both benign and malicious tools to complete their target tasks. In both of these use cases, it is important to capture the system behavior or interaction information in order to detect such event. Collecting logs is a well-adopted and old technique for ensuring system performance. Nowadays, it is popular to keep track of system events which are also useful for security purposes [27]. That is why in recent times, data provenance based detection of attack campaigns have become very popular [13,17,20,22,29]. Using system level raw data which are collected during system operation or interaction with the system, a meaningful depiction of the whole scenario is represented through a graph, which is known as a provenance graph [13]. But due to the fact that the bulk of provenance data is heavy to handle, it is necessary to process the data in a meaningful and efficient way. Moreover, attacks semantics are not platform invariant, thus significant domain knowledge is necessary to detect attacks on a specific platform (e.g. Linux, Windows, macOS). In our approach, we leverage domain-specific attack knowledge to simultaneously reduce noise from logs and create multiple versions of the same attack instance trace to incorporate limited attack traces in the learning process.

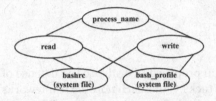

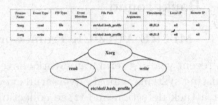

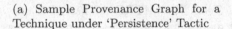

(a) Sample Provenance Graph for a Technique under 'Persistence' Tactic

(b) Sample Log and Generated Provenance Graph

Fig. 1. Provenance graphs

In this paper, we propose machine learning-based approaches to classify adversary tactics from provenance graphs. Generally, few tactics do not possess enough representative techniques which only yield a minority number of provenance graphs for those tactics. As a result, a class imbalance issue may emerge which weakens the performance of the learning model. We propose novel machine learning algorithms to efficaciously alleviate the class imbalance problem. To classify tactic, we first convert APT traces into a graph, and then using GraphSAGE [12], we generate node and eventually graph embeddings which will be treated as instances to train the machine learning models. Finally, we perform the prediction using advanced approaches to address the class imbalance issue. We compare our approaches with other baseline models and show the effectiveness of our approach. To the best of our knowledge, this is the first known approach to address class imbalance issue in identifying tactics of APT and to limit the attack traces for computational ease well before a provenance graph is generated.

To summarize, in this paper, we propose the following contributions.

- We identify different tactics using advanced machine learning models, e.g. SetConv [10] which is defined in Sect. 4.2 and OAML [9] which is defined in Sect. 4.1, to address class imbalance issue, and show the superiority of these models over the baseline models.
- We address the problem of overlapping common noisy system interaction behavior in different attack traces and process those traces to build a robust model.
- We propose to incorporate domain knowledge in attack trace processing which eventually produces different versions of attack traces.

The paper is organized as follows. Section 2 presents some background on MITRE framework and GraphSAGE. Section 3 talks about the data collection in details, and how the collected data is converted to graph. Section 4 provides the details of our machine learning models. Section 5 explains the experimental setup in detail and discusses the results. Finally, Sect. 6 presents related work and concludes our work.

2   Background

2.1   MITRE ATT&CK Framework

In recent years, several frameworks have been proposed to evaluate the defense of existing systems against adversarial cyberattacks. Some such notable frameworks for attack detection and trace collection are Red Team Automation (RTA) [8], Metta, CALDERA [4], and Atomic Red Team [2]. MITRE ATT&CK framework provides a knowledge base of threat models and practices by investigating real-world scenarios of different adversarial behavior. It provides an adversary tactic and technique taxonomy that could be utilized to assess a system's threat detection, response mechanism, and risk calculation and hence improve the effectiveness of cybersecurity solutions.

The framework contains a comprehensive matrix of tactics and techniques for multiple platforms. Some of the tactics are Defense Evasion, Discovery, Persistence, Privilege Escalation, Reconnaissance, and so on. Each of the tactics contains a list of techniques that refer to the method or type of attack. For instance, the Privilege Escalation tactic includes techniques such as Access Token Manipulation, Hijack Execution Flow, Process Injection, and the like. Each technique contains information on how to deploy the attack such as required platforms, required permissions, defenses bypassed, etc., and how to detect attacks from processes and mitigate the attacks with different strategies. The attack payloads are defined as TTP (Techniques, Tactics, & Procedures) and are numerically followed by mostly four digits to point to a specific type of technique. For example, T1046 refers to the attack or vulnerability technique named Network Service Scanning from the Discovery tactic class.

Moreover, each technique includes sub-techniques that explain different methods to implement that particular technique. For example, T1136 (i.e., Create Account) technique falls under the tactic class 'Persistence'. To maintain access to the victim system, adversaries may create accounts in the local system, within a domain, or in the cloud. Therefore, the technique T1136 contains sub-techniques Local Account, Domain Account, and Cloud Account. Thus all the sub-techniques under this TTP generate instances for the tactic 'Persistence' since they correspond to the same tactic class that the technique belongs to.

The Atomic Red Team framework supplies a collection of scripts for detection tests of certain attack techniques mapped to the MITRE ATT&CK Framework. It consists of the techniques and sub-techniques for the TTPs to be executed in Linux, Windows, or the macOS platform. In this paper, we incorporate the definition of the TTPs from the MITRE ATT&CK framework and emulate the attacks using Atomic Red Team's framework.

2.2   Graph Embedding and GraphSAGE

Graph embedding has become a well-known approach as graphs are adopted as a very popular data structure in different types of problem domains, such

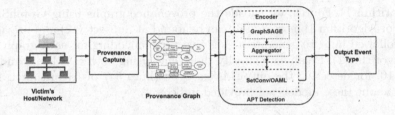

Fig. 2. System architecture

as protein-protein interaction systems, supply chains, knowledge graphs, social-network, and so on. A graph is a pair G = (V, E) where V is a set whose elements are called vertices, and E is a set of paired vertices, whose elements are called edges. A neural network architecture that operates on graph structures is known as the Graph Neural Network (GNN). Generally, GNNs are used for node classification purposes; that is, every node of the graph is assigned some features and a label and the GNN predicts the labels of the unseen nodes by leveraging the seen node information within a neighborhood. GNNs propose to address the challenging forecasting problem including both spatial and temporal dependencies and its recent advances greatly boost the ability of modeling data from the non-Euclidean space such as the graph structures [19]. Inspired by the mechanism of message passing in a graph, a variant of GNN known as Graph Convolutional Networks (GCN) is proposed that aggregates up to the n-hop spatial neighborhood to each location in the data.

In recent years, many algorithms for learning node representations of graphs have been proposed such as DeepWalk [30] and GraphSAGE [12]. GraphSAGE leverages graph structure to produce node embeddings in an inductive way. That is, GraphSAGE trains aggregator functions that aggregate a node's neighborhood rather than directly embedding vectors of nodes individually. This strategy makes it easy to generalize to unseen nodes given their features and neighborhood and avoids re-training the model for new nodes. The n-hop is used for controlling the coverage range of aggregation functions from selected neighbors. GraphSAGE is most appropriate for dynamic graphs, where the structure of the graph is always growing or changing. In this paper, we leverage GraphSAGE to generate node embeddings of the provenance graphs, which is then used with a global aggregator (which is usually permutation and order invariant) to generate a single graph embedding for the overall graph.

3   Architecture and Approach

The overall architecture of our system is illustrated in Fig. 2 and the approach can be summarized as given in the Algorithm 1. First, we execute the attack pay-loads in the victim's host network (more details can be found at Subsect. 3.1). Second, we capture the provenance information (i.e., logs) against the deployed attacks. Third, we generate provenance graphs from the captured logs (lines 1–2 of Algorithm 1). Fourth, we encode the provenance graphs using GraphSAGE (line 3 of Algorithm 1; more details can be found at Subsect. 3.2) and use aggregator followed by it to generate a single vector embedding for each graph (line 4 of Algorithm 1). Finally, we classify the events using both OAML [9] and SetConv [10] for detecting the output event type (lines 5–7 of Algorithm 1; more details about these models are provided in Sect. 4).

Algorithm 1: Steps of our Overall Approach

Input: Graph
Output: Label for the Graph as *'Benign'* or of any of the *Tactics*
1 Take raw log as input
2 Generate provenance graph from the log
3 Using GraphSAGE, generate the embedding for the overall graph
4 Using Aggregator, generate a single vector space embedding for each graph
5 Split the graphs into *train* and *test* set
6 Train the Machine Learning algorithms (Baseline Models including 'SetConv' and 'OAML') using the *training* set and test the models on the *test* set
7 Analyze the performance of the models

3.1 Data Collection

3.1.1 Attack Generation

As discussed in Sect. 2.1, MITRE ATT&CK framework provides a knowledge base of tactics and techniques generated from actual observations of adversarial behavior. Moreover, the Atomic Red Team provides a library that can be leveraged to execute disparate adversarial attacks that follow the tactic/technique taxonomy of MITRE ATT&CK framework to test system robustness against cyberattacks. Therefore, to emulate attacks in the victim's host network in our work, we exploit the attacks defined in the MITRE ATT&CK framework and execute them with the help of the Atomic Red Team framework.

3.1.2 Provenance Graph Generation

After the execution of attack payloads, we collect the log data of the attack traces that resembles the data provenance of the machine activities. To collect the log data, we use *Sysdig*, which is a system monitoring service. An example of the captured log data is represented in Fig. 1b. Next, we generate the provenance graphs from these captured logs by using *Apache TinkerPop* [35]. In the graph generation procedure, we follow a set of rules to achieve limited attack traces as well as ensure removal of noise from the logs (more details in Sect. 5.1.2). We write the rules with *Groovy* and execute these Groovy scripts using the *Gremlin Console*, which is a terminal that allows users to create and traverse graphs with the Apache TinkerPop. Later, the generated graphs are streamed to the graph visualization tool *Gephi* [11], which allows us to import a graph's nodes and edges as separate CSV files. These CSVs are then used to create our final provenance graphs. .

We first convert the different versions of the logs to provenance graphs. A very generic definition of such provenance graphs would be to include only the processes, files, and sockets as nodes of the graph. But we also incorporate the different system calls and how different processes make use of those different system calls into the graph. For file-level nodes, *read* and *write* type system calls are emphasized, whereas for network-level nodes special types of network-level system calls are handled such as *socket*, *connect*, and *bind*.

To generate the edges in the graph, we connect the nodes in the following ways: a process node responsible for a system call is connected by an edge with the system call node; a process node is connected by an edge with a filepath node if that process accesses that filepath; a filepath node is connected by an edge with a system call node if that system call node is either *read* or *write* type and thus is used for accessing that filepath by the process. A glimpse of the generated provenance graph is shown in Fig. 1b.

It is crucial to incorporate the edge weights in the graph as well. For this purpose, we identify attack trace windows using the start and end of events (using > and < symbols) from the field *Event Direction* of the log data. Then, we extract how many bytes are read or written for corresponding *read* and *write* system calls from the *Event Arguments* field of the log data for that trace window. The calculated byte amounts are then used as edge weights in the provenance graphs.

3.2   Graph Embedding Using GraphSAGE

From the provenance graphs, we need to create suitable representations that we can feed into the machine learning models for classification. As discussed in Sect. 2.2, we can utilize *GraphSAGE* to generate node embeddings of graphs. Although, in our work, we need graph embeddings rather than node embeddings. Therefore, we implement a global aggregator following the original GraphSAGE to create graph embeddings. That is, after the GraphSAGE creates node embeddings of a graph, these node embeddings are feed into the global aggregator that generates a single graph vector embedding for the whole graph. This aggregator could be permutation and order invariant.

Because of the supervised learning setting, we also need the embedding encoder to be trainable using labels. Therefore, we use a very simple neural network following the graph encoder. After the encoder training phase, we discard the simple neural network and keep the encoder only for following training phases and testing. Therefore, we can produce valuable embeddings from the generated provenance graphs for the given classification task.

4   Models

Supervised learning is utilized to incrementally learn from the data. For supervised learning, we learn accurate models by leveraging attack and benign data, which are initially gleaned from benign data, synthetic attacks and existing APT attack traces, and later from live attack detection for detecting the novel type of APT attack. We adopt two models from our previous works to be the classifiers, which are OAML [9] and SetConv [10]. The details of these two algorithms are in the Sect. 4.1 and Sect. 4.2.

4.1 Online Metric Learning

Online Metric Learning (OML) or otherwise said, Online Adaptive Metric Learning (OAML) [9] is based on a deep learning architecture that transforms an instance feature from an original feature space to a latent feature space. By transforming to a latent feature space, the metric distance between dissimilar instances is increased and distance between similar classes is reduced. The work leverages methods which use *pairwise* and *triplet* constraints. Our OAML method learns a non-linear similarity metric unlike others which use a preselected linear metric (e.g., Mahalanobis distance [36]). Our OAML method overcomes bias to a specific dataset by using an adaptive learning method. Our OAML leverages neural networks where the hidden layer output is passed to an independent metric-embedding layer (MEL). The MELs then generates an n-dimensional embedding vector as output in different latent space.

Problem Setting Let $S = \{(\boldsymbol{x}_t, \boldsymbol{x}_t^+, \boldsymbol{x}_t^-)\}_{t=1}^T$ be a sequence of triplet constraints sampled from the data, where $\{\boldsymbol{x}_t, \boldsymbol{x}_t^+, \boldsymbol{x}_t^-\} \in \mathcal{R}^d$, and $\boldsymbol{x}_t$ (anchor) are similar to $\boldsymbol{x}_t^+$ (positive) but dissimilar to $\boldsymbol{x}_t^-$ (negative) (see Fig. 3). The goal of online adaptive metric learning is to learn a model $\boldsymbol{F} : \mathcal{R}^d \mapsto \mathcal{R}^{d'}$ such that $||\boldsymbol{F}(\boldsymbol{x}_t) - \boldsymbol{F}(\boldsymbol{x}_t^+)||_2 \ll ||\boldsymbol{F}(\boldsymbol{x}_t) - \boldsymbol{F}(\boldsymbol{x}_t^-)||_2$. Given these parameters, the objective is to learn a metric model with adaptive complexity while satisfying the constraints. The complexity of $\boldsymbol{F}$ must be adaptive so that its hypothesis space is automatically modified.

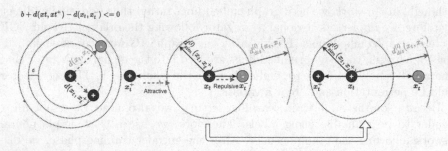

Fig. 3. Data instance before applying OML (left) and data instance after projection using OML (right).

Overview Consider a neural network with L hidden layers, where the input layer and the hidden layer are connected to an independent MEL. Each embedding layer learns a latent space where similar instances are clustered and dissimilar instances are separated.

Figure 4 illustrates our Artificial Neural Network (ANN). $E_\ell \in \{E_0, \ldots, E_L\}$ denote the ℓth metric model in OAML (i.e., the network branch from the input layer to the ℓth MEL). The simplest OAML model E_0 represents a linear transformation from the input feature space to the metric embedding space. A weight $\alpha^{(\ell)} \in [0, 1]$ is assigned to E_ℓ, measuring its importance in OAML.

At time t, the metric embedding $f^{(\ell)}(x_t^*)$ of an arrived triplet constraint (x_t, x_t^+, x_t^-) generated by E_ℓ is

$$f^{(\ell)}(x_t^*) = h^{(\ell)}\Theta^{(\ell)} \tag{1}$$

where $h^{(\ell)} = \sigma(W^{(\ell)}h^{(\ell-1)})$, with $\ell \geq 1$, $\ell \in \mathbb{N}$, and $h^{(0)} = x_t^*$. We use x_t^* to denote a anchor (x_t). It might be positive (x_t^+), or negative (x_t^-) instance. For the activation of the ℓth hidden layer, we use $h^{(\ell)}$ to denote. To reduce the search space and accelerate training, we limit theLearned metric embedding $f^{(\ell)}(x_t^*)$ to a unit sphere (i.e., $||f^{(\ell)}(x_t^*)||_2 = 1$)

In the training step, for every arriving triplet (x_t, x_t^+, x_t^-), we first retrieve the metric embedding $f^{(\ell)}(x_t^*)$ from the ℓth metric model using Eq. 1. A local loss $\mathcal{L}^{(\ell)}$ for E_ℓ is evaluated by calculating the similarity and dissimilarity errors based on $f^{(\ell)}(x_t^*)$. Thus, the overall loss is defined by following:

$$\mathcal{L}_{overall}(x_t, x_t^+, x_t^-) = \sum_{\ell=0}^{L} \alpha^{(\ell)} \cdot \mathcal{L}^{(\ell)}(x_t, x_t^+, x_t^-) \tag{2}$$

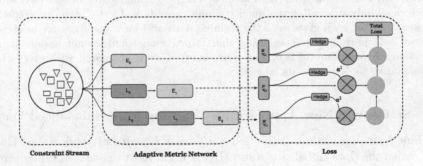

Fig. 4. OAML network structure consists of L_i linear layer and Embedding layers E_i layer.

Parameters $\Theta^{(\ell)}$, $\alpha^{(\ell)}$, and $W^{(\ell)}$ are learned during the online learning phase. The final optimization problem to solve in OAML at time t is therefore:

$$\underset{\Theta^{(\ell)}, W^{(\ell)}, \alpha^{(\ell)}}{\text{minimize}} \quad \mathcal{L}_{overall}$$
$$\text{subject to} \quad ||f^{(\ell)}(x_t^*)||_2 = 1, \forall \ell = 0, \ldots, L. \tag{3}$$

We evaluate the similarity and dissimilarity errors using an *adaptive-bound triplet loss* (ABTL) constraint [9] to estimate $\mathcal{L}^{(\ell)}$ and update parameters $\Theta^{(\ell)}$, $W^{(\ell)}$ and $\alpha^{(\ell)}$.

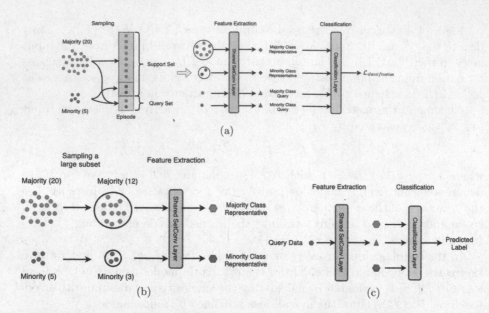

Fig. 5. Overview of the proposed approach. (a) The training procedure of SetConv. At each iteration, SetConv is fed with an episode to evaluate the classification loss for model update. Each episode consists of a support set and a query set. The support set is formed by a group of samples where the imbalance ratio is preserved. The query set contains only one sample from each class. (b) The post training step of SetConv, which is performed only once after the main training procedure. In this step, we extract a representative for each class from the training data and later use them for inference. Here we only perform inference using the trained model and do not update it. (c) The inference procedure of SetConv. Each query data is compared with every class representative to determine its label.

4.2   SetConv: a New Approach for Learning from Imbalanced Data

Machine Learning method finds its use in broad domains of applications. However, when the data Imbalance Ratio (IR) is high, most existing machine learning methods are biased towards the majority class and their performance deteriorates seriously. We use the set convolution (SetConv) [10] operation and a new training strategy named as episodic training to assist learning from imbalanced class distributions. SetConv is designed to alleviate the class imbalance by explicitly learning the weights of convolution kernels based on the intra-class and inter-class correlations, and uses the learned kernels to extract a single representative for each class. Thus, the subsequent classifier, which takes these class representatives as input, always perceives a balanced class distribution. As a naturally permutation-invariant operation, SetConv guarantees the uniqueness of the learned class representatives despite the order of input samples.

As shown in Fig. 5a, our model is composed of a SetConv layer and a classification layer. For simplicity, we first consider a binary classification problem and later extend it to the multi-class scenario. At each iteration during training, the model is fed with an *episode* sampled from the training data, which is composed of a support set and a query set. The support set preserves the imbalance ratio of training data, and the query set contains only one sample from each class. Once the SetConv layer receives an episode, it extracts features for every sample in the episode and produces a representative for each class in the support set. Then, each sample in the query set is compared with these class representatives in classification layer to determine its label and evaluate the classification loss for model update. We refer this training procedure as *episodic training*.

After training, a post training step is performed only once to extract a representative for each class from the training data, which later be used for inference (Fig. 5b). It is conducted by randomly sampling a large subset of training data (referred as S_{post}) and feeding them to the SetConv layer. *Note that we only perform inference using the trained model and do not update it in this step.* We can conduct this operation because the SetConv layer has learned to capture the class concepts, which are insensitive to the episode configuration during training.

The inference procedure of the proposed approach is straightforward (Fig. 5c). For each query sample, we extract its feature via the SetConv layer and then compare it with those class representatives obtained in post training step. The class that is most similar to the query is assigned as the predicted label.

4.2.1 SetConv Layer

In many real-world applications, the minority class instances often carry important and useful knowledge that need intensive attention by the machine learning models [6,16,33]. Based on this prior knowledge, we choose to design the SetConv layer in a way such that the *feature extraction process focuses on the minority class*. We achieve it by estimating the weights of the SetConv layer based on the relation between the input samples and a pre-selected minority class anchor. This anchor can be freely determined by the user. We adopt a simple option, i.e., *average-pooling* of the minority class samples. As shown in Fig. 6, this weight estimation method assists the SetConv layer in capturing not only the intra-class correlation of the minority class, but also the inter-class correlation between the majority and minority classes.

Suppose $\mathcal{E}_t = \{S_t, Q_t\}$ is the episode sent to the SetConv layer at iteration t, where $S_t = \left(X_{maj} \in \mathcal{R}^{N_1 \times d}, X_{min} \in \mathcal{R}^{N_2 \times d}\right)$ is the support set and $Q_t = \left(q_{maj} \in \mathcal{R}^{1 \times d}, q_{min} \in \mathcal{R}^{1 \times d}\right)$ is the query set. In general, $X_{maj}, X_{min}, q_{maj}$ and q_{min} can be considered as a sample set of size $N_1, N_2, 1$ and 1 respectively. For simplicity, we abstract this sample set into $X \in \mathcal{R}^{N \times d}, N \in \{N_1, N_2, 1\}$. We define the set convolution (SetConv) operation as:

$$
\begin{aligned}
h[Y] &= \frac{1}{N} \sum_{i=1}^{N} X_i \cdot g(Y - X_i) \\
&= \frac{1}{N}\left(X \circ g(Y - X)\right)
\end{aligned}
\tag{4}
$$

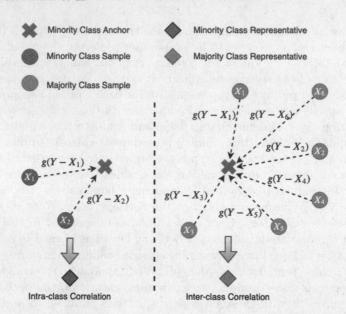

Fig. 6. Relations between the input samples and a pre-selected minority class anchor are used by SetConv to estimate both intra-class correlations and inter-class correlations.

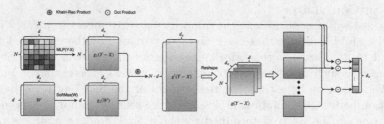

Fig. 7. The computation graph of the SetConv layer. Here Y is a minority class anchor. $W \in \mathcal{R}^{d \times d_o}$ is a weight matrix to learn that records the correlation between the input and output variables. Specifically, the i_{th} column of $g_2(W)$ gives the weight distribution over input features for the i_{th} output feature. It is indeed a feature-level attention matrix. In addition, we estimate another data-sensitive weight matrix $g_1(Y - X)$ from the input data. The final convolution weight tensor is simply the Khatri-Rao product of $g_1(Y - X)$ and $g_2(W)$.

where $Y \in \mathcal{R}^{1 \times d}$, $g(Y - X) \in \mathcal{R}^{N \times d \times d_o}$ and $h[Y] \in \mathcal{R}^{1 \times d_o}$ denote the minority class anchor, kernel weights and the output embedding respectively. Here, $\circ$ is the tensor dot product operator, i.e., for every $i \in \{1, 2, \ldots, d_o\}$, we compute the dot product of X and $g(Y - X)[:, :, i]$.

Unfortunately, directly learning $g(Y - X)$ is memory intensive and computationally expensive, especially for large-scale high-dimensional data. To overcome this issue, we introduce an efficient method to approximate these kernel weights.

Instead of taking X as a set of d-dimensional samples, we stack these samples and consider it as a giant dummy sample $X' = Concat(X) \in \mathcal{R}^{1 \times Nd}$. Then, Eq. 4 is rewritten as

$$h[Y] = \frac{1}{N}\left(X' \cdot g'(Y - X)\right) \tag{5}$$

where $g'(Y - X) \in \mathcal{R}^{Nd \times d_o}$ is the transformed kernel weights. To efficiently compute $g'(Y-X)$, we propose to approximate it as the *Khatri-Rao* product[1] [31] of two individual components, i.e.,

$$
\begin{aligned}
g'(Y - X) &= g_1(Y - X) \circledast g_2(W) \\
&= \mathrm{MLP}(Y - X; \theta) \circledast \mathrm{SoftMax}(W, 0)
\end{aligned} \tag{6}
$$

where $W \in \mathcal{R}^{d \times d_o}$ is a weight matrix that represents the correlation between input and output variables. $g_2(W)$ takes softmax over the first dimension of W, and is indeed a *feature-level attention* matrix. The i_{th} column of $g_2(W)$ provides the weight distribution over input features for the i_{th} output feature. On the other hand, $g_1(Y - X)$ is a *data-sensitive* weight matrix estimated from input data via a Multilayer Perceptron (MLP) by considering their relation to the minority class anchor. Similar to data-level attention, $g_1(Y-X)$ helps the model customize the feature extraction process for input samples, which potentially improves the model performance. Figure 7 shows the detailed computation graph of the SetConv layer.

4.2.2 Classification

Suppose the feature representation obtained from the layer for $X_{maj}, X_{min}, q_{maj}$ and q_{min} in the episode are denoted by $v^s_{maj}, v^s_{min}, v^q_{maj}$ and v^q_{min} respectively. The probability of predicting v^q_{maj} or v^q_{min} as the majority class is given by

$$P(c = 0|x) = \frac{\exp(x \odot v^s_{maj})}{\exp(x \odot v^s_{maj}) + \exp(x \odot v^s_{min})} \tag{7}$$

where $\odot$ represents the dot product operation and $x \in \{v^q_{maj}, v^q_{min}\}$.

Similarly, the probability of predicting v^q_{maj} or v^q_{min} as the minority class is

$$P(c = 1|x) = \frac{\exp(x \odot v^s_{min})}{\exp(x \odot v^s_{maj}) + \exp(x \odot v^s_{min})} \tag{8}$$

where $x \in \{v^q_{maj}, v^q_{min}\}$.

We adopt the well-known cross-entropy loss for error estimation and use the Adam optimizer to update model.

4.2.3 Extension to Multi-class Scenario

Extending SetConv for multi-class imbalance learning is straightforward. We translate the multi-class classification problem into multiple binary classification

---

[1] https://en.wikipedia.org/wiki/Kronecker_product.

problems, i.e., we create a one-vs-all classifier for each of the N classes. Specifically, for a class c, we treat those instances with label $y = c$ as positive and those with $y \neq c$ as negative. The anchor is hence computed based on the smaller one of the positive and negative classes. The prediction probability $P(y = c|x)$ for a given instance x is computed in a similar way as Eq. 7,

$$P(y = c|x) = \frac{\exp(x \odot v_{y=c}^s)}{\exp(x \odot v_{y \neq c}^s) + \exp(x \odot v_{y=c}^s)} \tag{9}$$

Therefore, the predicted label of the instance x is $\mathrm{argmax}_c P(y = c|x)$.

5   Experiments

5.1   Experiment Setting

5.1.1   Dataset

In our experiments, we use two datasets to evaluate our approach in the paper: DAPT 2020 [24] and the Graph dataset that we collect following the procedure described in Sect. 3.

DAPT 2020 is an APT dataset, which covers all attack stages of different aspects of the real-world APT. In this dataset, a total of 4 different APT phases are involved. Hence, it contains 5 different classes including the benign class. Although, two APT phases, which are the lateral movement and data exfiltration, only contain 6 and 4 malicious instances, respectively. Therefore, we discard these two classes, since their malicious instances only constitute 0.1% and 0.23% of the total instances, respectively. We run our experiments on the rest of the data with the other 3 classes. Table 1 shows the statistic information of the DAPT 2020 dataset, including the number of instances in each file and the percentages of malicious instances.

Graph Dataset includes different variations. It contains the graph embeddings generated from the collected original unmodified logs. Based on the original log file, three variations are constructed after filtering each log file leveraging the domain knowledge (filtering procedure is described in Sect. 5.1.2). This procedure extracts 1) one-third, 2) half and 3) two-third of the whole log file. The graph embeddings of these log variations are then generated and included with the graph embeddings of the original log files to make the entire graph dataset. This is how we achieve limited attack traces for each log executed against the techniques.

Table 2 provides the Graph dataset statistics. We have one benign tactic and the other nine being malicious tactics totaling ten classes. It is evident from the number of instances for each class that this dataset is imbalanced.

5.1.2   Filtration of Logs

For the filtering of logs, first, we generate *keywords* for each of the TTP that specify the TTP characteristics. For example, the attack payload T1546 accesses the *bash_profile* or *.bashrc* system files and eventually read or write them. Therefore, some keywords for T1546 would be bash_profile, bashrc, open, write, dup,

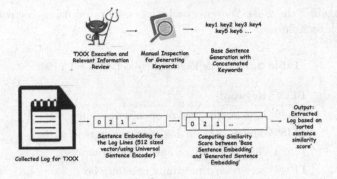

Fig. 8. Generating different version of logs

etc. Some sample *keywords* for some select TTPs are provided in Table 3. Thus leveraging domain knowledge, we generate a large number of keywords for each of the TTP which are considered constituents of a whole sentence. We define this sentence as the *Base Sentence* and use it to filter the logs. We consider each of the log lines as an individual sentence by taking three specific columns in the log file namely: *process name, filepath,* and *system call.* We generate sentence embeddings for every log line as well as the *Base Sentence* using the Universal Sentence Encoder [5]. Next, we calculate the sentence similarity score between each of the sentences generated from the log lines and the *Base Sentence.* We then sort the similarity scores and based on the sorted results, four different copies of each log file are generated. The schematic depiction of this whole process is provided in Fig. 8.

This filtration not only allows to generate graph instances with limited attack traces but also removes noise from the logs as we eliminate the part of logs that are less related to the particulars of some attack. The log lines which are not necessarily critical to some attack are discarded as the similarity scores are

Table 1. DAPT 2020 dataset statistics

File name	Total No.	Malicious No.	Benign No.	Malicious%	Benign%
custom_reconnaissance.csv	29254	4405	24849	15.06%	84.94%
custom_foothold.csv	17486	8632	8854	50.63%	49.37%
custom_lateralmovement.csv	4051	4	4047	0.1%	99.9%
custom_dataexf.csv	2617	6	2611	0.23%	99.77%
All Files	53408	13047	40361	24.43%	75.57%
First two files	46740	13037	33703	27.89%	72.11%

Table 2. Graph dataset statistics - Benign class is the 10th class

Class	0	1	2	3	4	5	6	7	8	9	10	Total
Number	32	16	84	44	476	16	16	32	112	124	408	1360
Percentage	2.35%	1.18%	6.18%	3.24%	35%	1.18%	1.18%	2.35%	8.24%	9.12%	30%	100%

calculated against the *Base Sentences* which is generated using *keywords* crucial to the attack techniques.

Table 3. Example keyword collection for TTPs

TTPs	Keywords
T1546	bash_profile bashrc open write dup
T1485	dd dev zero var log syslog open read write
T1529	shutdown reboot halt poweroff writev
T1049	access var run utmpx netstat who
T1148	HIST CONTROL echo export whoami

5.1.3   Baseline

We compare our algorithm with several traditional and state-of-the-art ML-based models for evaluation. For traditional ML-based methods, we utilize Decision Tree and Support Vector Machine. We briefly discuss the other utilized state-of-the-art models here.

EasyEnsemble [21] is an algorithm based on ensemble and under sampling. The random under sampling method is used to produce balanced bootstrap samples. Then, it utilizes AdaBoost learners to get a final ensemble model.

Multilayer Perceptron (MLP) [15] is a feedforward Artificial Neural Network (ANN). It comprises multiple layers, and each layer contains a number of perceptrons. Being a widely used model in the machine learning area, MLP shows competitive performance in many different practical applications.

KMeans-SMOTE [7] is a oversampling method to relieve the class imbalance problem. This method is based on kmeans clustering algorithm and SMOTE over sampling. The major advantage is generating effective instance avoided noise. We use a Support Vector Machine (SVM) to be a classifier after oversampling. We also use SVM itself to be a baseline. In both two settings, we use polynomial kernel in the SVM classifiers.

5.1.4   Evaluation Metric

There are many different metrics to evaluate classification problems like accuracy. For binary classification, precision, recall, and F1 score are very popular metrics to evaluate the performance of a model. However, they are not a credible metric for multi-class classification problems, although there exist variants of these metrics to deal with such problems. For a given class c, we have True Positive (TP), False Positive (FP), True Negative (TN), and False Negative (FN). The precision (P), recall (R), and F1 score (F1) are defined by following:

$$P = \frac{TP}{TP + FP} \tag{10}$$

$$R = \frac{TP}{TP + FN} \tag{11}$$

$$F1 = \frac{2 \times Precision \times Recall}{Precision + Recall} \tag{12}$$

Then, we choose the the Macro Averaging variants to evaluate multi-class classification problems.

$$P_{macro} = \frac{1}{m} \sum_{i=1}^{m} P_i \tag{13}$$

$$R_{macro} = \frac{1}{m} \sum_{i=1}^{m} R_i \tag{14}$$

$$F1_{Macro} = \frac{2 \times P_{macro} \times R_{macro}}{P_{macro} + R_{macro}} \tag{15}$$

where m is the number of classes. The macro averaging uses the same weight to every class even the instance numbers are imbalanced among different classes.

5.1.5 Experiment Setup

For DAPT 2020 and graph datasets, we design different setups to run the experiments due to different data structures. For DAPT 2020, we utilize the embedding method from the original paper [24]. Then, we normalize the feature vectors as the ranges of different features are very different. Because most of the algorithms are designed for taking feature vectors to be the inputs, graph data is hard to feed in these models directly. To solve this problem, we have two phases to train and predict data in graph format. The first phase is the embedding encoder. We utilize GraphSAGE [12] to convert the data from graphs to their feature embeddings. Second, we train a GraphSAGE model with GCN [19] to be the aggregator, and it produces node embeddings. The feature embedding of a given graph is the average value of its node embeddings. Third, we concatenate the GraphSAGE model with a simple MLP model to train with the training set. Finally, we discard the simple MLP part and use the intermediate output (graph embedding from GraphSAGE) to encode training and testing datasets for future works.

The imbalance of datasets is a general property in the cybersecurity scenario. Although some of the methods are designed to handle this problem, the embedding encoder still suffers from this problem because they are separate phases. Therefore, we design two different experiment setups. The first one keeps the same ratios among classes to train an encoder. Next, the dataset is balanced by re-sampling. An embedding encoder is trained based on the balanced dataset. Then, the training and testing datasets are encoded by the encoder, but it remains original inter-class instance ratios. In this way, the feature embeddings are more robust, and the evaluation focuses more on the following classifier rather than the encoder.

5.2 Result

In this subsection, we briefly discuss and compare the experimental results for both dataset.

5.2.1 Graph Dataset

The experiment results of the graph dataset are shown in Table 4 and Table 5. Table 4 shows the results when embedding encoder is trained without re-sampling and Table 5 shows the performances of models when embedding encoder is trained with re-sampling.

It is apparent from the Table 4 that *SetConv* achieves the best result compared to other methods in terms of the macro accuracy, precision, recall, and F1 score with 0.9228, 0.8022, 0.7163, and 0.7161 values, respectively. *KMeans-SMOTE* achieves an impressive accuracy of 0.9007, although it shows lower performance for other metrics with macro precision, recall, and F1 score of 0.7022, 0.7047, and 0.6894, respectively. Due to the data imbalance influence, *OAHU* shows substandard results. The accuracy is 0.8732 and the macro precision, recall, and F1 score are 0.674, 0.6448, and 0.6528, respectively. Overall, *SetConv* is better than other models under this experimental setup.

If we use a better embedding encoder (with re-sampling), absolute performances of every model are improved, but the relative performances do not exhibit much changes, as shown in Table 5. *SetConv* demonstrates that it exceeds other methods in terms of performance no matter which experiment setup is adopted. It achieves an accuracy of 0.9449 and obtains scores of 0.9674, 0.9196, and 0.9406 for macro precision, recall, and F1 score, respectively. *MLP* and *KMeans-SMOTE* still produce reasonable performances. On the other hand, the *EasyEnsemble* displays relatively low performance with an accuracy of just 0.864, and the macro precision, recall, and F1 score of 0.9047, 0.8479, and 0.8602, respectively.

Table 4. Results for the graph dataset **feature embedding encoder is trained without re-sampling method**

	DecisionTree	SVM	KmeansSMOTE	EasyEnsemble	MLP	OAHU	SetConv
Accuracy	0.8971	0.9136	0.9007	0.8088	0.8915	0.8732	**0.9228**
Macro precision	0.633	0.6162	0.7022	0.5475	0.4881	0.674	**0.8022**
Macro recall	0.6265	0.6212	0.7047	0.5617	0.5302	0.6448	**0.7163**
Macro F1	0.6292	0.6174	0.6894	0.526	0.5058	0.6528	**0.7161**

Table 5. Results for the graph dataset **feature embedding encoder is trained with re-sampling method**

	DecisionTree	SVM	KmeansSMOTE	EasyEnsemble	MLP	OAHU	SetConv
Accuracy	0.9136	0.9063	0.9283	0.864	0.9357	0.8382	**0.9449**
Macro precision	0.9305	0.9576	0.9149	0.9047	0.9638	0.7346	**0.9674**
Macro recall	0.9076	0.8515	**0.9511**	0.8479	0.9182	0.7923	0.9196
Macro F1	0.9171	0.8963	0.9281	0.8602	0.9357	0.7488	**0.9406**

5.2.2 DAPT 2020

In these experiments, we discard the severe imbalance classes. The dataset has few classes as compared to the graph dataset and easier to classify. As a result, most of the algorithms exhibit good performances on this dataset, as represented in Table 6. Even *OAHU* does not have a strong design for an imbalanced dataset, yet it achieves competitive performance with an accuracy of 0.9633. *EasyEnsemble* also shows a strong performance in this experiment setup, but *SetConv* slightly performs better than most of the algorithms with an accuracy of 0.986, and the macro precision, recall, and F1 score of 0.9779, 0.98, and 0.9789, respectively.

Table 6. Results for the DAPT 2020 dataset

	DecisionTree	SVM	KmeansSMOTE	EasyEnsemble	MLP	OAHU	SetConv
Accuracy	**0.9988**	0.9795	0.9721	0.8688	0.9583	0.9633	0.986
Macro precision	**0.9983**	0.9659	0.9507	0.9415	0.9467	0.9429	0.9779
Macro recall	**0.999**	0.9751	0.9667	0.7632	0.896	0.9643	0.98
Macro F1	**0.9987**	0.9704	0.9585	0.7897	0.9169	0.9531	0.9789

6 Related Works

There have been several works that exploit TTPs from the MITRE ATT&CK matrix to identify the tactics and stages of an APT attack. One such work is the RapSheet [14] that makes use of the rule matching capability of an endpoint detection response (EDR) tool to discover TTPs in system logs. From there, they build provenance graph, named initial infection point (IIP) provenance graph, that highlights the threat alerts discovered by the EDR tool. A tactical provenance graph is then generated that contains only the alerts, and a threat score is assigned to the graph. In our work, we attempt to identify different tactics of an APT attack through the use of TTPs, rather than an entire APT attack. Furthermore, we propose a method for identifying TTPs rather than relying on an EDR (Endpoint Detection and Response) tool. In addition, our approach does not rely on manually set rules in an EDR tool for discovering TTPs in system logs.

Holmes [23] generates a high-level compact graph to summarize ongoing attack campaign. The key technique is to map activities from the host logs which corresponds to the kill chain. Contrary to that, our approach focuses on cropped or trimmed parts of a system level log or scenario to identify the tactics. In a real time setting, the window for capturing provenance might shift in an unwanted way, which could result in missing information that can lead to false identification or no identification of attack tactics. Our approach shows that we can detect specific attack tactics with cropped provenance capture. Our approach also differs from this work in that it does not need a rule-based scheme to generate high-level scenario (HSG) graphs to map low-level activities to high-level attack tactics; rather it utilizes simple domain knowledge to learn a robust model and identify attack tactics. As such, the extension of our model is simple and easy with new evolving tactics and techniques.

Unicorn [13] generates a fixed sized graph sketch periodically through building a runtime in-memory histogram in a sequential process. It needs to process the graph sequentially to extract crucial information about an attack campaign. Ayoade et al. [3] propose an approach that adopts a provenance capture-based approach to detect different versions or parts of advanced persistent threats. To capture provenance, they use the Camflow [26] and CamQuery [28] tool. The limitation of their approach is that the data collection is limited in platform and also the provenance definition is not compatible with the notion of graph embedding for generating data instances. Our approach addresses this problem and also works on identifying different tactics of an advanced persistent threat attack campaign.

Sheyner et al. [32] introduce an automated way of generating attack graphs using symbolic model checking algorithms. In another work [18], a backtracking technique is used to identify processes and files which may have an impact on the detection point. This approach attempts to find out the chain of events which essentially leads to the intrusion from the entry point. Our approach adopts simple steps for generating provenance graph without any necessity of backtracking and generates data instances which are used for training the machine learning models.

Harmful Episode Reconstruction by Correlating Unsuspicious Logged Events (HERCULE) [29] uses multiple log in the system to generate a multi-dimensional weighted graph to run community detection algorithm on it. It is built on the observation of attack related log entries being heavily and densely connected. Our system only uses a single source log to identify different APT tactics which might or might not be interleaved with benign traces. Made: Security analytics for enter-prise threat detection [25] detects new malicious activities in enterprise networks and for addressing the issue of large data, they adopt a filtration process on the network communications data. But as this approach only attempts to see the start of a whole attack, e.g. detection of malicious domains which can cause the system to be compromised at the first place, it cannot detect whether a system has already been compromised and is in any intermediary tactical phase of an APT campaign.

7   Conclusion and Future Work

Our work mainly focuses on identifying different tactics of Advanced Persistent Threat based on logs that are reduced to make noise free, which also yields limited attack traces for such identification. Our approach generates single vector space embedding for each of the graphs necessary for supervised training setting of machine learning models. The data imbalance being prominently present in the Graph dataset, SetConv method performs well in handling this issue compared to other machine learning methods.

In the future, we plan to explore our approach for windows-based attacks. In addition, we plan to devise techniques to map appropriate responses to alerts of different attack tactics for the ease of system monitoring. To address the cropping or trimming problem of important provenance graphs (or otherwise said, important part of host logs), our future endeavor would be to incorporate a shifting window-based approach to accommodate crucial aspects of an attack into consideration while detecting an attack. Moreover, our future work will focus on incorporating diversified attribution of a graphical depiction into the embedding scheme so that the learning process can be aided for machine learning models.

Our approach can also detect novel attacks if the filtration of the logs is performed based on the common *'keywords'* for all the attacks. More specifically, the log lines related to common system calls for each of the Linux commands can be discarded and from those filtered logs, provenance graphs can be generated. We intend to apply our approach to identify novel techniques under the tactics in the future.

Disclaimer. This paper is not subject to copyright in the United States. Commercial products are identified in order to adequately specify certain procedures. In no case does such identification imply recommendation or endorsement by the National Institute of Standards and Technology, nor does it imply that the identified products are necessarily the best available for the purpose.

Acknowledgements. The research reported herein was supported in part by NIST award 60NANB20D178, NSF awards DMS-1737978, DGE-2039542; and an IBM faculty award (Research).

References

1. https://attack.mitre.org/groups/G0049/
2. Red Canary, September 2020. https://github.com/redcanaryco/atomic-red-team
3. Ayoade, G., et al.: Evolving advanced persistent threat detection using provenance graph and metric learning. In: 2020 IEEE Conference on Communications and Network Security (CNS), pp. 1–9 (2020)
4. CALDERA: Caldera. https://github.com/mitre/caldera. Accessed 10 June 2021
5. Cer, D., et al.: Universal sentence encoder. CoRR abs/1803.11175 (2018)
6. Chen, C., Shyu, M.: Clustering-based binary-class classification for imbalanced data sets. In: Proceedings of the IEEE International Conference on Information Reuse and Integration, IRI 2011, 3–5 August 2011, Las Vegas, Nevada, USA, pp. 384–389. IEEE Systems, Man, and Cybernetics Society (2011)
7. Douzas, G., Bacao, F., Last, F.: Improving imbalanced learning through a heuristic oversampling method based on k-means and smote. Inf. Sci. **465**, 1–20 (2018)
8. Endgameinc: Red team automation (RTA). https://github.com/endgameinc/RTA. Accessed 10 June 2021
9. Gao, Y., Li, Y.F., Chandra, S., Khan, L., Thuraisingham, B.: Towards self-adaptive metric learning on the fly. In: The World Wide Web Conference, pp. 503–513. ACM (2019)
10. Gao, Y., Li, Y.F., Lin, Y., Aggarwal, C., Khan, L.: SetConv: a new approach for learning from imbalanced data (2021)
11. Gephi: The open graph viz platform. https://gephi.org/. Accessed 10 June 2021

12. Hamilton, W., Ying, Z., Leskovec, J.: Inductive representation learning on large graphs. In: Guyon, I., et al. (eds.) Advances in Neural Information Processing Systems, vol. 30, pp. 1024–1034. Curran Associates, Inc. (2017)

13. Han, X., Pasquier, T., Bates, A., Mickens, J., Seltzer, M.: Unicorn: runtime provenance-based detector for advanced persistent threats. arXiv preprint arXiv:2001.01525 (2020)

14. Hassan, W., Bates, A., Marino, D.: Tactical provenance analysis for endpoint detection and response systems. In: 2020 IEEE Symposium on Security and Privacy (SP), pp. 1172–1189. IEEE Computer Society, Los Alamitos, CA, USA, May 2020

15. Hastie, T., Tibshirani, R., Friedman, J.: The Elements of Statistical Learning: Data Mining, Inference, and Prediction. Springer Science & Business Media, New York (2009). https://doi.org/10.1007/978-0-387-84858-7

16. He, H., Garcia, E.A.: Learning from imbalanced data. IEEE Trans. Knowl. Data Eng. **21**(9), 1263–1284 (2009)

17. Jiang, X., Walters, A., Xu, D., Spafford, E., Buchholz, F., Wang, Y.M.: Provenance-aware tracing ofworm break-in and contaminations: a process coloring approach. In: 26th IEEE International Conference on Distributed Computing Systems (ICDCS 2006), p. 38 (2006). https://doi.org/10.1109/ICDCS.2006.69

18. King, S.T., Chen, P.M.: Backtracking intrusions. SIGOPS Oper. Syst. Rev. **37**(5), 223–236 (2003)

19. Kipf, T.N., Welling, M.: Semi-supervised classification with graph convolutional networks. arXiv preprint arXiv:1609.02907 (2016)

20. Lee, K.H., Zhang, X., Xu, D.: High accuracy attack provenance via binary-based execution partition. In: NDSS (2013)

21. Liu, X.Y., Wu, J., Zhou, Z.H.: Exploratory undersampling for class-imbalance learning. IEEE Trans. Syst. Man Cybern. Part B (Cybern.) **39**(2), 539–550 (2008)

22. Ma, S., Zhang, X., Xu, D.: Protracer: towards practical provenance tracing by alternating between logging and tainting. In: NDSS (2016)

23. Milajerdi, S.M., Gjomemo, R., Eshete, B., Sekar, R., Venkatakrishnan, V.: Holmes: real-time APT detection through correlation of suspicious information flows. In: 2019 IEEE Symposium on Security and Privacy (SP), pp. 1137–1152. IEEE (2019)

24. Myneni, S., et al.: DAPT 2020 - constructing a benchmark dataset for advanced persistent threats. In: Wang, G., Ciptadi, A., Ahmadzadeh, A. (eds.) MLHat 2020. CCIS, vol. 1271, pp. 138–163. Springer, Cham (2020). https://doi.org/10.1007/978-3-030-59621-7_8

25. Oprea, A., Li, Z., Norris, R., Bowers, K.: Made: security analytics for enterprise threat detection. In: Proceedings of the 34th Annual Computer Security Applications Conference, pp. 124–136. ACSAC 2018. Association for Computing Machinery, New York, NY, USA (2018)

26. Pasquier, T., et al.: Practical whole-system provenance capture. In: Proceedings of the 2017 Symposium on Cloud Computing, pp. 405–418. SoCC 2017, ACM, New York, NY, USA (2017)

27. Pasquier, T., et al.: Runtime analysis of whole-system provenance (2018)

28. Pasquier, T., et al.: Runtime analysis of whole-system provenance. In: Proceedings of the 2018 ACM SIGSAC Conference on Computer and Communications Security, pp. 1601–1616. CCS 2018, ACM, New York, NY, USA (2018)

29. Pei, K., et al.: Hercule: attack story reconstruction via community discovery on correlated log graph. In: Proceedings of the 32nd Annual Conference on Computer Security Applications, pp. 583–595. ACSAC 2016, Association for Computing Machinery, New York, NY, USA (2016)

30. Perozzi, B., Al-Rfou, R., Skiena, S.: Deepwalk: online learning of social representations. In: Proceedings of the 20th ACM SIGKDD International Conference on Knowledge Discovery and Data Mining, pp. 701–710 (2014)
31. Rabanser, S., Shchur, O., Günnemann, S.: Introduction to tensor decompositions and their applications in machine learning. CoRR abs/1711.10781 (2017)
32. Sheyner, O., Haines, J., Jha, S., Lippmann, R., Wing, J.M.: Automated generation and analysis of attack graphs. In: Proceedings 2002 IEEE Symposium on Security and Privacy, pp. 273–284 (2002)
33. Sun, Y., Kamel, M.S., Wong, A.K.C., Wang, Y.: Cost-sensitive boosting for classification of imbalanced data. Pattern Recogn. **40**(12), 3358–3378 (2007)
34. Thakur, V.: The sykipot attacks (2011). https://www.symantec.com/connect/blogs/sykipot-attacks
35. TinkerPop, A.: Apache tinkerpop. https://tinkerpop.apache.org/. Accessed 10 June 2021
36. Xiang, S., Nie, F., Zhang, C.: Learning a mahalanobis distance metric for data clustering and classification. Pattern Recogn. **41**(12), 3600–3612 (2008)

WiP: Slow Rate HTTP Attack Detection with Behavioral Parameters

Shaurya Sood[1], Manash Saikia[2], and Neminath Hubballi[1(✉)]

[1] Indian Institute of Technology Indore, Indore, India
[2] Tezpur University, Tezpur, India
{phd1801201007,neminath}@iiti.ac.in, csb18020@tezu.ac.in

Abstract. Hypertext Transfer Protocol (HTTP) is vulnerable to slow rate Denial of Service (DoS) attacks. Here an adversary deliberately reads and sends data slowly thereby prolonging the connection duration. Multiple such slow connections will cripple the web server and prevent servicing legitimate requests. The simplest detection methods which use x number of malicious requests in y window period can be easily evaded. In this paper, we identify few behavioral parameters whose values change when such attacks are launched. We also identify the relationship between these parameters by estimating the correlation between them. Using these parameters and their correlation, we describe a detection method. In this detection method, evaluation is done based on the number of messages sent to prolong the connection. A very high number of such messages is a direct indication of an attack. When the number of such messages are in a range below this threshold, such intervals are verified with other behavioral parameters for detecting attacks. This two stage detection method will make the evasion harder for an adversary. We evaluate the proposed method with experiments done in a testbed and a live web sever and show that it has good detection performance.

Keywords: Application layer attacks · HTTP · Slow rate DoS

1 Introduction

Denial of Service (DoS) and its variant Distributed Denial of Service (DDoS) attacks are posing increased threat to the safety of networked services and applications. These attacks target the availability of services and render them not accessible to legitimate users. There are several mitigation and detection methods proposed in the literature for handling these attacks. However, these attacks continue to grow in scale and variety. Recently a new variant of DoS attacks known as application layer DoS attacks have surfaced. Unlike network based DoS attacks, these variants target specific applications. They exploit the operational behavior of applications. The goal is two-fold [22] i) to minimize the resource (network bandwidth, CPU and memory) requirements of attacker and ii) being low profile (stealthy) making it difficult to detect. Several popular application

© Springer Nature Switzerland AG 2021
S. Tripathy et al. (Eds.): ICISS 2021, LNCS 13146, pp. 26–37, 2021.
https://doi.org/10.1007/978-3-030-92571-0_2

layer protocols on the Internet like HTTP [21], SIP [11], DHCP [12], DNS [13] and NTP [23] have been shown to be vulnerable to these attacks.

HTTP is vulnerable to slow rate attacks where an adversary will exhaust the connection pool at the server and maintain them occupied for longer periods thereby denying service to legitimate users. These attacks can be generated using both HTTP Get and HTTP Post methods. There are several open source tools [20] for generating such attacks. Conventional detection methods count number of requests made in a time interval and flag an alert if count is more than a preset threshold. Such detection methods can be evaded. In this paper, we propose a two phase detection method to detect slow rate DoS attacks using behavioral parameters. Our contribution in this paper are as follows.

1. We identify four indicative parameters which aid in detecting slow rate HTTP attacks launched with slowloris. Few parameters are measured at the server and one using a designated set of client nodes.
2. We identify the correlation between the parameters and subsequently describe a method to detect such attacks.
3. We evaluate the proposed method with two experiments and show that proposed method is able to detect the attacks.

Background: Slowloris is a TCP based slow attack which exploits the working of HTTP. To begin with, it establishes multiple connections to exhaust all available connections at the server and subsequently prolong the connections by repeatedly sending incomplete requests. A constant arrival of header messages will hog the server and fresh connection requests by other genuine clients are not serviced. This attack can be mounted from a single machine and it affects all threaded variants of web servers. The number of requests is a configurable parameter and slowloris tool facilitates this. It is available as open source project and can be launched from different operating systems.

2 Related Work

In this section we briefly elaborate the detection and mitigation methods available for handling slowloris attacks.

i) Implementation Modules: There are few protection mechanisms that have been implemented to protect the web servers. These include modules - 'Core' [6], 'Antiloris' [17], 'Limitipconn' [18] and 'mod_reqtimeout' [19]. All the four implementation modules are available for Apache web server. 'Core' requires to buffer the HTTP request before it is forwarded to the web server for handling the request. Server receives only complete requests, hence it is protected from these requests. However, this solution requires enough space in the kernel to handle all the incomplete requests. 'Antiloris' [17], 'Limitipconn' [18] enforce a limit on the number of complete/incomplete HTTP requests per IP address. The fourth module 'mod_reqtimeout' [19] enforces the sender to send the entire request in a predefined amount of time.

ii) Overlay based Mitigation Techniques: These methods propose to have filters set away from the real servers. Filtering is done by dedicated services where HTTP requests are verified to find whether these are legitimate or generated by an attack source. Some overlay based methods perform client identification and other checks before the requests are sent to the server. Commercial solutions offered by CLOUDFLARE [5] and Akamai's Kona [1] protect against such malicious requests with filtering mechanisms. Few other works propose Software Defined Networking based solutions [16,25] to filter attack traffic. Jia et al. [14] propose to dynamically instantiate new mirror servers in cloud to take down the increased load. Dantas et al. [8] adopt Adaptive Selective Verification (ASV) method proposed for detecting network layer DDoS attacks to detect slow rate HTTP attacks. Some of these works require third parties to decrypt the HTTP requests hence compromise the end-to-end encryption security of communication. Recent works [9,10] proposed overlay based mitigation methods which preserve the end-to-end encryption security and yet achieve considerable reduction in attack traffic at the server.

iii) Traffic Profiles and Feature based Detection: These methods generate a profile of normal behavior of web server. This is typically done using network traffic or system resources. The work of Tripathi et al. [21] generates a profile from HTTP traffic and subsequently measures Hellinger Distance (HD) [4] between historic traffic profiles and a test interval. It detects an attack if this distance is beyond a preset threshold. Aqil et al. [2] argue that single threshold based detection methods can be easily evaded. Thus, a combination of features and characteristics are needed to detect these attacks. Authors showed that a combination of attacks each operating below the threshold levels can easily take down the target and yet not detectable. They showed the effectiveness of such attacks using TCP SYN flood and slowloris attacks in combination. Recently there are some efforts of using machine learning methods [3] to detect slow rate attacks.

3   Proposed Slow Rate Attack Detection Method

In this section, we describe the proposed method for detecting the slow rate HTTP DoS attacks.

3.1   Attack Indicators

The key to detecting attacks is identifying parameters which are relevant and can differentiate normal and attack scenarios. By carefully studying the normal and slowloris attack instances of a web server, we make following observations and select the required behavioral parameters.

(i) `Number of Incomplete Requests`: When the server is under attack, the number of incomplete requests obviously increase. Such incomplete requests are otherwise not seen in regular/normal requests from clients. Thus, we chose this as our first attack indicator.

(ii) `Response Time`: This is the time difference between a request made by a client to receiving a response. When a web server is experiencing slow rate attacks, all the available connections with server are utilized and hence it is likely that legitimate requests are not honoured or experience very slow response. It is worth noting that, response time is dependent on the load, the server is experiencing and the state of the network. If the load on the server is more, the response may be slower. Also if the network is experiencing congestion, then also there may be large delays. Thus, the response time is a good indicator; but insufficient on its own to detect attacks.

(iii) `Number of Response Messages`: With increase in the number of incomplete requests, the server response slows down and hence will send less number of bytes/responses than otherwise it is sending normally.

(iv) `Number of Context Switches`: Context switch happen when the Operating System switches from one process to another. This is different from an interrupt. Interrupt is a service request and the execution will resume from the state where it was left after servicing the interrupt. In case of slowloris attack, the number of context switches are likely to increase as new connections are made in short span of time.

3.2 How Different Parameters are Related?

In order to identify the relevance of the parameters described above, we compute the correlation between the parameters. In particular, we correlate the number of incomplete requests with the remaining parameters. This is due to the fact that, presence of incomplete HTTP requests is the starting point for the attack. We use the Pearson's correlation method to determine how the parameters correlate with the number of incomplete requests. The Pearson's correlation coefficient is calculated as in Eq. 1.

$$\rho_{ab} = \frac{Cov(a,b)}{\sigma_a \sigma_b} \qquad (1)$$

where
ρ_{ab} - is the Pearson coefficient
$Cov(a,b)$ - is the co-variance of the two variables a and b
σ_a and σ_b - are the standard deviation of variables a and b.

(i) We can see that as the number of incomplete requests increase, the connection response time increases and mostly no response is received from the server if all the TCP connections are occupied. Thus, these two are likely to be positively correlated.

(ii) Increasing number of incomplete requests to prolong the existing connections will decrease the number of responses from the server. Thus, these two are negatively correlated with each other.

(iii) Increase in the number of incomplete requests will increase the number of context switches. Thus, these two are positively correlated.

3.3 Slow Rate Attack Detection

Our detection method is based on the measurements of behavioral parameters. Some of these are measured in the server and one parameter is measured from few selected clients located remotely. In particular, we measure (i) number of incomplete HTTP requests (ii) number of server responses and (iii) number of context switches at the sever and (i) response time from few designated clients. Figure 1 depicts a server with two attackers and three clients from where response times are measured. Slow rate attack is detected using a combination of these four parameters.

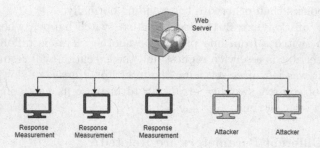

Fig. 1. Slow rate attack detection setup

Algorithm 1 shows the detection method using these parameters. It uses five thresholds; two for the number of incomplete requests and one for every other parameter. Unlike the previous methods which use a single threshold for detecting the attack, this algorithm has a two phase operation. First is a very certain stage and the other requires supplementary evidence. In the first/certain phase, it straightaway detects the attack if the number of incomplete HTTP requests are more than a preset threshold. If these requests are not crossing that threshold and there are incomplete requests above a second threshold, it uses secondary level check using a combination of other parameters. The thresholds for these parameters are set based on the correlation between the number of incomplete requests and these remaining parameters as outlined in the Subsect. 3.2. Parameters having positive correlation will have threshold values set higher to baseline normal operation and those having negative correlation will have thresholds lower than the normal operation.

4 Experiments

In this section, we describe the experiments done to evaluate the performance of the proposed slow rate attack detection method. We performed two experiments. First experiment is done in a testbed and second one with a real web server.

Algorithm 1: Detecting Slow HTTP Attack

Input: $\delta_{incomplete\ request}1$ - Number of Incomplete HTTP Requests 1
Input: $\delta_{incomplete\ request}2$ - Number of Incomplete HTTP Requests 2
Input: $\delta_{response\ time}$- Response time
Input: $\delta_{response\ message}$- Number of response messages
Input: $\delta_{context\ switch}$- Number of context switches
Result: Label Intervals as Attacks or Normal
while *! Interrupted* **do**

    Incomplete ← Count incomplete requests in a time window W;
    if *Incomplete* $\geq \delta_{incomplete\ request}1$ **then**
        | Declare attack;
    else if *Incomplete* $\geq \delta_{incomplete\ request}2$ *and*
    Incomplete $< \delta_{incomplete\ request}1$ **then**
        ResponseTime ← Avg(HTTP Response Time);
        ResponseMessage ← Count(HTTP Response Messages);
        ContextSwitch ← Count(Context Switch);
        if *ResponseTime* $\geq \delta_{response\ time}$ *and*
        ResponseMessages $\leq \delta_{response\ message}$ ||
        ResponseTime $\geq \delta_{response\ time}$ *and ContextSwitch* $\geq \delta_{context\ switch}$ ||
        ResponseMessages $\leq \delta_{response\ message}$ *and*
        ContextSwitch $\geq \delta_{context\ switch}$ **then**
            | Declare attack;
    else
        | Declare normal operation;
end

4.1   Experiment in a Testbed (Experiment-1)

Testbed Experimental Setup: We created a network setup similar to Fig. 1. We used four virtual machine (VM) instances in our testbed. In one of the VM, we deployed the Apache web server. In another VM, we deployed cURL script [7] for measuring the HTTP response time. In the third VM, we installed Kali Linux and we used slowloris from this machine to generate the attack. In the fourth VM, we deployed Jmeter [15] with which we generated the normal HTTP requests. We collected network traffic in the server. The number of context switches are measured with a bash script (which uses a Linux command) in the server. The cURL script periodically sent the requests to measure the response time. Number of incomplete requests and total responses from the server are derived by processing the traffic trace files collected in the server using tshark tool [24].

Evaluation of Parameters: In order to verify that the four parameters chosen are indeed valid and help in detecting the attack, we performed a small scale experiment of 10 min duration. After initialing the traffic collection, we started Jmeter which generated HTTP requests for the entire duration of 10 min. CURL script generated periodic requests and measured the response time. While the normal requests are on, we generated slowloris attack two times each lasting for a minute in the middle. By processing the trace file generated, we derived the number of incomplete requests and also the number of responses. Other two parameters were also measured as mentioned above for the same period.

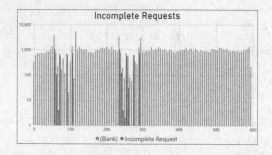

Fig. 2. Incomplete requests (slowloris attack) (Color figure online)

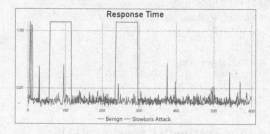

Fig. 3. HTTP response time (Color figure online)

We show these four parameters in Figs. 2, 3, 4 and 5. In Figs. 2, 3 and 5 blue colored lines correspond to normal HTTP requests and the red colored lines correspond to incomplete HTTP requests of slowloris attack. From Fig. 2, we can see that incomplete requests are seen only in two small patches corresponding to the time when attack was launched. The response times measured during the same period are shown in Fig. 3. We can see that during attack period, response time increases. Similarly, from Fig. 4 it is evident that the number of response messages from the server decreased when the attack is on. Figure 5 shows the number of non voluntary (red colored bars) and voluntary context switches (blue colored bars) happened during the 10 min period. We can see that the number of non voluntary context switches increase as the attack started. This experiment and corresponding diagrams show that the chosen behavioral parameters are indeed valid. We also measured the correlation values between the parameters chosen. Response time, number of responses and context switches have correlation values of 0.008, −0.022 and 0.012 respectively with the number of incomplete request values.

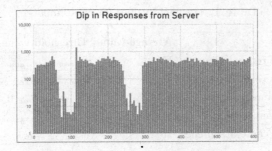

Fig. 4. Number of response messages from server

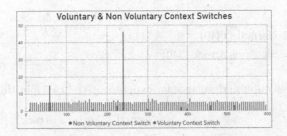

Fig. 5. Voluntary and non-voluntary context switches (Color figure online)

Detection Results: We performed an evaluation with a larger dataset collected with the same setup as described above. We collected nine hours of data (network traffic, context switches and response time) for evaluation by running the Jmeter and slowloris attack. Out of this, first two hours of data has only HTTP requests generated from Jmeter and this was used for deriving the thresholds and remaining seven hours of data was used for testing the detection performance. The second part of seven hours data also involves one hour of slowloris attack. We derived the threshold parameters by dividing the two hours data (of all parameters) into windows of sizes 15 s and calculated the average values of all parameters in that period. The average values of different parameters and thresholds used for attack detection are shown in Table 1. The threshold values are derived by adding and subtracting 20% to the averages depending on whether these values are positively or negatively correlated with the number of incomplete requests.

We evaluated the detection performance with different window sizes. We used the same method of adding and subtracting 20% to the average values of parameters seen during that window for deriving the threshold values. Table 2 and Table 3 show the detection performance for 15 s and 5 min intervals respectively. For the 15 s interval, there are 1440 normal (6 h out of 7 h) and 240 (1 h out of 7 h) intervals corresponding to slowloris attack. We can see from Table 2 that our algorithm is able to predict the two types of intervals with a correct attack prediction rate of 99.17%. Similarly from Table 3, we can notice that all 72

Table 1. Threshold values for experiment-1

Parameter	Average value	Threshold value
Incomplete request count 1	NA	$\delta_{incomplete\ request}1 = 100$
Incomplete request count l1	4	$\delta_{incomplete\ request}2 = 5$
Response time	0.34 s	$\delta_{response\ time}\ 0.4\,s$
Response messages	458	$\delta_{response\ message} = 412$
Number of context switches	25	$\delta_{context\ switch} = 30$

Table 2. Detection performance for experiment-1 with 15 s time window

	Normal	Slowloris attack
Normal (1440)	1440	0
Slowloris attack (240)	2	238

Table 3. Detection performance for experiment-1 with 5 min time window

	Normal	Slowloris attack
Normal (72)	72	0
Slowloris attack (12)	0	12

normal and 12 intervals corresponding to slowloris attack are correctly predicted by the detection method.

It is worth noting that our detection method is sensitive to window size or interval period used (for 15 s interval there are 2 false negatives and for 5 min interval there are no wrong predictions). In order to understand the variation of detection performance with interval time chosen, we performed a study by varying the window size using the test data of 7 h. Figure 6 shows the detection rate variation with window size. We can notice that beyond 20 s interval, the attack detection rate is 100%. The lower detection rate for smaller intervals is due to the fact that, slowloris does not send incomplete requests aggressively once it exhausts all connections with the server. After the connections are established, it only sends periodic incomplete requests and if the interval is too small, there may not be any incomplete or less number of HTTP requests in some of the intervals.

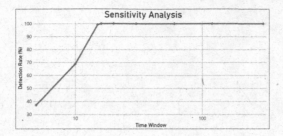

Fig. 6. Sensitivity analysis for experiment-1

4.2   Experiment with Real Web Server (Experiment-2)

This experiment was conducted with a web sever deployed in an academic institution. We collected network traffic and context switch data from this server and measured response time from a remote location using cURL. As in the previous case, in this experiment also we used 30 min normal HTTP traffic for deriving the thresholds and second portion comprising of 55 min of normal and 20 min of data where we launched slowloris attack against the server for evaluation purpose. The average values of different parameters and threshold values in this case are shown in Table 4. The detection performance using the algorithm is shown in Table 5. We can see that even in this case too the proposed two phase detection method is able to identify the attack and normal intervals with good accuracy. As in the previous experiment, we also did a sensitivity analysis by varying the window sizes. Figure 7 shows the variation of detection rate with window sizes. From this figure also we can observe that with increase in window size, the detection rate also increases.

Table 4. Threshold values for experiment-2

Parameter	Average value	Threshold value
Incomplete request count 1	NA	$\delta_{incomplete\ request}1 = 100$
Incomplete request count ll	8	$\delta_{incomplete\ request}2 = 11$
Response time	0.24 s	$\delta_{response\ time} = 0.3\,s$
Response messages	1470	$\delta_{response\ message} = 1103$
Context switch	10	$\delta_{context\ switch} = 12$

Table 5. Detection performance experiment-2 with 15 s Window

	Normal	Slowloris attack
Normal (220)	220	0
Slowloris attack (80)	4	76

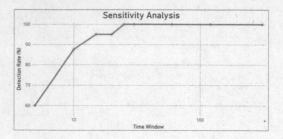

Fig. 7. Sensitivity analysis for experiment-2

5   Conclusion

Slow rate attacks exploit the HTTP operation and can take down web servers
with few customized HTTP messages. Single threshold based detection methods
are easier to evade. In this paper, we identified few behavioral changes which are
seen when such attack is mounted against a web server. We showed that, when
the number of such requests are within a range below the detection threshold,
these parameters can collectively help identifying low intensity attacks. We performed two experiments one in a testbed setup by generating slowloris attack
against a web server and the second one by launching attack against a live web
server. The evaluation results showed good detection performance in both the
cases.

Acknowledgement. This work is financially supported by funding through SPARC
project via grant number "SPARC/2018-2019/P448" by Government of India. Authors
thankfully acknowledge the funding received.

References

1. Akamai. https://www.akamai.com/us/en/products/security/kona-ddos-defender.
jsp. Accessed 25 July 2021
2. Aqil; A., et al.: Detection of stealthy TCP-based dos attacks. In: MILCOM 2015–
2015 IEEE Military Communications Conference, pp. 348–353 (2015)
3. Calvert, C., Kemp, C., Khoshgoftaar, T.M., Najafabadi, M.M.: Detecting slow
http post dos attacks using NetFlow features. In: FLAIRS 2019: Proceedings of
the Thirty-Second International Florida Artificial Intelligence Research Society
Conference, pp. 387–390 (2019)
4. Cao, X.: Model Selection Based on Expected Squared Hellinger Distance. Colorado
State University (2007)
5. CLOUDFLARE. https://www.cloudflare.com/en-in/learning/ddos/application-
layer-ddos-attack/. Accessed 25 July 2021
6. Core: (2019). https://httpd.apache.org/docs/2.4/mod/core.html. Accessed 8 Aug
2021
7. CURL. https://curl.se/docs/httpscripting.html. Accessed 25 July 2021

8. Dantas, Y.G., Nigam, V., Fonseca, I.E.: A selective defense for application layer DDoS attacks. In: JISIC 2014: Proceedings of the IEEE Joint Intelligence and Security Informatics Conference, pp. 75–82 (2014)
9. Eid, M.S.A., Aida, H.: Secure double-layered defense against HTTP-DDoS attacks. In: COMPSAC 2017: Proceedings of the 41st Annual Computer Software and Applications Conference, vol. 2, pp. 572–577 (2017)
10. EID, M.S.A., Aida, H.: Trustworthy DDoS defense: design, proof of concept implementation and testing. IEICE Trans. Inf. Syst. $\mathbf{D}(8)$, 1738–1750 (2017)
11. Golait, D., Hubballi, N.: Detecting anomalous behavior in VoIP systems: a discrete event system modeling. IEEE Trans. Inf. Forensics Secur. $\mathbf{12}(3)$, 730–745 (2017)
12. Hubballi, N., Tripathi, N.: A closer look into DHCP starvation attack in wireless networks. Comput. Secur. $\mathbf{65}(C)$, 387–404 (2017)
13. IMPERVA. https://www.imperva.com/learn/ddos/dns-flood/. Accessed 08 Aug 2021
14. Jia, Q., Wang, H., Fleck, D., Li, F., Stavrou, A., Powell, W.: Catch me if you can: a cloud-enabled DDoS defense. In: DSN 2014: Proceedings of the 44th Annual IEEE/IFIP International Conference on Dependable Systems and Networks, pp. 264–275 (2014)
15. Apache JMeter. https://jmeter.apache.org/. Accessed 25 July 2021
16. Lukaseder, T., Hunt, A., Stehle, C., Wagner, D., Van Der Heijden, R., Kargl, F.: An extensible host-agnostic framework for SDN-assisted DDoS-mitigation. In: LCN 2017: Proceedings of the 42nd Conference on Local Computer Networks, pp. 619–622 (2017)
17. mod_antiloris (2013). https://sourceforge.net/projects/mod-antiloris/. Accessed 8 Aug 2021
18. mod_limitipconn (2002). http://dominia.org/djao/limitipconn.html. Accessed 8 Aug 2021
19. mod_reqtimeout (2019). https://httpd.apache.org/docs/trunk/mod/mod_reqtimeout.html. Accessed 8 Aug 2021
20. Radware. https://www.radware.com/security/ddos-knowledge-center/ddos-attack-types/common-ddos-attack-tools/. Accessed 25 July 2021
21. Tripathi, N., Hubballi, N.: Slow rate denial of service attacks against HTTP/2 and detection. Comput. Secur. $\mathbf{72}(C)$, 255–272 (2018)
22. Tripathi, N., Hubballi, N.: Application layer denial-of-service attacks and defense mechanisms: a survey. ACM Comput. Surv. $\mathbf{54}(4)$, 1–33 (2021)
23. Tripathi, N., Hubballi, N.: Preventing time synchronization in NTP broadcast mode. Comput. Secur. $\mathbf{102}$, 102–135 (2021)
24. Tshark. https://tshark.dev/setup/install/. Accessed 8 Aug 2021
25. Yin, D., Zhang, L., Yang, K.: A DDoS attack detection and mitigation with software-defined internet of things framework. IEEE Access $\mathbf{6}$, 24694–24705 (2018)

Multi Layer Detection Framework for Spear-Phishing Attacks

Shivani Arya and Saurabh Chamotra[✉]

Cyber Security Technology Division C-DAC, Mohali, India
{shivania,saurabhc}@cdac.in

Abstract. With emails becoming prime communication medium across organizations, spear-phishing has become one of the most effective medium for attackers to breach enterprise network security. Latest targeted attacks which employ compromised email accounts for sending spear-phishing emails are almost impossible to detect using conventional security solutions. Attackers use contextual information of targeted entity to make the spear-phishing emails look legitimate. Convincing the victim to either click a malicious link or download and open a malicious attachment.

The Detection of spear-phishing email becomes more challenging when it has to be done in an enterprise network scenario. Factors such as nonavailability of training data, huge volumes of emails received and critical role of email in business operations makes detection a challenge. In the work presented in this paper we propose a multi-layer detection framework for the spear-phishing email detection. The proposed framework employs sentiment analysis, context-based behavior analysis along with deception technologies for the detection of spear-phishing emails.

Keywords: Spear-phishing emails · Deception technology · Sentiment analysis · Attack-analysis · Sandboxing

1 Introduction

Spear-phishing emails have become one of the most common propagation vectors employed by attackers to infiltrate organizational-network's perimeter security. As per a recent report published by cyber-security firm Group-IB [9], email-accounts of high-ranking executives of more than 150 companies have been breached by an adversary named PerSwaysion. In one of its threat reports [39] Proof-point stated that, every three out of four spam emails delivers a malware. In an another threat report [24] it was claimed that the spear-phishing emails are the most widely used infection method, employed by 71% of hacker groups. Spear-phishing attacks are so successful that state-sponsored hacking units popularly known as APTs are putting considerable amount of efforts in scanning and probing the internet for vulnerable email servers [19]. These discovered vulnerable email servers are later compromised and used as a platform

© Springer Nature Switzerland AG 2021
S. Tripathy et al. (Eds.): ICISS 2021, LNCS 13146, pp. 38–56, 2021.
https://doi.org/10.1007/978-3-030-92571-0_3

to launch spear-phishing email attacks. There are incidents publicly documented where APT groups such as GhostNet [21], Night Dragon [13], Operation Aurora [34] employed spear phishing emails for launching attack campaign. In a recent incident, an advisory [36] was issued by NSCS UK regarding the spear-phishing attacks launched by APT29 group targeting organisations involved in COVID-19 vaccine development. Spear-phishing attacks tends to be more successful than other attacks due to their targeted nature. The targeted nature of spear-phishing emails makes it extremely difficult for a target to differentiate or distinguish between spear-phishing email and benign email. This argument is supported by a published report [38] according to which 97% of people around the world cannot identify a sophisticated phishing email, 30% of phishing messages get opened by targeted users and 12% of those users click on the malicious attachment or link.

All the above-mentioned facts highlights the growing prevalence and potency of spear-phishing attacks. In the work presented in this paper we have proposed a framework for the detection of spear-phishing emails. The proposed framework uses a combination of detection engines targeting the identified key characteristics of the spear-phishing emails. The framework has two major components, one of which works at email level and the other at the network level. The first engine processes the organizational emails through multi layer detection engines. The multiple machine learning based and rule based engines assesses emails based upon characteristics such as, sentiments reflected, context and content associated with the email and allocates a score. The second mechanism uses deception along with sand boxing for detection of adversary performing lateral movement & credential harvesting. The proposed framework uses the results of these two components for the detection of the spear-phishing emails.

2 Characteristics of Spear Phishing Email

Over a period of time attackers have mastered the art of creating and launching spear-phishing email campaigns. Attackers launching such campaigns first segment their victims, personalize email contents, impersonate specific senders and use techniques to bypass traditional email defenses. Their goal is to trick the targets into clicking malicious links or opening malicious attachments. By mining social networks for personal information about a target, an attacker can easily write emails that are extremely accurate and compelling.

Researchers [26] have modeled these campaigns using three components 1) Lure, 2) Hook and 3) Catch. The "Lure" component of a phishing scheme is an email with carefully crafted content. Victims of spear-phishing email campaigns who fails to turn away from the "Lure" gets hooked. Here the "Hook" refers to exploit code embedded in the attachment or in malicious URL. The "Catch" phase involves communication with the master, performing credential harvesting from compromised system and using it for lateral movement inside the organization.

The first step towards development of a detection mechanism for such adversary is the characterization of the adversary. Based upon the threat reports and literature reviews [7,15,23,26,27,36] we have identified some of the key traits that characterise a spear-phishing emails. These identified characteristics forms the basis of the proposed detection mechanism. The identified key characteristic of spear-phishing email are as follows.

2.1 Reflects Sense of Urgency

Most of the spear-phishing email attacks are opportunistic hacking campaigns which monetise the latest issues difficult for victims to ignore. As per the threat report [5], subject lines of more than 70% of attack emails try to establish rapport or a sense of urgency. The reason why subject lines reflect some sense of urgency could be the fact that the attacker wants to ensure that the email must catch the attention of the target and he should open the email. Another reason could be the fact that the URLs and malicious links used in spear-phishing email have noticeably short life span and are taken offline by the defenders tracking the APT attack campaigns. In this paper we have tried to characterise spear-phishing emails based upon the sentiment reflected by their subject lines and contents.

2.2 Impersonation

In most cases, the source email addresses in a spear-phishing email are often spoofed or sent from a compromised email account. This is done for generating some sense of trust or authority at the recipient. The scammer impersonates a company employee or other trusted party and tries to trick the employees. Barracuda researchers evaluated more than 360,000 spear-phishing emails and discovered that 83% [5] of spear-phishing attacks involve brand impersonation thereby using name-spoofing techniques, to make the email appear to come from a known person. Apart from spoofing email addresses, spear-phishing emails also employ typo-squatting or Unicode characters to make the sender address look similar to the one t hey want to masquerade [3]. From the above-mentioned facts, it could be established that the presence of spoofing and other imperson-ation types in the sender address is a strong indication of spear-phishing email campaign and hence could be used to spot spear-phishing emails.

2.3 Malicious URLs and Attachments

The Malicious URLs or attachments act as a hook in spear-phishing email campaign. The hook plays the role of compromising the targeted system by either downloading a malware on the victim's system or exploiting a vulnerability and later downloading a malware. While trend-micro report [46] suggests that, most commonly used and shared file types in organizations accounted for 70% of the total number of spear-phishing email attachments. Attackers use VBA code from Macros or use DDE to deliver attacks with malicious Office attachments and in case of PDF attachments attacker exploits vulnerabilities in PDF JavaScript extensions to deliver and execute malicious payloads. Hence presence of malicious attachment or Mal-URLs in an email can be used as one of the characteristics to recognize spear-phishing emails.

2.4 Credential Harvesting and Lateral Movement

One of the recent trend observed in spear-phishing email attack campaigns is the use of credential stealing malware for credential harvesting [4,14,35]. The spear-phishing email campaigns specifically initiated by APT groups, employs credential harvesting techniques. The objective is to use the stolen credentials for performing "lateral movements" inside the organizational network. During lateral movement, an adversary searches for higher value assets inside the organizations. In the proposed framework we have used deception as a tool for detection of credential harvesting and Lateral Movement.

3 Related Work

The concept of targeted spear-phishing emails was first introduced in 2007 as social phishing or context-aware phishing by Jakobsson et al. [26]. Subsequently researchers have come up with many approaches to detect such emails. One of the most popular approach for detecting spear-phishing emails, adopted by many researchers [11,12,31,41] is based on the style of email writing, modelled through the characteristics of its text content. This approach is based on assumption that emails written by a user can be characterised by their writing style. Using this assumption Lin et al. [31] developed a spear-phishing email detection engine which uses stylometry features to check the authenticity of an email. Chandrasekaran et al. [6] presented an approach based on natural structural characteristics in email text contents. In their work Abu-Nimeh et al. [2] used "bag-of-words" based text mining approach and based upon the 43 identified keywords they developed a classifier for phishing emails. Some of the researchers experimented with the context-based email features in combination with the stylometry features for achieving higher accuracy. In this context Ma et al. [32] has developed a system for detection of phishing email using a hybrid feature set. In another similar work, Prateek et al. [11] has used a combination of social features from LinkedIn profiles, and stylometric features extracted from email subject, body, and attachments. Islam and Abawajy [25] proposed a multi-feature detection approach where they extracted features from the email header along with the email contents. In a similar approach Hamid et al. [20] proposed a hybrid feature selection approach where they modelled the attacker behaviour based on features extracted from email headers and contents. The Stylometric features were employed by many researchers for spear-phishing email detection but later it was felt that stylometric features are computationally expensive and requires considerable amount of training data. As a solution to this, researchers explored approaches where they looked for content-agnostic traits of a user for characterising an email written by the user. Based upon this concept H. Gascon et al.

[16] developed a spear-phishing email detection engine. They considered spoofing as a key characteristic of spear-phishing emails and employed content-agnostic traits left by the sender in the email as feature set to model the sender profile. In another approach Stringhini et al. [43] developed a spear-phishing email detection engine named IdentityMailer which detects spear-phishing emails by modelling the email sending behaviour for a user. Stolfo et al. developed Email Mining Toolkit (EMT) [41] which mines the email logs to find cliques of users who frequently contact each other and flags any anomalous communication.

The researchers have also explored approaches where they examined URLs contained in the email [7,15,45]. Chhabra et al. [8] have proposed an approach where they analysed the URL based features for detection of the phishing emails. In the work proposed in this paper we have adopted a hybrid approach, where we have used a combination of sentiment analysis, impersonation detection, URL analysis and attachment analysis along with deception based sand-boxing as a measure for the detection of the spear-phishing emails.

4   Proposed Solution

For the detection of spear-phishing emails the proposed framework employs, multi layer detection approach. The framework uses a combination of machine learning and rule based detection techniques customized to detect the identified characteristics of spear-phishing emails. A schematic overview of our analysis framework is depicted in Fig. 1. The proposed framework have following sub modules.

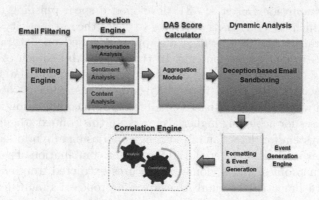

Fig. 1. Over all system block diagram

1. **Filtering Engine:** The main purpose of the filtering engine is to reduce the number of emails processed by the analysis engine. This is done by sifting out emails which are not having any embedded URL in its contents or not having any attachment. Only emails with either embedded URLs or the attachments are used as an input for detection engines.

2. **Detection Engine:** Filtered emails are further processed by multiple layers of detection engines. The proposed detection engine process every emails from 1) Impersonation analysis engine, 2) Sentiment analysis engine & 3) content analysis engine. These engines apply different detection techniques on content, header & attachment of the email and allocates a suspicion score based upon their analysis.

3. **DAS Score Calculator:** Based upon the scores allocated by detection engines in the previous step, a cumulative score is calculated for each email. We have named this cumulative score as Directed Anomaly Score(DAS). The emails with a higher DAS score are more likely to be malicious. Based upon this DAS score the emails are ordered and passed to the next stage.

4. **Dynamic Analysis:** As the business emails are crucial in maintaining the business process flow, therefore any false positive in email detection could leads to serious consequences. Hence a second layer of check is performed on the emails that have allocated high DAS score. We have created a customised sandbox named deception-sandbox for this purpose. The deception sandbox uses deception technology along with normal sand-boxing for analysis of URLs & attachments. The use of deception in conventional sand-boxing is a novel idea. The use of deception technology helps to optimise detection of activities such as credential harvesting, privilege escalation and lateral movement. The deception-sandbox system consists of a custom build cuckoo sandbox which is loaded with data capturing tools and deception elements. The use of deception elements such as honey-tokens, honey files, beacons and traps in sandbox is a novel idea proposed in this paper which makes deception-sandbox unique. Once the list of emails with high DAS score is received, dynamic analysis engine creates a sub-list based upon a cut-off value. This cut-off is selected biased upon the processing capability of deception-sandbox. The Emails with higher DAS score are prioritised and are processed first by deception-sandbox. Artifacts generated during the sandbox execution are collected and forwarded to the Event generation engine.

5. **Event Generation Engine:** The data generated and captured during deception-sandbox analysis is given as an input to the event generation engine. The event generation engine models the data as events. An event consists of attributes and objects. An objects further is a group of attributes which have a common context. The modeling is done in a way which enables the effective correlation based upon the key common attributes.

6. **Correlation Engine:** The correlation engine uses MISP Framework [47] for data enrichment and correlation. It not only performs automatic event correlation and enrichment but also provides users a platform for manually validating and cross-checking a correlated pattern of malicious events before declaring it as a possible attack campaign. The idea behind our approach is to collect alerts from various entities across the deception sandbox including deception elements and correlate them. The objective of correlation engine is to generate attack pattern and look for similarity among attack patterns.

5 Detection Engines

Filtered emails acts as an input to the Detection Engines. The proposed Detection module consists of multiple layers of detection engines. These layers access the email using underlying detection technique and allocates a score. The details of each such detection engine is as follows:

5.1 Impersonation Analysis Engine

Impersonation is one of the key characteristics of spear-phishing emails as it is a tool used by attackers to build trust. Although to counter email spoofing attacks, security standards such as SPF, DKIM & DMARC [10,28,29] have been laid but the adoption rate of these standards are far from satisfactory [1]. Also by conducting attacks such as a "cocktail joint attack" [27], an attacker can make a spoofing email completely bypass all these security protocols. Therefore one could not completely rely on theses measures for spoofed email detection. Hence the proposed detection framework employs a combination of a rule-based and an anomaly based detection for impersonation analysis. The framework segregates emails that are received from external domains from the one that are generated internally. Rule based detection engine processes emails received from external domains through 19 rules created by us. These rules checks email headers for various anomalies mentioned in literature [27,42]. The Table 1 shows the brief description of rules (R1 to R19) that are used by the detection engine. Anomaly based detection engine processes emails from organizational senders only. The anomaly based detection engine is based on the assumption [16] that senders have

Table 1. Header analysis rules

R1	Domain miss-match in the "message ID:" header (along with its MX Record) with the "From:" header field	R11	Use of invisible characters (U+0000-U+001F, U+FF00-U+FFFF) and semantic characters (@,:,;,") in the Headers
R2	"Return-Path" header mismatch with the "From:" header field	R12	Date header mismatch with the Received field
R3	Inconsistency between "Mail From" and "From" headers	R13	Encoded string and truncated email addresses in the "Mail form "headers
R4	Empty "Mail From" header	R14	"Reply-To" header mismatch with the "From" header field
R5	Multiple "Mail From" Headers in the email	R15	"X-Distribution" if this field's value is bulk
R6	Multiple Email Addresses in the "Mail From" Headers	R16	No match of "X-Mailer" header with popular clients
R7	"Mail form "headers with parsing inconsistencies	R17	Presence of "Bcc "or "X-UIDL" headers.
R8	Use of non-existent subdomain	R18	DMARC Fail
R9	Use of"RIGHT-TO-LEFT OVERRIDE" character, U+202E in the "Mail From" Headers	R19	SPF Fail
R10	DKIM Fail		

Table 2. Data set for model creation

Total email accounts	65
Observation period	3 months
Total number of emails	89037
Mails sent with in the organizational domain	25,350
Average mails sent with in organization per account	390
Average mail per day sent with in organization per user	9

characteristic traits embedded in the structure of an email. The emails sent by user accounts belonging to organization are processed to model user profiles. To model the profiles we have considered features suggested by Hugo Gascon et al. [16]. In their work Gascon et al. have used 46 features comprising 13 behaviour, 22 composition and 11 transport features. Further, we have used the concept of prototypes introduced by Rieck. K. et al. [40]. Prototypes are representative of a population as they represent a group of instances having similar characteristics. Prototypes calculation methods used, involves a linear-time algorithm proposed by Gonzalez et al. [17] which provably determines a set of prototypes only twice as large as the optimal solution. Once we obtain the prototypes, we calculate the distance of every email with all its prototypes and based on the cumulative average distance the possibility of an email being spoofed or not is decided. For the selection of the threshold value we have performed calibration experiment. Table 2 shows the details of the data-set used during this experiment. The performance of the engine was evaluated using the metrics: precision and recall. During calibration we look for the threshold values that maximise precision of the developed model. This calibration has to be done for each user account (65 accounts) as every account has its own set of prototypes and threshold values. The maximum number of mails sent were 548 mails from AC13 account followed by AC23 (425) & AC56 (398). Figure 2 shows the precision graph against different threshold values for account no AC13, AC23 & AC56.

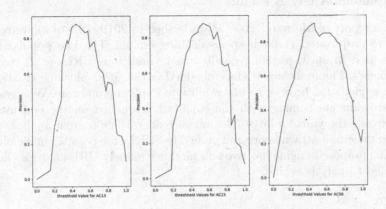

Fig. 2. Optimum threshold value

5.2   Sentiment Analysis Engine

Sentiment analysis engine processes the incoming email for sentiment reflected in its subject line or contents. One of the challenge in sentiment analysis is that, the people express their opinions in many complex ways and the presence of lexical content in text can give a more clear picture about the emotion involved. The words or short phrases are the building blocks of any sentiment expressed. Another aspect is to find the typical keywords to identify the sentiment reflected by them. One of the identified characteristics of spear-phishing email is the sentiment which reflects sense of urgency. The other side of the story is that not all the emails with such an intent are malicious. To curb this challenge we have referred the threat report of Symantec [44] in which it has published the popular lures with an intent of urgency (i.e. bill invoice, Email delivery failure, legal law enforcement, Scanned document, Package delivery etc.) used by spear-phishing attacks. For accessing an email we use these lures which reflect such sentiments and are popular among the attacker community. Ten classes of emotions mainly package delivery, legal law enforcement, scanned document, email delivery failed, joy, request, sad, payment, bill/invoice have been classified for all the emails. The proposed model banks on these identified lures to grade the emails. It is assumed that every email must have some probability of each sentiment. The proposed approach uses probabilistic modelling framework based on LDA (Latent Dirichlet Allocation) which detects sentiment and topic simultaneously from the text [37]. The idea is to associate a particular text (i.e. an input) to the corresponding sentiment (output). The model processes every email and tags it with multiple sentiments and their probability of occurrence. The one having the highest probability is considered as the most probable sentiment associated with an email. Unlike other machine learned based approaches for classification of sentiments which often require labelled corpora for classifier training, this model is fully unsupervised. Figure 3 showcases ROC curve for the chosen sentiments. Classifiers that give curves closer to the top-left corner like "email delivery failure", Bill, scanned document indicate a better performance.

5.3   Content Analysis Engine

As per a report of MalwareBytes [33] published in 2019, 79% of malware infections are propagated through spear-phishing emails. The two popular attack vectors used in spear-phishing emails are 1) malicious URLs & 2) malicious attachments. The malicious URLs embedded in the spear-phishing emails when clicked, exploits the browser's vulnerability to implant a malware. Whereas malicious attachments coming with the email when opened on the end user system, exploits the vulnerability of document readers. The content analysis engine assesses the email attachments and embedded URLs for possible malicious content. The proposed engine has two sub modules namely URL analysis engine & Attachment analysis engine.

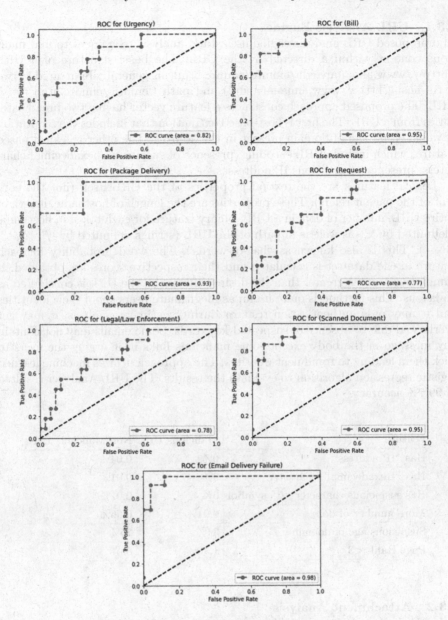

Fig. 3. ROC curve for various sentiments

5.3.1 URL Analysis Engine

The proposed URL analysis engine uses static analysis techniques to find malicious content within a directed by the URL. The basic structure of a URL ('http://www.annauniv.edu/emmrc/emmrc.html') is generally bifurcated in two parts host ('http://www.annauniv.edu') and path ('emmrc/emmrc.html') of a URL. The proposed approach constructs a feature vector having two broad categories from a URL. The first is host-based extraction that includes the reputation of website and age of domain present in the address. The other is lexical based features which include URL encoding, presence of suspicious/hexadecimal characters, presence of malicious IP addresses.

Lexical features are the textual properties of the URL itself (not the content of the page it refers). These properties are the length of hostname, length of entire URL, number of dots in a URL, binary feature for each token in hostname (delimited by '.') as well as in path of the URL (strings delimited by '/', '?', '.', '=','-'). This is also known as "bag-of-words". The word probability for each feature in the data-set is calculated and their respective scores are obtained. If cumulative score is greater than the desired threshold, the URL is considered as malicious. This method is quite useful as illegitimate users spoof their identities and it may pass authentication tests or during sentiment analysis, it may get overlooked due to absence of suspected keywords. Some emails may not contain any message in the body except some malicious links in it urging the users to click them leading to fraudulent websites. The approach utilizes machine learned logistic regression algorithm to evaluate the results. The URL Analyzer resulted in 99.7% accuracy.

Feature	Malicious Urls	Non-Malicious Urls
Has "IP address"	0%	0.04%
Has "Hexadecimal" character	0%	0.01%
Has suspicious character "@" symbol	0%	0.01%
More number of dots	0.01%	0.06%
Suspicious age of domain	34%	75%
Page Rank <3	1.30%	88%

5.3.2 Attachment Analysis

In its threat report Verizon [48] has reported that, 66% of malware were installed via malicious email attachments which includes back-doors, exploits, key-loggers, ransomware, downloaders, spyware etc. A lot of work has already been done to analyse malicious attachments. Attachment analysis adopts static analysis approach for the detection of malicious attachments. Different attachment types are handled in different ways. Initial filtering of attachments is done based upon a rule-based engine. These rules decide, what types of email attachments to allow and block on the mail server. A rule is composed of a) Attachment types to block, b) Action to be taken when a matching attachment is found and c) The users to which a rule applies. The first issue is addressed by looking for Executable attachments as they are the programs that launch immediately once the file is clicked. Running these programs enables the malware to take over. Usually executable files are considered quite suspicious and marked as malicious. The most common file types (like Word documents and PDF files) will not be blocked if they are attached in an archive file. For PDF document the approach followed is structure-based detection employed by PJScan [30]. This attachment analyzer utilizes a machine learning algorithm called a One-class Support Vector Machine (One-class SVM) to learn a model of malicious files to classify malicious & benign PDF files. This tool performs the lexical analysis of java script code embedded in the PDF files. The ultimate success of any learning-based approach mainly depends on the quality of data-set provided for training. For this purpose, we employ VIRUSTOTAL, which is a service allowing the users to scan suspicious documents through 70 antivirus engines. The data-set comprised of 10,324 PDF documents with a size of nearly 8 GB. To evaluate detection accuracy in our experiments, we have manually analyzed that among 883 benign files with JavaScript, we found 12 PDF documents that we believe have been incorrectly claimed as benign at Virus-Total. We trained our model with this data-set. Finally, when a total of PDF attachments of CDAC webmail server were passed through this analysis engine 510 files were discovered as malicious with an overall accuracy of 98%.

6   Aggregation Module

The above-mentioned detection engines label the emails with the score calculated by them. The labelled emails are further processed through deception-based sandbox. As sandbox analysis is a resource intensive and time-consuming process hence there is a need for a system which can prioritise emails based upon the degree of their maliciousness. The aggregation module is the module which implements the technique for selection of most suspicious emails form the corpus of the email labelled by detection engines. Each email is allocated an ID (i) and is represented as a feature vector.

$$E_i = (D_{i1}, D_{i2}, D_{i3}) \tag{1}$$

where D_1, D_2, D_3 represent scores allocated by the sentiment analysis, impersonation analysis, content analysis detection engines respectively. The input to the aggregation module is the feature matrix of size N × 3. Here N is the number of emails and column represents the score allocated by the respective detection engine. The aggregation module employs the algorithm devised by Ho, G. et al. [22] which they have named as Directed Anomaly Scoring (DAS). The Directed Anomaly Scoring or DAS algorithm ranks all emails by comparing how suspicious each email is in comparison to all other emails. Formally we consider email E_1 with feature vector $[D_{11}, D_{12}, D_{13}]$ to be at least as malicious as email E_2 with feature vector $[D_{21}, D_{22}, D_{23}]$ if $(D_{11} < D_{21}, D_{12} < D_{21}, D_{13} < D_{31})$. Based upon this comparison the DAS algorithm allocates an anomaly score to each email. The value of anomaly score allocated to each email lies within range of 0 to 1 with 1 being the most suspicious one. The aggregation module then arranges the emails with respect to the descending anomaly score allocated by the DAS algorithm. Once all the emails are sorted as per the anomaly score the dynamic analysis engine selects the N most suspicious emails, where N is the total budget of the dynamic analysis engine. Here the term 'budget'refers to the number of emails the dynamic analysis engine can process with the available resources and bandwidth in each cycle.

7   Dynamic Analysis Engine

The input to Dynamic analysis engine is the set of emails which are sorted based upon their DAS score. These emails are subsequently processed by the deception-based sandbox engine (Table 3).

Table 3. Honey entities along with their placement location

Honey entities	Type	Location and Value
Git Credentials	File	C:/Users//.gitconfig user.name= C:/Users//.gitconfig user.email=@xxx.com C:/Users//.gitconfig credential.helper=store
RDP Credentials	File	Default.rdp, is stored as a hidden file in My Documents
OpenVPN Scripts	File	C:\Program Files/OpenVPN/config
OpenVPN Scripts	File	/etc./openvpn/<filename.conf>
Network folder share	WCM	Windows credential manager entry
SSH Credentials	File	%HOMEDRIVE%%HOMEPATH%\.ssh\id_rsa.pub /home/<yourusername>/.ssh/id_rsa.pub
SSh PuTTY Credentials	Registry	HKCU\Software\SimonTatham\PuTTY\Sessions
MySQL Registry Entry	Registry	HKEY_LOCAL_MACHINE\SOFTWARE\odbc
MySQL server configuration	File	HKEY_CURRENT_USER\Software\Odbc\Odbc.ini\ Data sources /usr/local/etc./odbc.ini
pre-set web application MediaWiki	Cache	%systemroot%\System32\config\SECURITY
pre-set web application SugarCRM	Cache	%systemroot%\System32\config\SECURITY
pre-set web application phpMyAdmin	Cache	%systemroot%\System32\config\SECURITY
OneDrive	WCM	Windows credential manager
Homegroup	WCM	Windows Credential Manager
realVNC	Registry	HKEY_LOCAL_MACHINE\SOFTWARE\RealVNC- -\WinVNC4 /v
AWS S3 Bucket	File	Credential C:\Users\<USERNAME>\.aws\credentials Configuration: C:\Users\USERNAME \.aws\config
chrome credentials, Bookmarks, History	File	C:\Users\App Data\Local\Google\Chrome\- -User Data\Default

The input to Dynamic analysis engine is the set of emails which are sorted based upon their DAS score. These emails are subsequently processed by the deception-based sandbox engine. The behavioral analysis performed by deception-sandbox engine, on emails confirms the maliciousness based upon the malicious intent. Also, the artefacts captured during the dynamic analysis in the sandbox are used for the generation of Cyber threat intelligence. The deception sandbox framework is a comprehensive customized integrated system having deception elements portraying enterprise network I. T infrastructure and assets at the end user systems. The framework implements multiple layers of deception elements for interacting with the adversary at multiple levels of abstractions. The deception-based sandbox engine comprises of a customized cuckoo sandbox loaded with honey tokens, honey-files, honey-passwords, beacons and traps. These honey-entities are strategically placed in file system, system cache, registries and databases of the applications (i.e. web Browsers history, web-browser passwords database etc.). The honey-entities are strategically placed in the cuckoo sandbox file system, registry and memory to give the attacker an impression of real system with passwords, crypto wallets, confidential files and key system configuration files scattered across. The deception-sandbox also implants breadcrumbs which are synthetic credentials and passwords leading attacker to a decoy machine. On the cuckoo sandbox these breadcrumbs are placed in a natural manner such that they blend into the environment and do not raise suspicion. Each of these layers and deception elements serve as a deceptive lure aiding in the successful detection and capturing of attacker activity.

The events logged at each layer of the deception stack is collected, correlated, and analyzed. The logs collected during the sandbox analysis along with the alerts generated by deception elements are converted into generic events. These events along with their attributes are ingested into the event correlation engine. The correlation engine used in this project is the Open-source MISP (Malware Information Sharing Platform) platform. This platform enables sharing, storage and correlating IoCs of targeted attacks. Before submitting the events to the correlation engine, alerts are processed to do a first level filtering, augmentation with contextual informational and modelling them as per the requirement of the correlation engine.

8 Experiments and Results

We have tested our framework in the network of Centre for Development of Advanced computing (CDAC). The test deployment was done for six months duration. The email analysis engine was deployed in in-line mode with the local mail server. We hosted a POSTFIX mail server with DOVECOT on a virtual machine with 4 GB RAM and hard-disk 50 GB. The deployment duration was form 04-09-2019 to 04-03-2020 and during this duration we processed 150,000 emails. The filtering engine reduced this count to 68,000. These 68,000 emails were further processed through the detection engines where scores were allocated to the emails. Table 4 shows the results of sentiment analysis engine (Table 5).

During the analysis processes a total of 1,096 PDF documents were extracted as attachments and were analysed. Out of these 18 PDF documents were labelled as malicious. A total of 6000 zip and rar, RTF, word files were extracted as an attachment and were analysed, out of which 54 were flagged as malicious. More

Table 4. Sentiment analysis results

Key	Values
Sense of urgency	25%
Mail reply	22%
Information	21%
Request	17%
No label	10%
Greetings	5%

Table 5. Impersonation analysis

Key	Values
Mail Boxes	65
Mail received	68,000
Avg Mail per account	1450
Avg Mail received per day	2550
Avg Mail per day post filtering	1770
Avg Prototype per account	76

Table 6. Confusion matrix

		Actual diagnosis	
		Positive	Negative
Predicted	Positive	15	5
Behavior	Negative	2	450

Table 7. Accuracy result

Accuracy	$\frac{TP+TN}{Total}$	0.9851
Precision (P)	$\frac{TP}{TP+FP}$	0.75
Recall (R)	$\frac{TP}{TP+FN}$	0.882
F1-Score	$\frac{2*P*R}{P+R}$	0.8105

TP: True Positive, TN: True Negative,
FP: False Positive, FN: False Negative

than 15,000 URLS were extracted from the emails and URL analysis engine marked 178 URLS as malicious. Once the score from each detection engine was allocated to the email, the scores were normalized, and DAS score was calculated through aggregation engine. The email tagged with DAS score were sorted in descending order. To evaluate the effectiveness of the detection engine, we manually analysed the emails labelled malicious. Considering manual analysis as benchmark we calculated the true positives, false positives and accuracy of the system. Out of the 68,000 analysed emails we took a data for 3 days which was a total of 472 emails. These 472 mails were manually analysed by the team. Based upon the results of the manual analysis performed we have calculated confusion matrix as shown in Table 6, the precision and recall for the system and over all accuracy as shown in Table 7. Some of the cases detected by the spear-phishing email detection engine and were further confirmed using manual analysis are as follows.

8.1   Case I- Email ID 547

The email was received by one of the users in the purchase department. This email was having a legitimate source address and contained an purchase invoice file as Rich Text File (RTF) attachment. The impersonation analysis engine generated alert for violating the rule R1&R19. The attachment accompanied with the email targeted CVE-2017-0199 remote code execution vulnerability that allows it to exploit Object Linking and Embedding (OLE) interface of Microsoft Office to download a PE malware file. The malware downloaded post exploitation executes in the back-end and extracts 16 other executable files having bat, dll, exe file formats. Also it resolved "dfipha.mjkse.org" domain name and used HTTPS protocol for communication. Apart from extracting the information from system the malware generated large number of ARP scans to detect the network resources accessible from the local system. All these indicators were observed during the dynamic analysis of the email.

8.2   Case II-Security and Email ID 529

It was a forwarded email, having paper submission deadline information as the subject line. The email seemed to be legitimate and quite convincing as it has the conference details of an IEEE-Approved conference. The email was accompanied with a word document containing the details of the conference. Email was processed through our detection engines. The sentiment reflected by the email were reflecting a sense of urgency. The email id used seems to be a legitimate but anomaly detection engine generated an alert for this email. The content analysis engine flagged the word file attached with the email as malicious. Based upon the inputs of the detection engines the 0.079 DAS score was calculated. During the sandbox analysis of the email it was discovered that the word document exploits the CVE-2012-0158 vulnerability. It further downloaded a malicious HTA file and a PE file. The downloaded HTA file is launched automatically and executes the dropped PE file. The credential harvesting malware Pony was used in the attack. The malware searches for the crypto currency wallets and VPN passwords. While searching for the crypto currency wallets it hits our honey wallets which immediately generated alert.

8.3   Case III - Email ID 347

Another case detected, was an email that claims to be sent from a well known bank. In the mail, bank congratulated the customer and offered a credit of some amount as the loyalty benefit. The content of the email were very legitimate, reflecting sense of urgency and convincing the reader to click an embedded URL. The anomaly Score of this email was close to 0.081. The URL embedded in the email was a short-lived URL claiming to be from a banking website. The SPF status of the email was fail. The static analysis of the URL marked the URL as malicious. This URL once sent to the sandbox executes an malicious JavaScript.

8.4   Case IV - Email ID 448

Attacker impersonated as HR head and asked the employees to immediately upload personal details on web page the URL of which was embedded in the email. The spear-phishing email detection engine evaluated the email and calculated a DAS score of 0.080 because the URL redirects the user to a fake phishing website with fake login page.

9   Conclusion and Future Work

In this paper, we have presented a multi layered detection approach for the detection of spear-phishing attacks. In the proposed approach we introduced the idea of using deception as a tool while performing sandbox analysis of the spear-phishing emails. The deception-based sandbox employs honey entities which when strategically placed in sandbox environment increases the degree of interaction thus, improving the value and volume of the data captured by the sandbox engine. Such a system not only helps in the detection of spear-phishing email but also aids in the mitigation of related threat. In future we would work towards reducing the latency and improving the accuracy of the developed detection engines.

References

1. 250ok: Global dmarc adoption (2019). https://s3.amazonaws.com/250ok-wordpress/wp-content/uploads/2019/07/09140509/Global-DMARC-Adoption-2019.pdf
2. Abu-Nimeh, S., Nappa, D., Wang, X., Nair, S.: A comparison of machine learning techniques for phishing detection (2007)
3. Agten, P., Joosen, W., Piessens, F., Nikiforakis, N.: Seven months' worth of mistakes: a longitudinal study of typosquatting abuse. In: Proceedings of the 22nd Network and Distributed System Security Symposium (NDSS 2015). Internet Society (2015)
4. ieter Arntz: Lemonduck no longer settles for breadcrumbs (2021). https://blog.malwarebytes.com/botnets/2021/07/lemonduck-no-longer-settles-for-breadcrumbs/
5. BARRACUDA: Spear phishing:top threats and trends (2019). https://assets.barracuda.com/assets/docs/dms/Spear_Phishing_Top_Threats_and_Trends.pdf
6. Chandrasekaran, M., Narayanan, K., Upadhyaya, S.: Phishing email detection based on structural properties (2006)
7. Chen, J., Guo, C.: Online detection and prevention of phishing attacks. In: 2006 First International Conference on Communications and Networking in China, pp. 1–7 (2006)
8. Chhabra, S., Aggarwal, A., Benevenuto, F., Kumaraguru, P.: Phi.sh/$oCiaL: the phishing landscape through short URLs (2011)
9. Cimpanu, C.: Spear-phishing campaign compromises executives at 150+ companies (2020). https://www.zdnet.com/article/spear-phishing-campaign-compromises-executives-at-150-companies/
10. Crocker, D., Hansen, T., Kucherawy, M.: Domainkeys identified mail (DKIM) signatures (2011)
11. Dewan, P., Kashyap, A., Kumaraguru, P.: Analyzing social and stylometric features to identify spear phishing emails (2014)
12. Duman, S., Kalkan-Cakmakci, K., Egele, M., Robertson, W., Kirda, E.: Email-profiler: Spearphishing filtering with header and stylometric features of emails. In: 2016 IEEE 40th Annual Computer Software and Applications Conference (COMPSAC), vol. 1, pp. 408–416. IEEE (2016)

13. MFPS Firm: Global Energy Cyberattacks: Night Dragon. McAfee, Incorporated (2011)
14. Fishbein, N., Robinson, R.: Global phishing campaign targets energy sector and its suppliers (2021). https://www.intezer.com/blog/research/global-phishing-campaign-targets-energy-sector-and-its-suppliers/
15. Garera, S., Provos, N., Chew, M., Rubin, A.D.: A framework for detection and measurement of phishing attacks. In: Proceedings of the 2007 ACM workshop on Recurring malcode, pp. 1–8 (2007)
16. Gascon, H., Ullrich, S., Stritter, B., Rieck, K.: Reading between the lines: content-agnostic detection of spear-phishing emails. In: Bailey, M., Holz, T., Stamatogiannakis, M., Ioannidis, S. (eds.) RAID 2018. LNCS, vol. 11050, pp. 69–91. Springer, Cham (2018). https://doi.org/10.1007/978-3-030-00470-5_4
17. Gonzalez, T.F.: Clustering to minimize the maximum intercluster distance. Theor. Comput. Sci. **38**, 293–306 (1985)
18. Granger, S.: Social engineering fundamentals, part I: hacker tactics. Secur. Focus **18** (2001)
19. Hacquebord, F.: Pawn storm in 2019 (2019)
20. Hamid, I.R.A., Abawajy, J., Kim, T.: Using feature selection and classification scheme for automating phishing email detection (2013)
21. Han, K., Wang, Y., Tian, Q., Guo, J., Xu, C., Xu, C.: GhostNet: more features from cheap operations. In: 2020 IEEE/CVF Conference on Computer Vision and Pattern Recognition (CVPR), pp. 1577–1586 (2020)
22. Ho, G., Sharma, A., Javed, M., Paxson, V., Wagner, D.: Detecting credential spearphishing attacks in enterprise settings. In: Proceedings of the 26th USENIX Conference on Security Symposium, pp. 469–485. SEC 2017, USENIX Association, USA (2017)
23. Ho, G., Sharma, A., Javed, M., Paxson, V., Wagner, D.: Detecting credential spearphishing in enterprise settings (2017)
24. HOSTINGTRIBUNAL: 7+ stunningly scary phishing statistics- an ever-growing threat (2020). https://hostingtribunal.com/blog/phishing-statistics/#gref
25. Islam, R., Abawajy., J.: A multi-tier phishing detection and filtering approach (2013)
26. Jakobsson, M., Myers, S.: Phishing and Countermeasures: Understanding the Increasing Problem of Electronic Identity Theft. Wiley-Interscience, USA (2006)
27. Shen, K., et al.: Weak links in authentication chains: a large-scale analysis of email sender spoofing attacks. In: 30th USENIX Security Symposium (USENIX Security 21). USENIX Association, Vancouver, B.C., August 2021. https://www.usenix.org/conference/usenixsecurity21/presentation/shen-kaiwen
28. Kitterman, S.: Sender policy framework (SPF) for authorizing use of domains in email, version 1 (2014)
29. Kucherawy, M., Zwicky, E.: Domain-based message authentication, reporting, and conformance (DMARC) (2015)
30. Laskov, P.: Static detection of malicious javascript-bearing pdf documents (2011)
31. Lin, E., Aycock, J., Mannan, M.: Lightweight client-side methods for detecting email forgery. In: Lee, D.H., Yung, M. (eds.) WISA 2012. LNCS, vol. 7690, pp. 254–269. Springer, Heidelberg (2012). https://doi.org/10.1007/978-3-642-35416-8_18
32. Ma, L., Ofoghi, B., Watters, P., Brown, S.: Detecting phishing emails using hybrid features (2009)

33. MalwareBytesLabs: 2019 state of malware. (2019). https://resources. malwarebytes.com/files/2019/01/Malwarebytes-Labs-2019-State-of-Malware-Report-2.pdf

34. McClure, S., et al.: Protecting your critical assets-lessons learned from operation aurora (2010) ‹

35. Montalbano, E.: Email campaign spreads strrat fake-ransomware rat (2021). https://threatpost.com/email-campaign-fake-ransomware-rat/166378/

36. NSCS: Advisory: Apt29 targets COVID-19 vaccine development (2020). https://www.ncsc.gov.uk/files/Advisory-APT29-targets-COVID-19-vaccine-development.pdf

37. Onan, A., Korukoglu, S., Bulut, H.: LDA-based topic modelling in text sentiment classification: an empirical analysis. Int. J. Comput. Linguist. Appl. **7**(1), 101–119 (2016)

38. Paganini, P.: New intel security study shows that 97% of people can't identify phishing emails (2015). http://securityaffairs.co/wordpress/36922/cyber-crime/study-phishing-emails-response.html

39. Point, P.: Cyber security predictions 2017 (2016). https://www.proofpoint.com/us/threat-insight/post/cybersecurity-predictions-2017

40. Rieck, K., Trinius, P., Willems, C., Holz, T.: Automatic analysis of malware behavior using machine learning. J. Comput. Secur. **19**(4), 639–668 (2011)

41. Sheng, Y., Rong, J., Xiang, W.: Simulation of the users' email behavior based on BP-BDI model. In: 2015 International Conference on Cyber-Enabled Distributed Computing and Knowledge Discovery, pp. 16–22 (2015)

42. Shukla, S., Misra, M., Varshney, G.: Identification of spoofed emails by applying email forensics and memory forensics. In: 2020 the 10th International Conference on Communication and Network Security, pp. 109–114 (2020)

43. Stringhini, G., Thonnard, O.: That ain't you: blocking spearphishing through behavioral modelling. In: Almgren, M., Gulisano, V., Maggi, F. (eds.) DIMVA 2015. LNCS, vol. 9148, pp. 78–97. Springer, Cham (2015). https://doi.org/10.1007/978-3-319-20550-2_5

44. Symantec: Internet security threat report 2019 (2019). https://docs.broadcom.com/docs/istr-24-2019-en

45. Toolan, F., Carthy, J.: Feature selection for spam and phishing detection. In: 2010 eCrime Researchers Summit, pp. 1–12. IEEE (2010)

46. APT TrendLabsSM: Spear-phishing email: Most favored apt attack bait

47. Vandeplas, C.: Misp - open source threat intelligence platform & open standards for threat information sharing (2020). https://www.misp-project.org/

48. Verizon: Databreach investigation report 2017 (2017). http://www.verizonenterprise.com/verizon-insights-lab/data-breach-digest/2017/

Vulnerability Analysis and Detection Using Graph Neural Networks for Android Operating System

G. Renjith[✉] and S. Aji

Department of Computer Science, University of Kerala, Thiruvananthapuram,
Kerala, India
{renjithg,aji}@keralauniversity.ac.in

Abstract. Android operating system approximately contains around 93 million lines of code, mainly consisting of C, C++ and Java languages. There is no strict software engineering life-cycle followed during Android software development, and hence the design flaws and vulnerabilities are largely reported. Rising security attacks targeting Android manifests the importance of early detection of vulnerabilities in Android operating system. The existing mechanisms either focus on Android Apps or short code differences of the Android framework, and hence they are less effective for Android operating system. In this work, we extracted all the officially reported publicly accessible Android Java vulnerabilities in application and framework layers from 2015 till June 2021. The extracted vulnerable and corresponding fixed (secure) code are then converted into the graphical form using different intermediate graph representations, and then graph features are extracted. Vectorization techniques are used for converting node features of the graph into numerical formats. A vulnerability detection mechanism based on Graph Neural Network is designed and achieved an F1-score of 0.92. To the best of our knowledge, this will be one of the first works for Android operating system source code vulnerability detection technique exploiting the potential of Graph Neural Networks.

Keywords: Android operating system · Vulnerability analysis ·
Vulnerability detection · Graph neural networks · Intermediate graph

1 Introduction

Android is the most widely used multi-featured and multi-domain embedded operating system. Android Open Source Project (AOSP) [27] consists of an amalgamation of multiple programming languages. There are around 2.5 billion Android activated devices in the market. Apart from running in smartphones and tablets, Android is also widely deployed in other embedded domains like cameras, wearables, home appliances, IoT, Automotive etc. Attacks targeting Android operating system are increasing day by day, which proves the inefficiency of existing vulnerability detection and malware detection techniques. Hence it

© Springer Nature Switzerland AG 2021
S. Tripathy et al. (Eds.): ICISS 2021, LNCS 13146, pp. 57–72, 2021.
https://doi.org/10.1007/978-3-030-92571-0_4

is very important to have an efficient vulnerability detection engine to early detect the AOSP source code vulnerabilities so that all the impending risks and losses due to malware attacks could be reduced. Early detection of vulnerabilities during the software development stage itself safeguards the Android devices more efficiently from exploiting the vulnerabilities by the attackers.

In this work a deeper analysis of the vulnerability trends in the Android operating system has been done. The statistics presented depicts the current trend of all the publicly accessible vulnerabilities in Android operating system from 2015 to April 2021. Figure 1, represents the vulnerability type and year-wise distribution of vulnerabilities. From the statistical analysis of vulnerability types, it is found that Escalation of Privilege (EoP) is the most common vulnerability type present, followed by Information Disclosure (ID). The least common type of vulnerability is Denial of Service (DoS), followed by Remote Code Execution (RCE). A significant number of vulnerabilities reported do not have enough of meta-data associated with it to determine its type, and hence they are labeled as Not-Specified for now. In the year-wise distribution analysis, we have observed that, more than 30% of the vulnerabilities are reported post-2018 targeting the newer versions of Android. None of the vulnerabilities reported in 2020 and 2021 affects Android version 6 and 7. In the severity wise analysis captured in Fig. 2, we have observed that most of the vulnerabilities reported are categorized into High severity, followed by Critical severity vulnerabilities. Reported vulnerabilities with moderate and low severities are less. The existing Android operating system vulnerability detection mechanisms are found to be not effective because of less considerations of the following aspects.

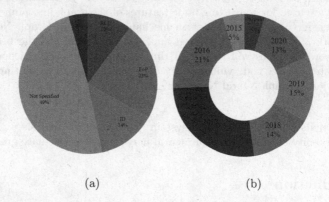

(a)   (b)

Fig. 1. (a) Vulnerability types. (b) Year-wise distribution of vulnerabilities

Android operating system and Android Apps have two entirely different prospects in terms of their functionality. The vulnerabilities in the Android OS source code are much less explored in the literature compared to vulnerabilities in Android Apps. This can mostly be due to the complexity of the heavy Android OS source tree. Since the Android applications (APKs) are packaged

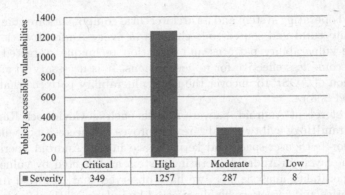

■ Severity	Critical	High	Moderate	Low
	349	1257	287	8

Fig. 2. Severity-wise distribution of publicly accessible vulnerabilities

only with uniform and limited intermediate byte code files, it is fairly easy to design vulnerability analysis systems that accepts the intermediate byte codes and then convert into feature vectors. However, Android OS contains diverse and huge number of raw source code files from C, C++ and Java languages, it is not that easy to design systems that directly accept and convert into intermediate graph format and feature vectors from those raw source codes. Hence designing a system that can directly analyse the Android OS source code and vulnerabilities is important.

In order to analyse the source code, a proper intermediate representation is very much essential. Only limited information could be represented using individual intermediate graph structures, like Control Flow Graph (CFG), Control Dependence Graph (CDG) and Data Dependence Graph (DDG). The combined graphical representations like Program Dependence Graph (PDG), Code Property Graph (CPG) allow different combinations of information available in a single graph and are proved to be much effective. Hence designing a system which processes the rich intermediate graphs is very important.

Synthetic vulnerable program suites available in OWASP Benchmark project [30] are developed by domain experts and can be easily analysed and converted to intermediate graph representations and can be directly given as input to deep learning based vulnerability detection engines. The major limitation of these detection engines is that, they cannot be directly applicable to real-world vulnerable programs such as Android operating system source code because of the irregular nature of the real-world vulnerable programs. Hence the neural networks designed for synthetic vulnerable programs will fail to detect the actual behavior of real-world vulnerable programs.

Analysis of the short code differences for a vulnerability will not give the actual context of the vulnerability and hence it will be less effective if we design a vulnerability detection. For a more reliable design, we should consider the vulnerable code fragment and its corresponding fixed code at least the function or class level to get the actual context and behavioral difference of the vulnerability. This will help the neural network to properly capture the actual behavior of the vulnerability patterns.

Android operating system and its architectural components are going through many architectural and source code changes in every Android version release. Hence, the vulnerability patterns and detection techniques targeted for older versions become less effective for newer versions. It is necessary to analyse the latest version of AOSP to uncover the new vulnerability patterns that may not have existed before.

The most recent Android malware attacks such as CovidLock Ransomware [28] and StrandHogg evil twin malware [29] proves the necessity of vulnerability detection for both user-space and kernel-space in the Android operating system. All the layers in Android operating system are affected by vulnerabilities. In our vulnerability analysis step, we have observed that, Android framework, native libraries and kernel are highly affected by vulnerabilities but the Android Runtime (ART) and HAL layers reported less number of the vulnerabilities. A layer-wise vulnerability analysis and detection would be necessary because of the distribution of different programming languages in different layers in AOSP.

In the proposed work, we have tried to properly consider all these important aspects. We have taken the latest Android 11 & 12 operating system versions and conducted a comprehensive vulnerable source code analysis. The code is then converted to rich intermediate graph formats for Application and Framework layer vulnerabilities. We designed a graph neural network based vulnerability detection engine. We have obtained an F1-score of 0.92 with 10-fold cross-validation in the experiments with more than 1600 vulnerable samples.

Section 2 provides the study on related works in vulnerability analysis and detection in Android. The proposed method is discussed in Sect. 3. Section 4 describes the performance evaluation carried out to measure the effectiveness of our proposed method. Finally Sect. 5 concludes our work by giving an insight towards the future work.

2   Literature Review

Some of the techniques used for vulnerability detection for Android are based on Android Apps (APKs) and not directly on the source code; hence they are not suitable for vulnerability detection for AOSP source code. In [1], where the dataset of APKs were taken from various app stores and corresponding APK byte code is analysed. In [2], static analysis is done on APKs by reverse engineering to obtain its intermediate code. Both techniques are not applicable to the Android OS vulnerability analysis and detection.

Till date there are only two notable literature that targeted the Android operating system source code vulnerabilities. Both these papers only conducted an in-depth vulnerability analysis of existing vulnerabilities in Android and defined the major vulnerability patterns and coding mistakes that lead to a vulnerability. Neither of two define a system for the detection of vulnerabilities in Android OS. In [3], conducted an analysis on vulnerabilities reported up to November 2016 from Android Security Bulletin. These vulnerabilities were analysed manually, which may cause the results to be unreliable as it was prone to human error, furthermore the authors were not able to determine the type of some of the vulnerabilities during manual analysis and hence these had to be excluded from some of the results. In [4], conducted a more in-depth study on vulnerabilities reported up to June 2018 from Android Security Bulletin [13] using an automated approach for extraction and analysis of the vulnerabilities. They extracted the short code differences from the patch files and used a clustering algorithm to reveal vulnerability patterns. The drawback to this approach is, they have only analysed the vulnerabilities which have short code differences; hence a major portion of the vulnerabilities having longer code differences were not considered for the pattern generation algorithm. Both these papers only considered the publicly accessible vulnerabilities.

In [5], the source code of synthetic vulnerable programs (OWASP Benchmark Project) [30] are taken for analysis are represented as multiple types of graphs such as AST, CFG, DDG and CDG. They have not considered other rich intermediate graphs. Their detection mechanism based on graph neural networks is not validated in any real-world vulnerable programs. [6] uses AST representation of vulnerable source code, which is then converted to a complete binary AST by inserting null nodes at each level to make them complete, which leads to the unwanted increase of the size of the binary tree and also leads to many zero values when converting to an array. In [7], dynamic behavior features of source code are extracted by first classifying the source code into a set of behaviors such as file operation, network operation, registry, hooking etc., and the API calls related to each of these behaviors are identified and analyzed. The API call sequences are vectorized and passed to the Neural Network model for training, and based on these features, vulnerability is detected. A drawback of this method is that all the different behaviors should have a certain API sequence associated with them. Apart from these, other literature such as [8–12] also use intermediate graph representation techniques for converting vulnerable code but none of these proposed systems focused on AOSP source code.

Although there are many literature over the years for vulnerability detection, there are only two papers that focuses on source code of AOSP for vulnerability analysis till 2018. This paper will be a unique attempt in this sense as we propose a mechanism for vulnerability analysis and detection using Deep Learning techniques exclusively for the AOSP source code vulnerabilities from 2015 till June 2021.

3   Proposed Methodology

The overall work-flow of our proposed vulnerability analysis and detection mechanism is presented in Fig. 3. The first step is the extraction of vulnerabilities from the Android Security Bulletin [13]. We then analyse the patches provided for the vulnerabilities to identify the vulnerable code segment and its corresponding fixed code segment. The extracted code segments can then be converted to various intermediate graph representations such as AST, CFG, PDG, CPG. These intermediate graphs are then vectorized and converted to matrices in a format

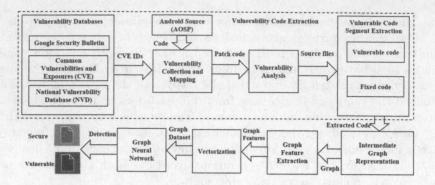

Fig. 3. Proposed vulnerability detection framework

that are supported for graph neural networks. The graph data of both vulnerable and corresponding fixed code are used to train the Graph Neural Networks so that it can identify the vulnerabilities in new pieces of code.

3.1 Vulnerability Code Extraction

Google releases monthly Android Security Bulletin, which reports a list of security vulnerabilities that affect the Android operating system and also updates the security patches in order to fix these issues. Vendors partnered with Android are notified at least a month before this list is made public. The vulnerabilities are solved in the Android Open Source Project (AOSP) repository, and the hyperlinks to the patch (actual code differences) are updated in the bulletin.

We manually extract the vulnerabilities corresponding to the CVE ID from the monthly Android Security Bulletin. After that the CVE ID is used to extract additional metadata about the same vulnerability from CVE [14] and NVD [15] websites. As a crucial step, each of these extracted vulnerabilities are manually analysed and then categorized according to various factors such as vulnerability type, affected Android versions, severity type, design aspects and corresponding software architecture layer it belongs to etc. We need to process the extracted vulnerabilities to obtain both its vulnerable code sections and its corresponding fixed code. To do this, we make use of the patch links provided for the vulnerabilities in the Android Security Bulletin; we analyse the patches differences in the code to identify the vulnerable code segment at a function level. The patch also contains the before and after fix versions of the vulnerable files that are changed; using this, we can manually create the code snippets at the function level that contain the vulnerable code and corresponding fixed code in separate files along with their enclosing class. Detailed analysis of the code snippets instead of just the patch differences provide better context about the vulnerability, and it is also easier to represent such function level code snippets as an intermediate graph.

3.2 Intermediate Graph Representation

Abstract Syntax Tree (AST) is a graph representation of source code written in any programming language by the structure of its syntax in the form of a tree. Each node in the tree denotes a statement or line of code that occur in a program source [16]. The AST does not represent the actual syntax or statement; but instead, it denotes its structure and hence becomes 'abstract'.

Control Flow Graph (CFG) is a graph representation of all paths through which the flow of control will pass through the program when it is executed. In a CFG, each node denotes a basic statement or line of code. Directed edges are used to denote the flow control from one node to another.

Program Dependence Graph (PDG) [18] combines both the data dependencies and the control dependencies of each operation in a program. Data dependencies denote the relevant relationships of data flow in a program. Control dependences denote the essential flow of control relationships of a program.

Code Property Graph (CPG) is a combination of three different graph representations of source code, namely the abstract syntax trees, control flow graphs and program dependence graphs [19]. In CPG, distinct program graph representations are merged into a single property graph that contains the information about the syntax, control and intra-procedural data flow of the program. CPG was first introduced in [12] as a graph representation for vulnerability discovery of C code and in the Linux kernel.

3.3 Feature Extraction

The actual graph data such as adjacency matrix, node attributes, edge attributes, graph indicator, graph label and graph list are extracted from the intermediate graphs using a parser program developed by us. The node attributes in our case are the code present in each line which is represented as nodes. By default, node attributes are in textual format, and hence these must be formatted to vectors by replacing each word with a numerical value using any vectorization methods such as TF-IDF and Doc2Vec.

TF-IDF [21] is a statistical measure that evaluates the relevance of a word to a document in a collection of documents. This is obtained by finding the product of the frequency of appearance of the word in a document and the inverse document frequency of the word across a set of input documents.

Doc2Vec [22] is a generalized form of Word2Vec [23] and is also a popular tool used in NLP for the vectorization of documents. The objective of Doc2Vec is to represent a document by its numerical value, regardless of its length. Doc2Vec is an enhanced version of the Word2Vec algorithm. Larger blocks of text such as sentences, paragraphs and entire documents are learned in an unsupervised manner in this algorithm.

3.4   Graph Neural Network

Neural network architectures specially designed for graph structured data namely Graph Convolution Network (GCN) and Graph Attention Network (GAT) are used in this work.

$$V^{(l+1)} = F(V^{(l)}, A) \tag{1}$$

The V^l represents the vertex attributes of the lth layer of the network, A represents the adjacency matrix which is represented as edge index. $F()$ is a nonlinear function. The output feature matrix at the last layer of the network is basically used for the node level prediction; graph-level predictions is introduced by adding some form of operation which performs the pooling, which is mostly summation, average, mean etc. [5].

Graph Convolution Network. GCN [25] performs the convolution as a function that integrates the normalized sum of node attributes at a distance of one-hop from the node. The function is performed on all nodes.

$$V_i^l = R\left(\sum_{j \in N(i)} \frac{1}{C_{ij}} W^{(l)} V_j^{(l)}\right) \tag{2}$$

$$C_{ij} = \sqrt{|N(i)|}\sqrt{|N(j)|} \tag{3}$$

Where V_i^l is the feature tensor for the ith unit of the lth layer of the GCN. $N(i)$ is the set of nodes which comes under the radius of one-hop distance for i^{th} unit in the layer. C_{ij} is a normalization factor. W^l is a weight matrix for units of the lth layer of the GCN, and $R()$ is the Relu non-linear activation function. A learnable weight matrix is used by each node to compute the embedding of the nodes at a one-hop distance. The embeddings contain the information of the relationship between each node in a graph, so these are passed to the next layer. The output from the GCN layer is then passed to the dense layer which is basically a feed-forward layer whose output is passed to the SoftMax layer to give probability of prediction [5]. The loss is calculated by comparing the output from SoftMax layer and the actual output by the defined loss function also known as cost function. The loss is propagated back to the GCN layers by the back-propagation method. Thus, the weights of the layers are modified to reduce the loss.

Graph Attention Network. GAT [24] is similar to the GCN but has an attention score between the units of GNN. The propagation equation consists of the attention score of the unit instead of the normalization present in GCN.

$$V^{(l+1)} = R\left(\sum_{j \in N(i)} \alpha_{ij} W^{(l)} V_j^{(l)}\right) \tag{4}$$

$$\alpha_{ij}{}^{(l)} = SoftMax_{(i)} \left(e_{ij}^{(l)} \right) = \frac{\exp^{(e_{ij}^{(l)})}}{\sum_{j \in N(i)} \exp^{(e_{ij}^{(l)})}} \tag{5}$$

$$e_{ij}{}^{(l)} = Leaky\_Relu \left(\overrightarrow{a}^{(l)^T} . [W^{(l)} V_i^{(l)} \| W^{(l)} V_j^{(l)}] \right) \tag{6}$$

α_{ij}^l is the normalized attention score between i^{th} unit from the lth layer and its jth neighboring unit, computed by applying a SoftMax on un-normalized pairwise attention score e_{ij}, and e_{ij} is computed by first concatenating the linear transformations of previous feature embeddings. $\overrightarrow{a}$ is the learnable weight vector for updating the attention score between i^{th} and j^{th} node in l^{th} layer. GAT is enhanced with the capacity and expressiveness through multi-head additive attention technique incorporated in the model compared to GCN, but the model compromises on the time taken for training and training convergence on the other hand.

3.5 Proposed GNN Architecture for Vulnerability Detection

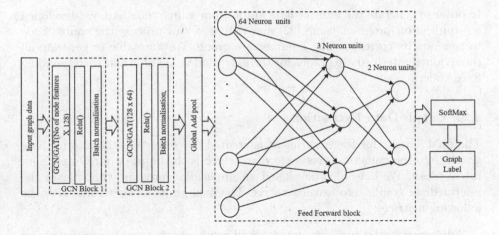

Fig. 4. Proposed GNN architecture for vulnerability detection

The proposed architecture of graph neural network for vulnerability detection is given in Fig. 4. The GNN accepts the extracted input graph data such as edge indices, node attributes and the batch information for predicting the graph label as output. In the architecture, there are two GCN blocks, a global add pool block, one feed forward block and a SoftMax block.

The first block consists of a GCN layer, ReLU function and a batch normalization function. The GCN layer consists of 128 units, it performs the feature expansion of the node feature matrix and the aggregation of the node features. The output of the GCN layer is passed to the ReLU which activates the neuron units that has values greater than zero. The output of the ReLU is passed to Batch Normalization which performs the similar function of the normalization and also helps to stabilize the network and increasing the converging speed. The output from first GCN block is passed to second GCN block.

The second GCN block is similar to first block and it performs node feature dimension reduction which consist of 64 units. The output from the second GCN block is pooled using global add pool which integrates the node feature map of each graph in the batch and then given to a feed forward block. The feed forward block consists of an input layer with 64 units, a hidden layer with 3 units and an output layer with 2 units. The output of feed forward layer is given to Softmax block which converts the feature map into probability. The output is calculated by finding the label which has the highest probability value from the softmax output. The GAT architecture and flow are exactly similar to the GCN architecture, except GCN blocks are replaced with GAT blocks.

4   Results and Discussion

4.1   Intermediate Graph Representation

In order to generate the intermediate graph from source code files, we developed an application program using [32] and [33] that can process the source code to generate its corresponding intermediate graph. We were able to generate all the required intermediate graphs for the extracted vulnerable and corresponding fixed code.

4.2   Graph Data Extraction

The final dataset for the experiment is created by converting the intermediate graphs into the numerical vectors format, which is the input of our Graph Neural Network. We have also developed an application program that parses the intermediate graphs into feature matrix. The final graph dataset consists of the following matrices:

- Adjacency matrix contains matrix for all subgraphs denoted by the 'from' and 'to' nodes. Each row specifies an edge of the graph, with the first value denoting the 'from' node and the second value denoting the 'to' node separated by a comma.
- Edge attributes contains the weight of each edge specified in the adjacency matrix. The weight value specified at each line corresponds to the edge denoted at the same line in the adjacency matrix. The normal edges have a weight of 0, edges that have a true or false control flow will have a weight of +1 or −1, respectively.
- Graph indicator shows to which graph or subgraph each of the listed node belongs to. Each row represents a node in the graph, and the corresponding value at each line represents the ID of the graph that contains that node.

- Graph labels contains a specific label for each subgraph so that it can be differentiated based on some category or attribute.
- Graph list contains the name of the graph for a corresponding source code; if source code contains multiple graphs, then each name is listed.
- Node attributes represents the textual information as each node represents each line of code in the input code snippet. This is converted to numerical feature vectors by TF-IDF and Doc2Vec64 vectorization techniques using a program developed by us utilizing TfidfVectorizer [26] and Gensim [17] packages.

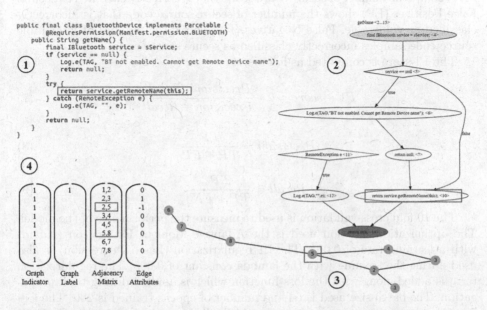

Fig. 5. Example walk-through of vulnerability ID CVE-2018-9432 of Type "EOP" (Color figure online)

The Fig. 5 shows the example walk-through of the feature extraction process of an officially published vulnerability ID CVE-2018-9432 [31] of severity type "High" and vulnerability type "EOP". First, the class containing the vulnerable source code corresponding to the vulnerability ID is extracted. Here, the return value of the getName() statement in BluetoothDevice class inside BluetoothDevice.java is not validated and it is a violation. The vulnerable source code further converted into the CFG intermediate graph format. Finally, it is vectorised and converted to graph data format. The graph data can be verified by any graph visual representation tools. The vulnerable code segment and corresponding nodes in graph are highlighted in red color.

4.3   Performance Evaluation of GNN

The deep learning with graph dataset is implemented using python library PyTorch Geometric, also known as geometric deep learning [20], an exclusive library for deep learning on graph datasets. It contains methods for deep learning on graphs and irregular structures.

To measure the efficiency of our proposed method, F1-score is used. True Positives (TP), True Negatives (TN), False Positives (FP) and False Negatives (FN) are needed to measure the F1-score. True Positives (TP) shows the number of vulnerable source code that is correctly classified as vulnerable. True Negatives (TN) shows the number of secure source code that is correctly classified as secure. False Positives (FP) shows the number of secure source code that is incorrectly classified as vulnerable. False Negatives (FN) shows the number of vulnerable source code samples incorrectly classified as secure source code.

The F1-score is computed as follows:

$$F1 - score = 2 * \frac{Precision * Recall}{Precision + Recall} \tag{7}$$

$$Precision = \frac{TP}{TP + FP} \tag{8}$$

$$Recall = \frac{TP}{TP + FN} \tag{9}$$

The 10-fold cross-validation is used to measure the performance of the model. The optimization function used is the Adaptive Moment Estimation (Adam) with a learning rate of 0.001. The L1 regularization (Lasso Regression) is also used during the training with the lambda constant of 0.005. The regularization term is added along with the loss function which is applied during back propagation. The batch size used is 64 and number of epochs trained is 200. The loss function used is cross entropy loss. For GAT, all the settings are similar to GCN except the learning rate of 0.045.

During our experiment, as tabulated in the Table 1, it is observed that F1-score for PDG and CPG are very close, and CPG results are just slightly below PDG results. The configuration of intermediate graph representation as PDG, vectorization technique as Doc2Vec64 and the graph neural network as GCN gives the best performance compared to other combinations. The maximum F1-score of 0.92 is reported with PDG, Doc2Vec and GCN configuration. The PDG type rich intermediate graph has obtained consistent performance throughout different configurations of vectorization and neural network types. This proves that, our proposed system can effectively classify the vulnerabilities. We have plotted ROC curve in Fig. 6 and measured the area under the ROC curve as 0.918. The training and validation losses are also represented in the Fig. 6 and it shows the expected trend as both the losses are significantly reduced when the epoch reaches 200 from the start. This result indicates that, graph neural network can be used as one of the best mechanism to classify the vulnerabilities

Table 1. Performance matrix

GNN Type	Vectoriser	Graphical type	F1-score
GCN	Doc2Vec64	AST	0.82
		CFG	0.90
		PDG	0.92
		CPG	0.91
		AST	0.84
GCN	TF-IDF	CFG	0.89
		PDG	0.91
		CPG	0.90
		AST	0.84
GAT	Doc2Vec64	CFG	0.87
		PDG	0.91
		CPG	0.90
		AST	0.82
GAT	TF-IDF	CFG	0.86
		PDG	0.90
		CPG	0.90

as it can properly understand the properties of the rich intermediate graphs. The experimental evaluation is conducted on MSI GF63 (Intel Core i7 processor, 9th generation, 16 GB memory, NVIDIA GeForce GTX 1650 with Max-Q design, 4 GB GDDR6) laptop. The operating system used is Ubuntu 18.04.

To assess the efficiency of our proposed method, a comparison of our method with related literature has been made in the Table 2. The first two methods listed, Daoyuan et al. [4] and Mario et al. [3] purely focused on vulnerability analysis, and no detection methods are involved, and hence no performance evaluation for vulnerability classification has been published in their work. The next set of methods listed, [1] and [2] proposed the vulnerability detection of Android Apps by extracting the byte code and not for Android operating system. [1] reported an F1-score of 0.83 for the Android Apps vulnerability detection and [2] didn't publish their results. Our mechanism gives a commanding performance in both analysis and detection of Android operating system vulnerability with an F1-score of 0.92.

It is observed from the TPs and TNs that, the model could successfully detect all the specific types of vulnerabilities reported in Android as mentioned in the Fig. 1(a). During the closer analysis on the FPs and FNs, it is observed that, the network has failed to properly detect some of the vulnerabilities which are categorized as type "Not Specified" by Google Security Bulletin. The network is also validated with the newest vulnerabilities reported (till June 2021) in the latest Android versions (V11 & V12), it found that, the network could

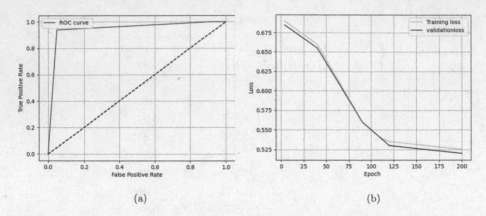

(a)   (b)

Fig. 6. (a) ROC curve. (b) Training/Validation loss plot for proposed method

successfully detect all the vulnerabilities except one vulnerability from "Not Specified" category.

Table 2. Comparison of proposed method with existing vulnerability analysis and detection methods

Work	Target	Problem	Samples	Method	F1-score
[4]	Android OS	Analysis	Security Bulletin 2015-18	Similarity Score	NA
[3]	Android OS	Analysis	Security Bulletin 2015-16	NA	NA
[1]	Android Apps	Detection	AndroZoo, F-droid	Static analysis	0.83
[2]	Android Apps	Analysis	AndroZoo	NA	NA
Proposed	Android OS	Both	Security Bulletin 2015-21	GNN	0.92

5   Conclusion and Future Work

One of the major challenges that we faced is the longer time duration taken while extracting and analysing the vulnerabilities from Android operating system source code. This task involves heavy manual work of going through each of the vulnerabilities and analyzing every patch, and then extracting the code for vulnerable and corresponding fixed code snippets from the GIT repository. This could be one of the major reasons for lesser literature around the vulnerability analysis and detection for Android operating system. This work has covered all the application layer and framework layer Java vulnerabilities of the latest Android 11 & 12 operating system versions and modeled a GNN based deep neural network and obtained a significant detection performance. In future, we will fine tune the current feature set construction process and machine learning algorithms to improve our performance. Also, we have observed that Android stack, system libraries, native layer, HAL and Android kernel are also affected with vulnerabilities which can lead to severe malware attacks. These layers and components are mostly written in C and C++ programming languages. This work also opens up a future direction for developing an end-to-end comprehensive vulnerability detection engine for Android operating system.

References

1. Namrud, Z., Kpodjedo, S., Talhi, C.: AndroVul: a repository for Android security vulnerabilities. In: Proceedings of the 29th Annual International Conference on Computer Science and Software Engineering, pp. 64–71 (2019)
2. Gao, J., Li, L., Kong, P., Bissyandé, T.F., Klein, J.: Understanding the evolution of android app vulnerabilities. IEEE Trans. Reliab. 212–230 (2019)
3. Linares-Vásquez, M., Bavota, G., Escobar-Velásquez, C.: An empirical study on android-related vulnerabilities. In: IEEE/ACM 14th International Conference on Mining Software Repositories (MSR), pp. 2–13 (2017)
4. Wu, D., Gao, D., Cheng, E. K., Cao, Y., Jiang, J., Deng, R. H.: Towards understanding Android system vulnerabilities: techniques and insights. In: Proceedings of the 2019 ACM Asia Conference on Computer and Communications Security, pp. 295–306 (2019)
5. Ghaffarian, S. M., Shahriari, H. R.: Neural software vulnerability analysis using rich intermediate graph representations of programs. In: Information Sciences, pp. 189–207 (2021)
6. Bilgin, Z., Ersoy, M.A., Soykan, E.U., Tomur, E., Çomak, P., Karaçay, L.: Vulnerability prediction from source code using machine learning. IEEE Access **8**, 150672–150684 (2020)
7. Li, Y., Ma, L., Shen, L., Lv, J., Zhang, P.: Open source software security vulnerability detection based on dynamic behavior features. PloS One **14**(8), e0221530 (2019)
8. Li, X., Wang, L., Xin, Y., Yang, Y., Chen, Y.: Automated vulnerability detection in source code using minimum intermediate representation learning. Appl. Sci. **10**(5), 1692 (2020)
9. Suneja, S., Zheng, Y., Zhuang, Y., Laredo, J., Morari, A.: Learning to map source code to software vulnerability using code-as-a-graph. arXiv preprint arXiv:2006.08614 (2020)
10. Iadarola, G.: Graph-based classification for detecting instances of bug patterns. Master's thesis, University of Twente (2018). http://essay.utwente.nl/76802/
11. Russell, R., et al.: Automated vulnerability detection in source code using deep representation learning. In: 17th IEEE International Conference on Machine Learning and Applications (ICMLA), pp. 757–762 (2018)
12. Yamaguchi, F., Golde, N., Arp, D., Rieck, K.: Modeling and discovering vulnerabilities with code property graphs. In: IEEE Symposium on Security and Privacy, pp. 590–604 (2014)
13. Google Android Security Bulletin. https://source.android.com/security/bulletin. Accessed 10 July 2021
14. CVE - Home. https://cve.mitre.org/index.html. Accessed 10 July 2021
15. NVD - Home. https://nvd.nist.gov/. Accessed 10 July 2021
16. Liang, H., Sun, L., Wang, M., Yang, Y.: Deep learning with customized abstract syntax tree for bug localization. IEEE Access **7**, 116309–116320 (2019)

17. Gensim. https://radimrehurek.com/gensim/models/doc2vec.html. Accessed 10 July 2021
18. Ferrante, J., Ottenstein, K.J., Warren, J.D.: The program dependence graph and its use in optimization. In: Paul, M., Robinet, B. (eds.) Programming 1984. LNCS, vol. 167, pp. 125–132. Springer, Heidelberg (1984). https://doi.org/10.1007/3-540-12925-1_33
19. The Code Property Graph. https://plume-oss.github.io/plume-docs/plume-basics/code-property-graph/. Accessed 10 July 2021
20. Pytorch Geometric. https://pytorch-geometric.readthedocs.io/en/latest/. Accessed 10 July 2021
21. Schütze, H., Manning, C.D., Raghavan, P.: Introduction to Information Retrieval. Cambridge University Press, Cambridge (2008)
22. Le, Q., Mikolov, T.: Distributed representations of sentences and documents. In: International Conference on Machine Learning PMLR, pp. 1188–1196 (2014)
23. Mikolov, T., Sutskever, I., Chen, K., Corrado, G., Dean, J.: Distributed representations of words and phrases and their compositionality. In: Proceedings of the 27th Annual Conference on Neural Information Processing Systems (NIPS), pp. 3111–3119 (2013)
24. Velickovic, P., Cucurull, G., Casanova, A., Romero, A., Lio, P., Bengio, Y.: Graph attention networks. In: Proceedings of the 6th International Conference on Learning Representations (ICLR) (2018)
25. Kipf, T.N., Welling, M.: Semi-supervised classification with graph convolutional networks. arXiv preprint arXiv:1609.02907 (2016)
26. Scikit-learn TfidfVectorizer. https://scikit-learn.org/stable/. Accessed 10 July 2021
27. Android Open Source Project (AOSP). https://source.android.com/. Accessed 10 July 2021
28. CovidLock: Android Ransomware Spreading Amid COVID-19 Epidemic. https://cyware.com/research-and-analysis/covidlock-android-ransomware-spreading-amid-covid-19-epidemic-4a5b/. Accessed 10 July 2021
29. The StrandHogg vulnerability. https://promon.co/security-news/strandhogg/. Accessed 10 July 2021
30. OWASP Benchmark Project. https://owasp.org/www-project-benchmark/. Accessed 10 July 2021
31. Google Security Bulletin. https://source.android.com/security/bulletin/2018-07-01. Accessed 10 July 2021
32. TinyPDG. https://github.com/YoshikiHigo/TinyPDG/. Accessed 10 Oct 2021
33. Joern Documentation. https://docs.joern.io/home. Accessed 10 Oct 2021

Malware Identification

Origin Information Assisted Hybrid Analysis to Detect APT Malware

Tejpal Kumar and Gaurav Somani[✉]

Department of Computer Science and Engineering, Central University of Rajasthan,
Ajmer, India
gaurav@curaj.ac.in

Abstract. Recently, the sophistication and varieties of advanced persistent threat (APT) based attacks have risen exponentially on global scale. Accurate prediction decisions related to the detection of APT malware are an ongoing challenge due to the use of zero-day attacks to exploit target assets. Signatures of zero-day malware are mostly non-existent and APT-based attacks remain undetected under the scanning of standard signature based methods. We require a set of distinguishable features of APT malware as traditional hybrid analysis techniques may not identify zero-day vulnerabilities. In this paper, we prepare a novel feature-set of malware having both traditional "static" and "dynamic" features and an additional novel feature of "Origin information". We argue that the additional information regarding the source of the executable, running on the target system provides important information about the activity of the malware in the initial penetration phase. With adequate experimentation, we evaluated the performance of the proposed approach using Support Vector Machines (SVM), Random Forest (RF), K-nearest Neighbors (KNN), Decision Tree (DT), and Gradient Boosting (GB) and achieved up to 92.31% prediction accuracy.

Keywords: Advanced persistent threat (APT) · Zero-day attacks · Vulnerabilities · Machine learning algorithms

1 Introduction

Organizations across the globe face security breaches such as malware-driven attacks, social-engineering based attacks, and Denial of Service (DoS) attacks on their IT infrastructure. Much recently the world has saw strategically planned, targeted and sophisticated attacks involving a detailed execution plan in the form of advanced persistent threats (APT) based attacks [14].

Advanced Persistent Threats based attack is a novel class of cyber threats that can not be detected with the traditional detection systems. APT-based attack is an attack class which include stealthy attacks where attackers move slowly to gain unauthorized entrance to the target network without revealing itself for an extended period of time. APT malware would overcome security mechanisms placed at the victim organization with major goals of cyber spying

© Springer Nature Switzerland AG 2021
S. Tripathy et al. (Eds.): ICISS 2021, LNCS 13146, pp. 75–93, 2021.
https://doi.org/10.1007/978-3-030-92571-0_5

and stealing critical information that belongs to individuals, organisations or even government institutions.

Many of the past contributions in this area focus on machine learning methods to detect and show the anomalous traffic behavior and system call or event patterns, and other static and dynamic approaches [26,32,48]. We observe that most of these contributions do not consider the zero-day nature of such attacks which target the unearthed vulnerabilities of the target system or network. We list contributions of this work in the following:

1. We propose a hybrid evaluation model of malware using a feature-set having static features, dynamic features, and a novel feature of "origin information" to train our machine learning model. We show that origin information combined with other static and dynamic features become a distinguishable feature-set to classify executables more accurately.
2. There are no readily available APT malware datasets. We prepare a dataset by collecting APT-based malware samples from a number of sources having 60 malware samples. In addition, we collect a dataset of genuine software having 40 samples.
3. We evaluate our hybrid analysis approach using Random Forest (RF), K-Nearest Neighbors (KNN), Decision Tree (DT), Support Vector Machine (SVM), and Gradient Boosting (GB). Our experimental evaluation shows detection accuracy of upto 92.31%.

We outline the remaining sections of this paper as follows: In Sect. 2, we give a comprehensive coverage related to defense mechanisms used in APT-based attacks. Section 3 details an overview of APT-based attack flow. Section 4 showcase our proposed approach. In Sect. 5, we present the experimental results and salient features of our detection method. Finally, we conclude this paper in Sect. 6.

2   Related Work

Many researchers describe and analyze the intrusion through anomaly-based, signature-based, or by pattern matching intrusion detection system (IDSs). These traditional defense mechanisms fail to detect sophisticated attacks like APTs which make use of system vulnerabilities. Organizations such as Fire-Eye [9], Kaspersky [10], Mitre [11] provide guidelines on different hardware and software resources and web-services to assess APT based sophisticated attacks. Most of these contributions present a vast array of solutions for APT detection. Some of the common solution categories include network traffic analysis, event association, threats mining, and Game-theory based solutions.

Many past contributions [22,32,48] proposed to monitor enormous amount of network traffic to detect malicious DNS requests and suspicious IPs involved in data exfiltration related to APT-based attacks. Contributions such as [24,26,35] proposed to perform anomaly detection through context and logical analysis of application logs, system logs, system call traces, and other host-based logs to detect APT-based malware.

Ghafir et al. [24] had developed a ML based system, which was referred to as MLAPT to detect APT-based threats. Their proposed system executes through three stages which includes threat detection, correlation, and prediction of APT-based attack. In the threat detection stage, they detect threats using eight detection modules. In the second stage, they decrease the false alarms by correlating the alert which is triggered by individual modules in the first stage with one APT-based scenario. In the last stage, they implement a prediction module through an existent record of the monitored network traffic to determine the probability of the early alerts. Shang et al. [41] used deep learning to detect the hidden communication channel between malware and C&C server and showed maximum F1 score of 0.968.

In [33], the authors had developed a system to detect suspicious activities related to an APT campaign. Their proposed system uses information flow between low level entities that may be files, processes, or any other entity in the system and generates a detection signal that maps to the ongoing stages of an APT campaign through analysis of host audit data. Qamar et al. [37] introduced the OWL (Web Ontology Language) based threat detection system. They perform semantic reasoning and contextual analysis to detect network threats. There is a range of contributions [29,31,46,47] in the area of Game-theory based solutions modeling the APT-based attack as a game between attackers and defenders. In [46], the authors use a node-level expected state evolution model with spontaneous lateral movement to study the defence as an repair problem of APT. In this contribution, the repair issue was modelled as a static Nash game [36].

Insider threat modeling and detection [15] has resemblance with the APT attack analysis. The goal of APT attacker is to gain control of authorised host inside the target network and attempt to mimic the normal behavior in order to bypass the detection system. There are a range of contributions which focus towards detection of insider threat using analysis of Fast-flux [20,28], Honeypot [19,30], host logs [25].

Traditional defense mechanisms [15,24,26,48] use signature matching or heuristic algorithms to detect anomaly behavior of a system by focusing on collecting, dissecting, and recording malware structure and behavior. They do not consider the aspect of zero-day attack. Therefore, they are inadequate against sophisticated attacks. In this work, we use hybrid analysis through fusion of static and dynamic characteristics that provide almost comprehensive information about the PUI's behavior. In addition, we consider a very important as well as differentiable feature related to origin of the executables. This helps us to make comparatively better and accurate detection decisions as most of the static, dynamic, and hybrid features do not address zero-day vulnerabilities.

3 Attack Flow of APT-Based Attacks

In this section, we provide stage-wise generic attack flow of APT-based attack. Many attackers use automated scanning mechanisms to find vulnerabilities over a large set of victims. Advanced Persistent Threats serve a most threatening category as these attacks involve constant information warfare to damage the high value assets. The attacker launches and executes an APT-based attack at many different levels. Figure 1 depicts the stages of a typical APT-based attack. These stages are based on the attack-cycle described in [14, 18, 32].

Stage 1 **Reconnaissance:** The attacker makes multiple attempts to gather the information about the victim and it's assets using social engineering or drive-by download. For this, the attacker may get DNS and whois information related to the target organization. Second part of this stage is "compromise", in which the attacker crafts spear phishing emails to mention specific topics (lures) relevant to the organization. These emails, if accessed, infect the victim with zero-day attacks.

Stage 2 **Foothold:** In this stage, the attacker tries to decide how the attack is to be carried out? For this, the attacker chooses their payload and techniques for delivering the exploit to the victim's machine.

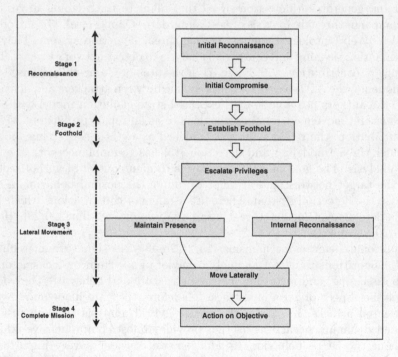

Fig. 1. Stage-wise generic attack flow of APT-based attack [14, 18, 32]

Stage 3 **Lateral Movement:** At this stage, the attacker utilizes various attack surfaces like payload and exploitation of known and unknown vulnerabilities of known applications to gain unauthorized access for sensitive resources and construct a connection with command and control servers to hide and control the activities related to the APT campaign.

Stage 4 **Complete Mission:** At this stage, the attacker achieves it's goals through the uses of payload that was downloaded during the stage 3 above.

4   Proposed Methodology

APT-based detection methods in general use heuristic analysis, behavior analysis, or a combination of both techniques [27,39]. A major challenge with these methods is that they are not able to detect zero-day vulnerabilities. Therefore, malware designers focus on writing newer forms of malware using zero-day exploits to evade existing malware detection systems. These malware utilizing zero-day exploits are mostly used in launching advanced persistent threat based attacks. Detecting such APT malware requires differentiable features helping accurate detection decisions as most of the static, dynamic, and hybrid features do not address zero-day vulnerabilities.

To address the fundamental issue of detecting APT malware utilizing zero-day vulnerabilities, we anticipate that some additional differentiable attributes of APT-based attacks may help in providing important information assisting overall malware analysis and subsequent detection. We argue that one of the important stages of APTs movement is initial penetration. We show this stage in Fig. 1 in Sect. 3. The initial penetration may happen through a range of mechanisms including spear-phishing, drive-by-download, Tor networks, USB, or by exploiting a zero-day vulnerability of a known application at the victim end. This phase of initial penetration aims to deliver the attack malware to the victim machine or the network. We observe that most of the known APT malware such as APT28 [3], APT29 [4], and APT34 [5] are delivered to the victim machines using such mechanisms without any knowledge to the system administrator about such software getting downloaded or installed. We believe that this additional information about the origin or source information about each executable getting installed on a victim machine may provide an important aid to the existing malware detection systems to detect APT-based malware.

APT-based malware is a kind of malware which may change its internal structure in each infection, but their functionality may not change [14,32]. This makes it harder for analysts to monitor such malware. Therefore, we envision that only static or dynamic, or a combination of these approaches in the form of hybrid features will not be able to detect advanced-type of malware. It is also important to note that the origin or source of the executable is neither a static feature nor a dynamic feature. The origin information has to be collected by the existing environment using browser and operating system support. We argue that the domain of origin information of PUI may help in creating an assistance to create a feature-set distinguishing APT malware from genuine software. For this, we inspect how the PUI gets installed on the system to penetrate the network of a target. In following subsections, we discuss the origin, delivery, and installation aspects in detail.

4.1   How Does the PUI Get Installed on the System?

Software installation makes software ready for execution, that is, it makes programs usable for users using the operating system. For each software and for machine programs including the operating system, the process of installing software varies. A code or program originated from installation files by copying it or generating a new file on the local system to increase accessibility for the OS. Installation files also provide un-installation features that include deletion of necessary directories. Once the program gets installed then it can be run multiple times without being required to reinstall before each execution. During installation of software, operating system performed some common operations like update program files and software versions, add configuration data, check exist software versions, and many more.

4.2   How to Get the PUI's Origin Information

As per [3–5], APT-based attacks established their campaigns by using different initial penetration methods. Therefore, we will inspect the program before installing it into the system so that we can get origin details of the PUI. To get the origin information of each executable getting downloaded, we may use different tools keeping a tap on such information. Different tools providing origin information include download managers, package managers, browsers, and anti-virus software. In addition, sandboxes such as Cuckoo [8] and Any.run [1] may also help in providing such information by keeping a tap on all downloaded files.

4.3   Feature Engineering

Feature engineering is a core input for machine learning models that influence the accuracy and coverage of malware detection systems [27, 40]. In this section, we present a set of features which we use in our proposed approach for the purpose of detecting suspicious activities related to the initial penetration phase of APT-based attacks. We show different set of features we use for the training and testing against different machine learning methods in Table 1. These features are collected using either automated mechanisms or manual mechanisms. Automated features are collected using different tools mentioned in the Table 1. We use manual mode of feature collection for origin information which may also be done automatically using tools while the installation starts. In Table 2, we show features in each of these three categories with their relevance in malware analysis.

Table 1. Different set of features and their collection mechanism

Feature engineering	Analysis approach	Tool	Feature types
Automated	Static	Cuckoo [8] and Any.run [1]	Portable executable (PE) entropy sections based information (.text, .data, .rdata, .rsrc, .edata, .idata, .reloc)
	Dynamic	Yara Signature [6], Virustotal [12], Cuckoo [8], and Any.run [1]	Cuckoo-status, Virustotal-status API-status for NtAllocateVirtualMemory, GetDiskFreeSpaceExW, GlobalMemoryStatusEx, and LookupPrivilegeValueW based function call data, Files, Registry, and Process-based data
Manual	Origin based information	Data of origin collected from various documents. List is annexed at Sect. A.2 in Appendix A	In what mode PUI gets entry onto the system? (Mean of penetration: Spear phishing, USB attached, exploitation of known application, Drive-by download, and tor network)

Table 2. Different features and their importance in malware analysis

Feature categories	Feature types	Contributions	Feature importance
Statistical features	PE-section entropy	[16,17,38]	Portable executable (PE) structures have standard format for Windows system executable. Therefore, entropy based detection method discovers malware by comparing changes in the original program before and after the implantation of malicious code
Behavior driven features	System calls, and Interaction of PUI with OS	[26,34,44,45]	These features detect maliciousness of the PUI by capturing the interaction behavior between the program and the OS. In addition the system call sequence is most intuitive way to reflect the behavior of the PUI
Origin-driven features	Spear phishing, USB attached, exploitation of known application, Drive-by download, and Tor network	Our work	Most of the known APT malware such as APT28, APT29, APT34, and APT37 established their campaigns by using different initial penetration methods. This includes methods such as uploading a malicious code segment into a web-based systems, exploitation of known application vulnerabilities, malicious USB attachment, and spear-phishing emails to infect the target rather than mass mailing campaigns with the goal of stealing intellectual property

4.4 Dataset Construction

Dataset contributes a major role in developing a strong training data for machine learning models to detect sophisticated threats like APT-based attacks. However, there are no specific datasets of APT malware available to serve the needs of our proposed detection approach. Many authors use CAIDA [43], NSL-KDD [21], and CICIDS 2017 [42] to detect APT-based attacks. As per [35] these datasets have some limitations like they do not deliberate over the aspect of stealthiness and persistent nature that are key features of APT. These datasets do not identify correlation between multiple phases of an APT and the distinctiveness between normal and abnormal behavior is so minute that it fails to showcase the sophisticated attacks.

To address the aforementioned issues, we prepare a comprehensive dataset of PUIs that may help us in collecting static features, dynamic features, and origin-based information from three types of PUIs. These PUIs are benign binaries, portable benign binaries, and APT-based malware collected from different sources. Our dataset of executables has a total of 104 samples with 30 benign software samples, 41 APT malware samples, and 33 portable benign binaries. We show Table 3 having a list of all these samples, their type and how we collected them.

Table 3. Details about the dataset samples and their collection

Sample	Sample type	Sample count	Sample collection sources
Benign	Benign binaries (non-portable)	30	Benign exectable samples collected from various sources. List is annexed at Sect. A.1 in Appendix A
	Benign binaries (portable)	33	Portable benign exectable samples collected from various sources. List is annexed at Sect. A.1 in Appendix A
Malware	Known APT binaries (APT 28 [3] and APT 29 [4])	41	APT malware executable sample from [7] and annexed at Sect. A.2 in Appendix A

5   Experiments and Performance Analysis

In this section, we first present an outline of the experimental set-up to run different ML algorithms to perform the hybrid analysis of APT-based malware. We then describe our data-acquisition process by which we prepare the training data covering different features. Later, we show different performance and evaluation metrics depicting the efficiency of our approach.

5.1   Experimental Setup

We perform our analysis experiments by utilizing VMWare servers to host the virtual machines. We also integrate Virustotal API [12] and Yara signature [6] on a sandbox with the latest malware signature. In Table 4, we provide detailed information about experimental setup.

Table 4. Experimental setup

Resource type	Resource details
Operating system	Windows 64-bit
Main memory	6 GB
Virtualization environment	VMware V.8.0.0-471780 [13]
Sandbox	Cuckoo [8], any.run [1], and Virustotal [12]
Programming language	Python 3.0+
Machine learning libraries	sklearn, pandas, numpy, matplotlib
Source of data	Malware executable samples from [7] and annexed at Sect. A.2 in Appendix A. Benign executable samples collected from various sources. List is annexed at Sect. A.1 in Appendix A

5.2   Data-Acquisition Process: Acquiring Features

We perform static and dynamic analysis of each executable available in our dataset as annexed at Appendix A. For this, we keep each PUI inside a sandbox and then record the behavior by logging different features and activities. Sandbox tool records all system calls that were invoked by PUI during its execution.

We generate a trace file for each PUI. After running each PUI, we revert the sandbox environment to a clean snapshot to analyze the next PUI in the data-set. We perform this important activity so that a clean environment for executing the next PUI is ready and the behavior of last PUI does not affect the trace. We show the overall working model having training and testing of PUIs in Fig. 2. After recording the traces of each file having different features of each PUI, we train different machine learning algorithms. Later, we use a matcher module using different algorithms to compute similarity between an unknown PUI and the already recorded PUI features. With the help of matcher module, classification algorithms classify an unknown PUI into a malicious, benign, or suspicious class.

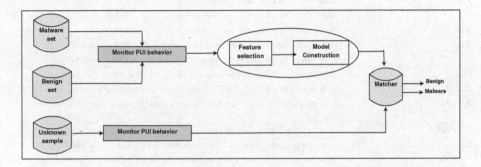

Fig. 2. Training and testing of PUIs using proposed approach

5.3 Experimental Details

APT malware get unauthorized control to the target's machine through exploitation of known platform vulnerability, by stealing critical user information or through delivery of payload. Our proposed feature-set contains recorded static, dynamic, and origin-based features of benign as well as malware PUIs as listed in Table 5. We performed following different set of experiments using five ML algorithms:

1. **Experiment 1:** Train and test using static and dynamic features of benign samples dataset.
2. **Experiment 2:** Train and test using static and dynamic features of dataset having both benign and malware samples.
3. **Experiment 3:** Train and test using static, dynamic and origin-information features of dataset having both benign and malware samples.
4. **Experiment 4:** Train and test using static, dynamic and synthetic origin information features of dataset having both benign and malware samples.

Above four experiments testify our feature-set against different sample size and sample type. We introduced this variability for better coverage and visualize the effect of different training and testing sample data. To address the problem of zero-day vulnearabilities, we need proactive approach to detect the initial phase

Table 5. List of various features used for training and testing

Feature	Feature description
Name	Name of the PUI
CS	Score generated by Cuckoo sandbox
VTS	Score generated by Virustotal API
SA	Whether the PUI is showing Suspicious activity?
MA	Whether the PUI is showing Malicious activity?
NT	Whether the PUI is showing No threats?
TP	Total number of processes accessed by an PUI during its execution
MoP	Number of monitored processes accessed by an PUI during its execution
MaP	Number of malicious processes accessed by an PUI during its execution
SP	Number of suspicious processes accessed by an PUI during its execution
TE	Total number of events occur when a PUI executes
RE	How many times can read events occur when a PUI executes?
WE	How many times can write events occur when a PUI executes?
DE	How many times can delete events occur when a PUI executes?
GMSE	How many times does the GlobalMemoryStatusEx API invoke by a PUI?
NPVM	How many times does the NtAllocateVirtualMemory API invoke by a PUI?
GDFSEW	How many times does the GetDiskFreeSpaceExW API invoked by a PUI?
CGK	How many times does the CryptGenKey API invoke by a PUI?
P32FW	How many times does the Process32FirstW API invoke by a PUI?
LPVW	How many times does the LookupPrivilegeValueW API invoke by a PUI?
Error	Whether the sandbox is showing error?
Executable files	Number of executable file touched by an PUI during its execution
Suspicious files	Number of suspicious files touched by an PUI during its execution
Text files	Number of text files touched by an PUI during its execution
Unknown types	Number of unknown-type files touched by an PUI during its execution
.text	Entropy related to .text section
.itext	Entropy related to .itext section
.data	Entropy related to .data section
.idata	Entropy related to .idata section
.rdata	Entropy related to .rdata section
.rsrc	Entropy related to .rsrc section
.upx1	Entropy related to .upx1 section
.reloc	Entropy related to .reloc section
.didata	Entropy related to .didata section
.edata	Entropy related to .edata section
Yara.rules.events	How many yara signature found?
Spear phishing	Whether the PUI penetrates the system by spear phishing mode?
Exploitation of known vulnerability of an known application	Whether the PUI penetrates the system by zero-day exploit mode?
Drive-by download	Whether the PUI penetrates the system by drive-by download?
Tor network	Whether the PUI penetrates the system by tor network?
USB attached	Whether the PUI penetrates the system by USB attachment?
Class	Class label (0 for benign, 1 for suspicious, and 2 for malicious class)

of penetration in an APT-based attacks. For experiment 3 and 4, we collect "origin information" of APT malware by reading in-depth information available in literature. The origin information make use of one or more of mechanisms such as spear phishing, drive-by-download, Tor network, or installed from USB. We did this manually because there is no specific APT dataset available and information of APT-malware was spread across various sources.

For experiment 4, we generated the synthetic information related to "origin information" of benign binaries available in our dataset as in experiment 3, we did not consider origin information for benign PUIs. In experiment 4, we generate the origin information for benign samples in the following manner:

1. For feature "**install from USB**", we assign 1 (to represent 'true') to benign executable as it may be installed from a USB device. Benign executable dataset also has many portable executables which make them USB installable.
2. For feature "**drive-by-download**", we assign 1 (to represent 'true') to benign executables as attacker/insider might use them for injecting malicious code inside a benign software.

5.4   Model Training

We split the dataset with the aspect of 3:1 to train and test the ML models respectively. This dissection keeps the representation of each class in both training and testing sets. We perform K-fold cross validation [23] on a training set to evaluate machine learning models. We randomly partition the training data into "K" different subsamples having equal size. Now, we select a random subsample and label it as a validation set and all K subsamples are used as training data. We repeat this process K-times (in our case, the value of K is 10) for each different subsample taken as validation data. Later, we test the model on the testing set to evaluate its performance.

5.5   Discussion

In this section, we discuss different aspects of our experimental results. We show resulting metrics in Table 6 and Table 7 which indicate a strong predictive performance in terms of accuracy, recall, precision, f1-score, and ROC-AUC score for each of the classes. These classes are: benign, suspicious, and malicious. Many researchers use only two classes to detect anomalous behavior in a system. One is a benign class and the other is a malicious class. But in our experiments, we use one more additional class which is referred to as suspicious. APT malware may uses zero day vulnerabilities to exploit target assets. In case a PUI is classified as suspicious then the system adiministrator will may use this information to futher investigate the PUI. Therefore, we use three class labels to classify the anomaly behavior in the datasets. These class labels are as follows: class 0 indicates benign, class 1 indicates suspicious, and class 2 indicates malicious class.

We also show the AUC-ROC (Area under Curve Receiver Operating Characteristics) curve of true positives against false positives for all classifiers in Fig. 3. For better classification, we attempt to achieve the value of AUC-ROC as close as possible to 1 [35].

Table 6. Experimental evaluation of our feature-set against five ML algorithms showing various performance metrics.

ML algorithm	Performance criteria	Experiment											
		Experiment 1			Experiment 2			Experiment 3			Experiment 4		
		Class labels			Class labels			Class labels			Class labels		
		0	1	2	0	1	2	0	1	2	0	1	2
K-Nearest Neighbor (KNN)	Precision	0.50	0.62	1.00	0.86	0.33	0.69	0.62	1.00	0.82	0.62	1.00	0.82
	Recall	0.60	0.62	0.67	0.75	0.17	0.92	1.00	0.33	0.75	1.00	0.33	0.75
	F1-score	0.55	0.62	0.80	0.80	0.22	0.79	0.76	0.50	0.78	0.76	0.50	0.78
Support Vector Machine (SVM)	Precision	0.57	0.71	1.00	1.00	0.67	0.61	1.00	0.67	0.65	1.00	0.67	0.65
	Recall	0.80	0.62	0.67	0.62	0.33	0.92	0.75	0.33	0.92	0.75	0.33	0.92
	F1-score	0.67	0.67	0.80	0.77	0.44	0.73	0.86	0.44	0.76	0.86	0.44	0.76
Decision Tree (DT)	Precision	1.00	0.71	0.00	0.62	0.00	1.00	0.62	0.00	1.00	0.62	0.00	1.00
	Recall	1.00	1.00	0.00	1.00	0.00	1.00	1.00	0.00	1.00	1.00	0.00	1.00
	F1-score	1.00	0.83	0.00	0.76	0.00	1.00	0.76	0.00	1.00	0.76	0.00	1.00
Random Forest (RF)	Precision	0.89	0.80	0.50	0.90	0.80	0.91	0.90	0.86	1.00	0.90	0.83	1.00
	Recall	1.00	0.67	0.50	1.00	0.67	0.91	1.00	1.00	0.82	1.00	0.83	0.91
	F1-score	0.94	0.73	0.50	0.95	0.73	0.91	0.95	0.92	0.90	0.95	0.83	0.95
Gradient Boosting (GB)	Precision	1.00	0.80	1.00	1.00	1.00	0.80	1.00	1.00	0.80	1.00	1.00	0.80
	Recall	0.60	1.00	1.00	1.00	0.50	1.00	1.00	0.50	1.00	1.00	0.50	1.00
	F1-score	0.75	0.89	1.00	1.00	0.67	0.89	1.00	0.67	0.89	1.00	0.67	0.89

In experiment 1, we train and test using static and dynamic features of dataset having samples of benign executables. We observed that the Decision Tree (DT) model outperforms all other algorithm by achieving 91.01% AUC-ROC value with 87.5% accuracy. In addition, Gradient Boosting (GB) also achieved similiar accuracy. However, AUC-ROC score of GB was less as compared to AUC-ROC value of Decision Tree.

Table 7. Performance metric in term of accuracy and ROC-AUC score

Experiment number	Performance criteria	ML-based algorithm				
		KNN	SVM	DT	RF	GB
1	Accuracy	0.625	0.6875	0.875	0.8125	0.875
	ROC-AUC	0.7073	0.7945	0.9101	0.8873	0.8735
2	Accuracy	0.6923	0.6923	0.7692	0.8846	0.8846
	ROC-AUC	0.7201	0.8186	0.8777	0.9703	1.0
3	Accuracy	0.7308	0.7308	0.8077	0.9231	0.8846
	ROC-AUC	0.8370	0.8211	0.8902	0.9821	1.0
4	Accuracy	0.7308	0.7378	0.8077	0.9231	0.8846
	ROC-AUC	0.8370	0.8186	0.8902	0.9896	1.0

In case of experiment 2, we train and test both benign and malware samples using hybrid features. In this case, Gradient Boosting algorithm showed better performance by obtaining a 88.46% accuracy score whereas Random Forest method also acquired the same accuracy value but with low AUC-ROC value. In experiment 3 and 4, we use static, dynamic, as well as origin-information features. In both cases, we train and validate the benign and malware samples using five machine learning models (KNN, DT, SVM, RF, GB). For experiment 3 and 4, ML algorithms showed accuracy between 73.08% to 92.31%. In these experiments, the Random Forest model showcased highest accuracy of 92.31%.

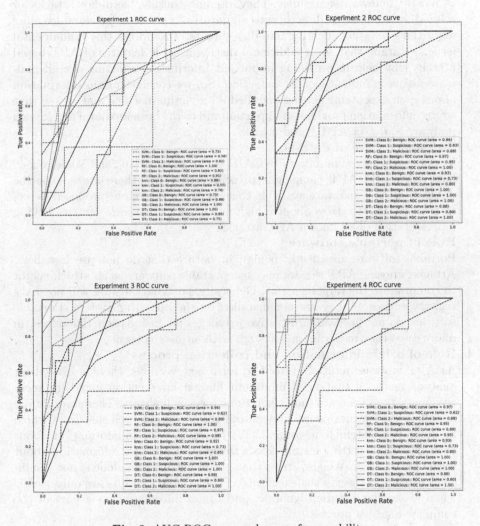

Fig. 3. AUC-ROC curve: degree of separability

We observe that the analysis of origin information of executables can assist to extract robust signatures which may subsequently enhance the detection efficacy. Using static and dynamic analysis, we get the accuracy of upto 88.75% as shown in Table 7. However, when we add one more additional feature "origin-information of executable", the accuracy rate get enhanced and reached upto 92.31%. There are some additional points which are important to ponder while analyzing the APT malware using our proposed methods.

1. **Suitability of machine learning algorithms**
   The accuracy of ML algorithms depends mostly on the training data which is mostly malware signatures. They do not consider zero-day attacks or related vulnerabilities directly into signatures. Therefore, machine learning algorithms may not identify zero-day threats. To address this fundamental issue, we argue that some additional distinguishable features of APT-based attacks may help in providing important information assisting overall malware analysis and subsequent detection. So, we consider origin information about each executable getting installed on a victim machine and we see that source information provides an important aid to the both unknown and known malware to detect APT-based attack.

2. **Size and nature of dataset**
   Various security communities like CAIDA [43], FireEye [10], and Mandiant [2] lists a range of APT campaigns presence. However, there are no specific datasets of APT malware available to serve the needs of our proposed detection approach. We stress about a high need of APT malware samples having representation of all known APT attacks.

3. **Role of portable software**
   Portable software are mostly benign in nature that do not use installers. Attackers posing APT threats may use portable software as an attack vector to compromise the target's assets. Generally, portable software will not have registry entries as they are not installed on the operating system. Portable software do not need administrative privileges for installation. Therefore, in many cases they may run on a system without user consent.

4. **Role of origin information and collection process**
   As APT malware multiplies itself to form new versions, there is a need for analysis methods that need minimum human intervention and help security analysts to generate timely solutions for new malware. Therefore, Before installing the executable, we understand the executable well that from which mode of the system it is entered. We considered origin-information about each executable getting installed on a target as it provides information about initial penetration. We also stress that origin information alone is not a sufficient feature to classify the executable. The accuracy results are only visible when we combine static, dynamic, and origin information as a part of the complete analysis process.

We show the set of features we use for the training and testing against five machine learning methods in Table 1 of Sect. 4. We collect static and dynamic features using automated mechanisms and we use manual mechanism for origin information. Even origin information may be collected automatically while the executables starts its execution in case of portable software or start doing installation in case of installable executables and these two events can be captured using operating system controls, download managers, package managers, or other antivirus and sandbox tools.

6   Conclusion and Future Work

APT malware indicates persistent and multistage attack with the goal of compromising the target. In this work, we proposed a APT malware analysis approach in which we combine novel distinguishable feature "origin information of executable" with hybrid features to enhance the APT-based attack detection efficiency. With the help of origin information, we classify the executables depending on their penetration method. Origin information with static and dynamic features become an important distinguishable matrix which helps to make accurate detection decisions.

With experimentation, we evaluate the performance of our proposed approach against five machine learning algorithms (KNN, SVM, DT, RF, and GB). Evaluation results show that proposed approach shows detection accuracy upto 92.31%. APT malware analysis and APT attacks are emerging fields in cyber security. There are number of research directions related to our work where a lot of work is still needs to be contributed. Preparing extensive data-sets having real attacks traces, inclusion of newer APT malware samples in such datasets, and techniques involving other novel features for the detection of such attacks, are few important directions.

A   Appendix

A.1   List of Sources: Benign Executable Samples

See Tables 8 and 9.

Table 8. List of various sources used for collection of benign executable samples

Non-portable benign executable		
Sr. No.	Non-Portable benign executable	Source
1	Shareit	https://shareit.en.softonic.com/
2	SunBird	https://mozilla-sunbird.en.softonic.com/
3	zoom	https://zoom.us/download
4	RssOwl	http://www.rssowl.org/
5	opera	https://www.opera.com/download
6	7zip	https://www.7-zip.org/download.html
7	musicbee	https://getmusicbee.com/downloads/
8	Dropbox	https://www.dropbox.com/desktop
9	keepass	https://keepass.info/download.html
10	treesize	https://www.jam-software.com/treesize_free
11	ProcessExplorer	https://docs.microsoft.com/en-us/sysinternals/downloads/process-explorer
12	Chrome	https://www.google.com/intl/en_in/chrome/
13	Cisco_WebEx_Add-On	https://www.webex.com/downloads.html
14	notepad++	https://notepad-plus-plus.org/downloads/
15	Avira	https://www.avira.com/en/free-antivirus-windows
16	produkey	https://www.nirsoft.net/utils/product_cd_key_viewer.html
17	malwarebytes	https://www.malwarebytes.com/mwb-download
18	rufus	https://rufus.ie/en_US/
19	defraggler	https://www.ccleaner.com/defraggler
20	speccy	https://www.ccleaner.com/speccy
21	handbrake	https://handbrake.fr/downloads.php
22	picasa	https://picasa.en.uptodown.com/windows
23	rainmeter	https://www.rainmeter.net/
24	sharex	https://getsharex.com/
25	folder lock	https://folder-lock.en.softonic.com/download
26	Paint	https://ms-paint.en.softonic.com/download
27	winrar	https://www.win-rar.com/start.html?&L=0
28	Filezilla	https://filezilla-project.org/
29	adobe acrobat reader dc	https://get.adobe.com/reader/otherversions/
30	anydesk	https://anydesk.com/en/downloads/windows
Portable benign executable		
Sr. No.	Portable benign executable	Source
1	ClamWinPortable	https://clamwin-portable.en.uptodown.com/windows
2	7-ZipPortable	https://7-zip-portable.en.softonic.com/
3	CarryItEasyPackage	https://www.softpedia.com/get/PORTABLE-SOFTWARE/
4	KasperskyTDSSKillerPortable	https://portableapps.com/apps/
5	PortableApps	https://portableapps.com/
6	Network Assistant	https://www.softpedia.com/get/PORTABLE-SOFTWARE/
7	DVDRepair	https://www.portablefreeware.com/index.php?id=1626
8	mtputty	https://ttyplus.com/downloads/
9	cpuz	https://portableapps.com/apps/
10	HWMonitor	https://hwmonitor-portable.en.softonic.com/
11	VirusTotalScanner	https://www.softpedia.com/get/PORTABLE-SOFTWARE/
12	DontSleep	https://www.techspot.com/downloads/5953-dont-sleep.html
13	AppReadWriteCounter	https://www.portablefreeware.com/index.php?id=2943
14	ProcessHacker	https://portableapps.com/apps/
15	WizTree	https://diskanalyzer.com/download
16	ZintPortable	https://portableapps.com/apps/
17	msdStrongbox	https://www.softpedia.com/get/PORTABLE-SOFTWARE/
18	WiseDiskCleanerPortable	https://www.wisecleaner.com/download.html
19	On-ScreenKeyboardPortable	https://on-screen-keyboard-portable.en.softonic.com/
20	PeerBlockPortable	https://portableapps.com/apps/
21	EraserDropPortable	https://eraserdrop-portable.en.softonic.com/
22	TCPViewPortable	https://portableapps.com/apps/
23	NSISPortable	https://portableapps.com/apps/
24	Allwaysync-n-go	https://allwaysync.com/ngo
25	SIWPortable	https://portableapps.com/apps/
26	WhoDatPortable	https://whodat-portable.en.uptodown.com/windows
27	WinMTRPortable	https://portableapps.com/apps/
28	winMd5SumPortable	https://portableapps.com/apps/
29	WindowsErrorLookupToolPortable	https://portableapps.com/apps/
30	ArthaPortable	https://portableapps.com/apps/
31	DiaPortable	https://portableapps.com/apps/
32	TypeFasterPortable	https://portableapps.com/apps/
33	DspeechPortable	https://portableapps.com/apps/

A.2 List of Sources: APT Malware Executable Samples

Table 9. APT malware executable samples from [7]

APT version	APT malware executable	Sources
APT28 (Number of samples = 18)	APT28_2011-09_Telus_Trojan.Win32.Sofacy.A	http://telussecuritylabs.com/threats/show/TSL20110908-01
	APT28_2014-08_MhtMS12-27_Prevenity	http://malware.prevenity.com/2014/08/malware-info.html
	APT28_2015-09_Sfecure_Sofacy-recycles-carberp-and-metasploit-code	https://labsblog.f-secure.com/2015/09/08/sofacy-recycles-carberp-and-metasploit-code/
	APT28_2014-10_TrendMicro Operation Pawn Storm	http://blog.trendmicro.com/trendlabs-security-intelligence/new-adobe-flash-zero-day-used-in-pawn-storm-campaign/
APT29 (Number of samples = 23)	APT29_2015-09_FSecure_THE DUKES7 years of Russian cyberespionage	https://www.f-secure.com/documents/996508/1030745/dukes_whitepaper.pdf
	APT29_2014-11_FSecure_OnionDuke APT Attacks Via the Tor Network	https://www.f-secure.com/weblog/archives/00002764.html OnionDuke: APT Attacks Via the Tor Network
	APT29_2014-04_FSecure_Targeted Attacks and Ukraine	https://www.f-secure.com/weblog/archives/00002688.html Targeted Attacks and Ukraine
	APT29_2016-12_Chris_Grizzly SteppeLighting up Like A Christmas Tree	https://fauie.com/2016/12/30/grizzly-steppe-lighting-up-like-a-christmas-tree/ Grizzly Steppe
	APT29_2014_FSecure_Cosmicduke Cosmu with a twist of MiniDuke	https://www.f-secure.com/documents/996508/1030745/cosmicduke_whitepaper.pdf Cosmicduke Cosmu with a twist of MiniDuke
	APT29_2015-07_PaloAlto_Tracking_MiniDionis	http://researchcenter.paloaltonetworks.com/2015/07/tracking-minidionis-cozycars-new-ride-is-related-to-seaduke/Tracking MiniDionis: CozyCar's New Ride Is Related to Seaduke

References

1. Any.run sandbox: Interactive malware Hunting service. https://any.run/. Accessed 12 Apr 2021
2. APT1- Mandiant report. https://www.fireeye.com/blog/threat-research/2013/02/mandiant-exposes-apt1-chinas-cyber-espionage-units.html. Accessed 08 May 2021
3. APT28. https://www.fireeye.com/content/dam/fireeye-www/global/en/current-threats/pdfs/rpt-apt28.pdf. Accessed 11 Feb 2021
4. APT29. https://attack.mitre.org/groups/G0016/. Accessed 11 Feb 2021
5. APT34. FireEye.Advancedpersistentthreats/apt-groups.html. Accessed 11 Feb 2021
6. Chronicle. Yara signature: The pattern matching swiss knife for malware researchers. https://virustotal.github.io/yara/. Accessed 22 June 2021
7. Contagio APT-malware. http://contagiodump.blogspot.com/. Accessed 11 Dec 2020
8. Cuckoo sandbox. https://cuckoo.cert.ee/. Accessed 12 Apr 2021
9. FireEye. https://www.fireeye.com/. Accessed 18 May 2021
10. Kaspersky Lab: Targeted cyberattacks logbook. https://apt.securelist.com/. Accessed 03 May 2021
11. Mitre-Attack. https://attack.mitre.org/groups/. Accessed 19 May 2021
12. Virustotal. https://www.virustotal.com/gui/. Accessed 12 Apr 2021
13. VMware server. https://my.vmware.com/web/vmware/details/wkst_800_win/dCVkYnQqdGhiZEBAdA==. Accessed 30 Mar 2021
14. Alshamrani, A., Myneni, S., Chowdhary, A., Huang, D.: A survey on advanced persistent threats: techniques, solutions, challenges, and research opportunities. IEEE Commun. Surv. Tutor. **21**(2), 1851–1877 (2019)

15. Azaria, A., Richardson, A., Kraus, S., Subrahmanian, V.: Behavioral analysis of insider threat: a survey and bootstrapped prediction in imbalanced data. IEEE Trans. Comput. Soc. Syst. **1**(2), 135–155 (2014)
16. Bai, J., Wang, J., Zou, G.: A malware detection scheme based on mining format information. Sci. World J. **2014**, 1–11 (2014)
17. Bat-Erdene, M., Park, H., Li, H., Lee, H., Choi, M.-S.: Entropy analysis to classify unknown packing algorithms for malware detection. Int. J. Inf. Secur. **16**(3), 227–248 (2017). https://doi.org/10.1007/s10207-016-0330-4
18. Bhatt, P., Yano, E.T., Gustavsson, P.: Towards a framework to detect multi-stage advanced persistent threats attacks. In: 2014 IEEE 8th International Symposium on Service Oriented System Engineering, pp. 390–395. IEEE (2014)
19. Bowen, B.M., Hershkop, S., Keromytis, A.D., Stolfo, S.J.: Baiting inside attackers using decoy documents. In: Chen, Y., Dimitriou, T.D., Zhou, J. (eds.) SecureComm 2009. LNICST, vol. 19, pp. 51–70. Springer, Heidelberg (2009). https://doi.org/10.1007/978-3-642-05284-2_4
20. Caglayan, A., Toothaker, M., Drapeau, D., Burke, D., Eaton, G.: Behavioral analysis of botnets for threat intelligence. IseB **10**(4), 491–519 (2012). https://doi.org/10.1007/s10257-011-0171-7
21. Dhanabal, L., Shantharajah, S.: A study on NSL-KDD dataset for intrusion detection system based on classification algorithms. Int. J. Adv. Res. Comput. Commun. Eng. **4**(6), 446–452 (2015)
22. Friedberg, I., Skopik, F., Settanni, G., Fiedler, R.: Combating advanced persistent threats: from network event correlation to incident detection. Comput. Secur. **48**, 35–57 (2015)
23. Garcia, F.C.C., Muga II, F.P.: Random forest for malware classification. arXiv preprint arXiv:1609.07770 (2016)
24. Ghafir, I., et al.: Detection of advanced persistent threat using machine-learning correlation analysis. Futur. Gener. Comput. Syst. **89**, 349–359 (2018)
25. Greitzer, F.L., Frincke, D.A.: Combining traditional cyber security audit data with psychosocial data: towards predictive modeling for insider threat mitigation. In: Probst, C., Hunker, J., Gollmann, D., Bishop, M. (eds.) Insider Threats in Cyber Security. ADIS, vol. 49, pp. 85–113. Springer, Boston (2010). https://doi.org/10.1007/978-1-4419-7133-3_5
26. Han, W., Xue, J., Wang, Y., Zhang, F., Gao, X.: APTMalinsight: identify and cognize APT malware based on system call information and ontology knowledge framework. Inf. Sci. **546**, 633–664 (2021)
27. Han, W., Xue, J., Wang, Y., Zhu, S., Kong, Z.: Build a roadmap for stepping into the field of anti-malware research smoothly. IEEE Access **7**, 143573–143596 (2019)
28. Hsu, C.-H., Huang, C.-Y., Chen, K.-T.: Fast-flux bot detection in real time. In: Jha, S., Sommer, R., Kreibich, C. (eds.) RAID 2010. LNCS, vol. 6307, pp. 464–483. Springer, Heidelberg (2010). https://doi.org/10.1007/978-3-642-15512-3_24
29. Khouzani, M., Sarkar, S., Altman, E.: A dynamic game solution to malware attack. In: 2011 Proceedings of the IEEE INFOCOM, pp. 2138–2146. IEEE (2011)
30. Li, F., Lai, A., Ddl, D.: Evidence of advanced persistent threat: a case study of malware for political espionage. In: 2011 6th International Conference on Malicious and Unwanted Software, pp. 102–109. IEEE (2011)
31. Lin, J.-C., Chen, J.-M., Chen, C.-C., Chien, Y.-S.: A game theoretic approach to decision and analysis in strategies of attack and defense. In: 2009 Third IEEE International Conference on Secure Software Integration and Reliability Improvement, pp. 75–81. IEEE (2009)

32. Marchetti, M., Pierazzi, F., Colajanni, M., Guido, A.: Analysis of high volumes of network traffic for advanced persistent threat detection. Comput. Netw. **109**, 127–141 (2016)
33. Milajerdi, S.M., Gjomemo, R., Eshete, B., Sekar, R., Venkatakrishnan, V.: HOLMES: real-time apt detection through correlation of suspicious information flows. In: 2019 IEEE Symposium on Security and Privacy (SP), pp. 1137–1152. IEEE (2019)
34. Mohaisen, A., Alrawi, O., Mohaisen, M.: AMAL: high-fidelity, behavior-based automated malware analysis and classification. Comput. Secur. **52**, 251–266 (2015)
35. Myneni, S., et al.: DAPT 2020 - constructing a benchmark dataset for advanced persistent threats. In: Wang, G., Ciptadi, A., Ahmadzadeh, A. (eds.) MLHat 2020. CCIS, vol. 1271, pp. 138–163. Springer, Cham (2020). https://doi.org/10.1007/978-3-030-59621-7_8
36. Osborne, M.J., et al.: An Introduction to Game Theory, vol. 3. Oxford University Press, New York (2004)
37. Qamar, S., Anwar, Z., Rahman, M.A., Al-Shaer, E., Chu, B.-T.: Data-driven analytics for cyber-threat intelligence and information sharing. Comput. Secur. **67**, 35–58 (2017)
38. Radkani, E., Hashemi, S., Keshavarz-Haddad, A., Haeri, M.A.: An entropy-based distance measure for analyzing and detecting metamorphic malware. Appl. Intell. **48**(6), 1536–1546 (2018). https://doi.org/10.1007/s10489-017-1045-6
39. Roundy, K.A., Miller, B.P.: Hybrid analysis and control of malware. In: Jha, S., Sommer, R., Kreibich, C. (eds.) RAID 2010. LNCS, vol. 6307, pp. 317–338. Springer, Heidelberg (2010). https://doi.org/10.1007/978-3-642-15512-3_17
40. Sabir, B., Ullah, F., Babar, M.A., Gaire, R.: Machine learning for detecting data exfiltration: a review. ACM Comput. Surv. (CSUR) **54**(3), 1–47 (2021)
41. Shang, L., Guo, D., Ji, Y., Li, Q.: Discovering unknown advanced persistent threat using shared features mined by neural networks. Comput. Netw. **189**, 107937 (2021)
42. Sharafaldin, I., Habibi Lashkari, A., Ghorbani, A.A.: A detailed analysis of the CICIDS2017 data set. In: Mori, P., Furnell, S., Camp, O. (eds.) ICISSP 2018. CCIS, vol. 977, pp. 172–188. Springer, Cham (2019). https://doi.org/10.1007/978-3-030-25109-3_9
43. Shiravi, A., Shiravi, H., Tavallaee, M., Ghorbani, A.A.: Toward developing a systematic approach to generate benchmark datasets for intrusion detection. Comput. Secur. **31**(3), 357–374 (2012)
44. Stiborek, J., Pevný, T., Rehák, M.: Multiple instance learning for malware classification. Expert Syst. Appl. **93**, 346–357 (2018)
45. Tajoddin, A., Jalili, S.: HM3alD: polymorphic malware detection using program behavior-aware hidden Markov model. Appl. Sci. **8**(7), 1044 (2018)
46. Yang, L.-X., Li, P., Yang, X., Tang, Y.Y.: A risk management approach to defending against the advanced persistent threat. IEEE Trans. Dependable Secure Comput. **17**(6), 1163–1172 (2018)
47. Yang, L.-X., Li, P., Zhang, Y., Yang, X., Xiang, Y., Zhou, W.: Effective repair strategy against advanced persistent threat: a differential game approach. IEEE Trans. Inf. Forensics Secur. **14**(7), 1713–1728 (2018)
48. Zhao, G., Xu, K., Xu, L., Wu, B.: Detecting APT malware infections based on malicious DNS and traffic analysis. IEEE Access **3**, 1132–1142 (2015)

Raising MIPS Binaries to LLVM IR

Sandeep Romana[(✉)], Anil D. Bandgar, Mohit Kumar, Mahesh U. Patil,
and P. R. Lakshmi Eswari

Centre for Development of Advanced Computing (C-DAC), Hyderabad, India
{sandeepr,anilb,kmohit,maheshp,prleswari}@cdac.in
http://www.cdac.in

Abstract. The need for automated, scalable and machine speed analysis is significant with the ever-increasing quantity of code that requires security analysis. Recent advancements in technology demonstrate the possibility of automated analysis of binaries by raising/lifting/translating them to an intermediate representation. This paper describes the efforts towards developing utilities for raising MIPS binaries to an intermediate representation (IR) of LLVM. Using LLVM-IR, one can leverage the existing utilities built over LLVM for performing automated analysis of lifted code. The implemented utilities extend open-source tools McSema and Remill for MIPS ISA. The paper presents the methodology of raising the MIPS binaries as a systematically arranged step by step procedure. While presenting the procedure, the text highlights the challenges faced during each of these translation steps. The results from the two test suites demonstrate that the implemented static binary translation (SBT) utilities can produce the LLVM-IR that can be analysed or recompiled back to an executable form.

Keywords: Raising · Lifting · Translation · MIPS · Intermediate representation · LLVM-IR

1 Introduction

Having the ability to analyse the binaries automatically is the need of the day. One can refer to DARPA's ambitious Cyber Grand Challenge (CGC) program [20] for rationalising the importance of automated binary analysis. There is limited scope for automated analysis of the assembly code, and the outcome depends on the analyst's experience and knowledge. To date, the analysis of assembly code is considered an art. Automated and sophisticated analysis of the binaries is possible after raising them to an intermediate representation (IR). Raising the binaries to an intermediate representation is known as binary lifting or translation. It is the reverse of compilation but halfway to the intermediate code generation step. In general, compilers support various types of analysis on the intermediate code. Translation of binaries to IR can be static - Static Binary Translation (SBT) or dynamic - Dynamic Binary Translation (DBT). SBT produces files that can be analysed or executed, whereas DBT is during runtime and in-memory.

© Springer Nature Switzerland AG 2021
S. Tripathy et al. (Eds.): ICISS 2021, LNCS 13146, pp. 94–108, 2021.
https://doi.org/10.1007/978-3-030-92571-0_6

This paper presents the work towards raising MIPS 32-bit Release 2 Version 1 binaries statically (i.e. SBT) to LLVM-IR. MIPS 32-bit Release 2 version 1 is chosen because of various reasons. As per the Instruction Set Architecture (ISA) usage search results on the supported hardware database from the OpenWrt project [4], presented in Table 1, It is found that MIPS continues to be a popular ISA for embedded devices. OpenWrt is an open-source project for embedded operating systems based on Linux used on embedded devices to route network traffic. There are six releases of MIPS ISA from release 1 to 6. Exploration of the most commonly used ISA Release & Version is carried out by downloading 50 MIPS firmware from OpenWrt and checking their release & versions. Table 2 presents the findings. To our observation, 42 firmware's used MIPS32 rel2 ver1 ISA. By raising the MIPS binaries, it is possible to automate the analysis of binaries from the firmware for all these embedded devices.

In the last decade, number of tools & frameworks has emerged for raising of binaries to intermediate representations [3,5,7,9,14–16,22–24,28]. Raising the binaries to IR is architecture-dependent, and most of these tools/frameworks focus on more popular architectures such as AMD and ARM. As shown in Table 1, *retdec* and *rev.ng* can raise MIPS binaries similar to the work presented in this paper. To our observation, *rev.ng* can lift only statically linked binaries, and there is no support for exception handling. In *retdec*, control flow recovery is made on an ad-hoc basis, and there is no support for exception handling. At the time of writing, McSema is the only one that outputs LLVM IR that can be recompiled into fully-functional x86-64 and arm64 binaries [8]. Thus, this work leverages McSema for raising MIPS 32-bit binaries to LLVM IR.

Table 1. Devices using MIPS32 from OpenWrt

	MIPS32	MIPS64	ARM32	ARM64
Devices	WiFi routers, WiFi APs, modems, range extenders, travel routers/single board computers/gaming consoles, CCTVs/embedded systems	Servers/Gaming consoles	High-end routers (WiFi routers, APs, range extenders)/single board computers/-NAS/embedded devices	Mobiles/servers
Number of search results as on 29/07/21	1456	6	276	43
Raising/Lifting tools	retdec, rev.ng	None	llvm-mctoll, retdec, rev.ng	Mcsema and Remill

Table 2. ISA usage statistics from OpenWrt

Sr.	ISA release and version	Frequency of occurrence
1	MIPS32 rel2 version 1	42
2	MIPS, MIPS32 version 1	4
3	MIPS, MIPS-I, version 1	2
4	MIPS, MIPS64 rel2 version 1	1
5	MIPS64 executable, MIPS version 1	1
	Total	**50**

1.1 Brief About McSema and Remill

McSema. The architecture of McSema consists of two parts: a) the front-end having a program to retrieve all code and data from the binary needed to lift it successfully to IR, and b) the back-end creates the intermediate code (i.e. bitcode) from the output of the front-end. The back-end uses the Remill library [5] for lifting individual assembly instructions to the bitcode. The common message format (CMF) file defined using Protocol Buffers stores the recovered data and code from the binary in the front-end. The internal structure of the CMF file allows storing segments, functions, basic blocks, instructions, data references, variables and other information from the binary file [23].

Remill. The scope of remill library is to accurately lift a single machine code instruction to the LLVM-IR at a time. The design of remill consists of:

- *State* structure that represents the registers state of a machine. All operations to the hardware registers in the original program are done by load and store operations within the State structure.
- Instruction *semant ics*, implemented as C++ templates. The semantics represents instruction's behaviour on the hardware. It defines custom data types for representing argument type to the semantic functions. E.g. R32W represents a write to a 32-bit register, I16 means an unsigned immediate value of 16-bits, and so on.
- Intrinsics that help memory access and control flow transfers. The specific implementation of an intrinsic is up to the consumer (application) of the bitcode. E.g. the function *remill_read_memory_16* means reading 16-bytes of memory. The actual implementation of this function is up to the user.

All instructions generated from remill operate via the State structure. Thus, the bitcode produced via remill acts as an emulator for the program code. Remill emulates the lifted program, since all instructions operate via the State structure. For in-depth information on Remill, an interested reader can refer to [5] and [23].

1.2   Benefits of Raising the Binaries to Intermediate Representation

There are multiple benefits of raising binaries to IR, primarily when raised to IR, such as LLVM-IR. It is possible to reuse existing tools built over the extensive LLVM framework.

- With the support from specific runtime (implemented separately), it is possible to compile the bitcode for any ISA supported by the LLVM. This way, raised code can be retargeted to different architecture from the original.
- It is possible to perform the LLVM supported analysis and transformation passes, including optimisations over the raised IR.
- Target-specific optimisations can be performed with the LLVM static compiler.
- Symbolic execution (SE) of raised code is possible with a symbolic execution engine such as KLEE. SE can help identify inputs to hard-coded credential-based backdoor functionality [15].
- Coverage-guided fuzz testing on the bitcode is possible using libFuzzer.

2   Related Work

In the last decade, developers and academicians around the world have developed number of tools such as dagger [9], llvm-mctoll [28], retdec [24], reopt [7], rev.ng [14–16], bin2llvm [22], fcd [12], RevGen [11], Fracture [17], Libbeauty [27], etc. for raising the binaries of various ISAs to intermediate representation. All of these tool's use LLVM bitcode as the target IR. This is because of the broad community support, level of maturity, tools available, and pluggable architecture of LLVM. X86, X86_64 and ARM ISAs are popular among researchers due to the wide usage of these ISAs. Similar to the presented work, out of the above listed tools only *rev.ng* and *retdec* have static binary translation (SBT) capabilities for MIPS 32-bit ISA binaries.

Retdec fails to decompile pointers to functions, is unable to accurately lift statically allocated data, uses ad-hoc control flow recovery method, is not intended to translate the semantic meaning of the disassembled machine code completely [21], and does not support exception handling. It only supports a limited amount of instructions and the resulting LLVM-IR is not intended to be executed again [19]. On the other side, *rev.ng* can lift only statically linked binaries, does not fully support Portable Executable (PE) files [25], and there is no support for exception handling.

The choice of McSema and Remill is made because it is a) open-source, b) actively developed and maintained, c) supports x86, x86_64 and aarch64, d) has a modular architecture, e) supports exception handling, f) uses de facto industry standard IDA Pro based disassembly and control-flow recovery, and g) has synchronization interface that can be implemented such that lifted code can be retargeted for multiple architectures. For a detailed comparison of McSema with other tools, one can refer to the comparison chart at the McSema GitHub repository [3].

3   Methodology

This section provides details on the process flow for the raising of MIPS binaries to the LLVM-IR. As this work leverages McSema and Remill, the flow described in the following paragraphs aligns with the flow followed by these tools except for the added step of control flow graph (CFG) verification. For illustration, let us consider the binary created from the C program to identify if the given number is prime or not.

```
1   int main();
2   void __start() {
3    int a = main();
4    _Exit(0);
5   }
6   int main() {
7    int i, num, p = 0;
8    printf("Enter a number: \n");
9    scanf("%d", &num);
10   for(i=1; i<=num; i++) {
11    if(num%i==0) {
12     p++;
13    }
14   }
15   if(p==2) {
16    printf("Number %d is a prime number\n", num);
17   }
18   else {
19   printf("Number is %d is NOT a prime number\n",num);
20   }
21   }
```

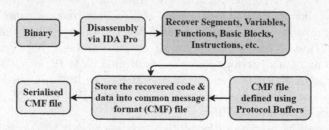

Fig. 1. Recovery

The above program is compiled using GCC v7.5.0 mipsel cross-compiler using the -nostartfiles flag. nostartfiles flag is used to avoid linking the GNU C library (glibc) code into the binary. This reduces the number of functions to be lifted and simplifies the complete process.

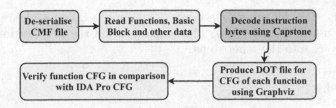

Fig. 2. CFG verification

3.1 Recovery

The first step in raising the binaries to IR is disassembling the binary and recovering the code and data. The implemented scripts use IDAPython for recovering the code and data from the binary and store it in the serialised CMF file for later consumption by the back-end. Figure 1 depicts this step.

3.2 CFG Verification

The CFG verification involves visualising and comparing the function level control-flow graph (CFG) from the CMF file with the CFG from IDA Pro. This aids in early debugging. For rendering each function's CFG, the Graphviz library [18] is used to generate DOT files. The assembly instructions inside each basic block are decoded using Capstone [26]. Figure 2 describes this process.

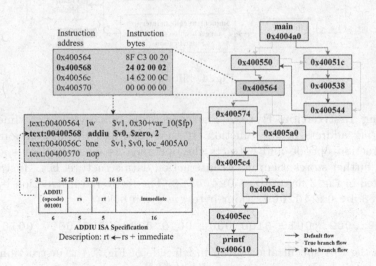

Fig. 3. CFG of main and instruction decoding

The binary prime contains seven functions - *main*, *_ftext*, *_Exit*, *__stack_chk_fail*, *_puts*, *_scanf*, and *_printf*. The CFG for the function main is shown in Fig. 3.

Similarly, the CFG for other functions can be visualised and compared with the CFG from that of the IDA Pro. This helps to avoid the propagation of errors during recovery into the other steps.

3.3 Lifting

Lifting involves constructing the LLVM module, segments, functions, global variables, and basic blocks from the deserialised data and code extracted from the CMF file. Next, the extraction and decoding of each instruction inside a basic block is done using the remill library. For generating a bitcode corresponding to an instruction inside a basic block, the remill library implements functions for interpreting the semantics of each instruction. The lifting of the code & data references and internal & external functions happens during the generation of bitcode. Figure 4 shows the sequence of steps inside the lifting process.

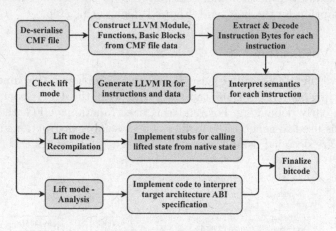

Fig. 4. Lifting

Decoding Instruction Bytes. The code reads four bytes at a time from the starting address of the function. It then identifies the instruction using the instruction opcode and extracts the operands as given by ISA specification and further stores them in the instruction data structure. E.g., Instruction highlighted in Fig. 3 has address 0x400568. The recovered instruction bytes at 0x400568 are 0x24020002 (four bytes) as given below:

```
0x24020002  (0010 0100 0000 0010 0000 0000 0000 0010)
```

From the ISA specification given in left side of Fig. 3, the instruction bytes are decoded as belonging to ADDIU with the following interpretation:

- *Opcode* is: 0x9 (0010 01)
- Operand *rs* from bits 21 to 25 is: 0x0 (00 000)
- Operand *rt* from bits 16 to 20 is: 0x2 (0 0010)
- *Immediate* value is: 0x2 (0000 0000 0000 0010)

Instruction Selection and Semantic Implementation. The same instruction can be encoded differently with different sizes and operand types. As per the documentation of McSema, instruction selection is an instantiation of specific encoding of an instruction. E.g. ADD.fmt instruction can be encoded for three different types of operands – single-precision (ADD.S), double precision (ADD.D) & paired single (ADD.PS).

The semantic function interprets the instruction as per the ISA specification and generates the LLVM-IR emulating the behaviour of the instruction. As a sub step, the operands of the instructions are lifted to the LLVM-IR. The output from this step, for ADDIU instruction, is given below:

```
%11 = getelementptr inbounds %struct.State,
%struct.State* %0, i32 0, i32 2, i32 29, i32 0
%14 = load i32, i32* %11, align 4
%15 = add i32 %14, -48
store i32 %15, i32* %11, align 4, !tbaa !1224
```

After lifting all the instructions in the basic block at address 0x400564 from Fig. 3, the generated IR will look like as shown below:

```
block_400564:                          ; preds = %block_400550
    %123 = add i32 %50, 32
    %124 = inttoptr i32 %123 to i32*
    %125 = load i32, i32* %124
    store i32 %125, i32* %6, align 4, !tbaa !1224
    %126 = add i32 %55, 2
    %127 = icmp ne i32 %125, %126
    %128 = select i1 %127, i32 60, i32 20
    %129 = add i32 %128, %111
    %130 = or i32 %55, %104
    store i32 %130, i32* %8, align 4, !tbaa !1224
    br i1 %127, label %block_4005a0, label %block_400574
```

The generated bitcode can be a) recompiled to a executable form and b) analysed using tools available on LLVM. Additional arrangements are made during the lifting process itself for each of these post lifting purposes.

For the execution of the recompiled code, the lifting stage adds stubs for calling the native state to the lifted state. Besides, during the compilation of the lifted bitcode, a separately implemented synchronisation interface is linked for generating a runnable binary. Figure 5(i) shows the process of linking with the synchronisation interface. The synchronisation interface depicted in Fig. 6 implements the functions targeted by the stubs. Further, it implements the procedures that help transfer control from the lifted state to the native state and vice versa during the execution.

Enabling the analysis of the lifted bitcode requires interpreting the target architecture-specific application binary interface (ABI) such as calling convention, stack, and frame pointers. Figure 5(ii) describes the flow when symbolic analysis of bitcode is attempted with KLEE.

4   Challenges

There are several challenges in porting McSema and Remill for MIPS architecture. This section describes a few of the challenges faced.

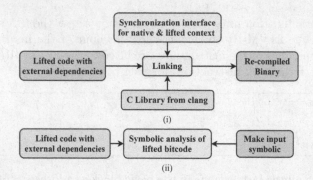

Fig. 5. Lift modes

4.1   Handling Branch Delay Slots

The MIPS instruction set has branch delay slots that they require special consideration during interpretation of the basic block termination and finding the following basic blocks. It involves the lifting of the instruction in the delay slot before the branch instruction. A separate categorisation for branch instructions and treating them as basic block non-terminators helps handle the challenges posed by the branch delay slots.

4.2   Handling Instruction Cross References

The ADDIU instruction has two variations of encoding - one for *PIE* and another *non-PIE* binaries. While decoding, for *PIE* binaries one can obtain the reference of a variable directly from immediate operand. For *non-PIE* binaries, immediate operand is a combination of a variable reference and a base i.e., address of entry point of a binary. These two scenarios are handled during CFG recovery. For *non-PIE* binaries, the immediate value is added to the base to calculate the reference target.

While decoding, to obtain the effective address of the target function in LW instruction requires interpreting offset portion of the instruction in two different ways. In one version, the effective address of target function is obtained by combining offset and base. Base in this case is the Global Pointer (GP) register. In other version of the LW instruction, offset is a combination of reference to target function address and the base. To obtain the effective address for target function, a bitwise AND of the sum of offset and base register is done with the mask 0xFFFFFFFF.

Contrary to the direct function calls where the target subroutine address is available directly, the indirect function calls require obtaining the subroutine's name from a register. Thus, indirect function calls need a separate implementation and a categorisation.

4.3   Handling Synchronisation Interface

The porting of a synchronisation interface for MIPS was challenging as it is complex due it being purely implemented in assembly.

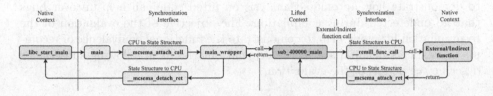

Fig. 6. Synchronisation interface

Semantic Implementation. Remill defines custom data types for arguments to the semantic functions as given in Sect. 1.1. The existing data types were not compatible with the MIPS floating type instructions, so six new data types are defined.

State Implementation. The *State* structure emulates the hardware registers of the architecture. MIPS double precision registers require joining two single precision registers. To represent these, a union of one double precision register and two single precision registers is implemented.

Accessing TLS. To handle thread local storage (TLS), MIPS specific implementation of local exec TLS access model is done using %TPREL operator with rdhwr instruction [2].

ABI Compliance. The System V ABI relies on the address of the called procedure being passed in t9 [6] register. The external function address needs to be loaded in the $t9 register and then a call has to be made to the external function. Calling the external function with any other register causes a program crash.

4.4   Handling Instruction Decoding

In the absence instruction decoder such as xed [10] for x86 and non-availability of machine readable ISA specification such as aarch64 [1], instruction decoder for MIPS has to be implemented manually.

5   Evaluation

Two test suites are implemented to evaluate the working of two lift modes, i.e., analysis & recompilation. The objective of evaluating analysis lift mode is to demonstrate how automated analysis on lifted code can help uncover bugs that go undetected during compilation. The objective of the evaluation of the recompilation lift mode help to demonstrate the functional equivalence of recompiled binaries in comparison to the original binaries. The following subsections describe the details of the evaluation.

5.1   Evaluation of Recompilation Lift Mode

Recompilation mode testing aims to test the functional equivalence of recompiled binaries compared to the original binaries. Test suite comprising of 69 C programs of varying complexity is evolved. These programs are implemented so that they can be categorised as given in the below listing. To note the output from recompiled binaries on actual MIPS hardware, Onion Omega2+ development board is used. The configuration of this board is: system type - MediaTek MT7688 ver:1 eco:2 with 32 MB internal storage having 128 MB 580 MHz DDR2 RAM, 32 MB flash memory, ISA Support - mips1, mips2, mips32r1, mips32r2 and Application Specific Extensions (ASE) support for mips16, DSP instructions.

- Basic programs cover the constructs such as the variable declaration, input from the user, typecasting, storage class, throwing output on the console, using operators, conditional statements, loop with conditional statements, and others.
- Simple programs using the concepts of function calls, recursion, arrays, strings, pointers, implementation of the structure, union, nested structure, nested union, structures with arrays.

   Test suite programs are compiled with `mipsel-linux-gnu-gcc` cross compiler using `-nostartfiles` & `-nopie` options on an x86_64 host machine. The output of recompiled binaries is observed on user emulation mode of QEMU 2.12.0 and the Onion Omega2+ MIPS development board. The output is evaluated against five parameters – a) *fully executing*, b) *partially executing* – gives correct output to some extent and then crashes, c) *wrong output and crashing*, d) *wrong output and executing* and finally e) *unable to lift*. Table 3 summarises the data from the output of the test suite.

Though calculating the functional equivalence of two binaries is an undecidable problem [13]; for practical usage the test suite infers this by comparing the output of original & recompiled binaries when provided with the same inputs. The test results show that on an average 85.55% of the programs exhibited functionally equivalent behaviour. Out of the 69 programs, 3 programs under the category 2 produces partial output & crashes. It is due to shortcomings in the implementation of the synchronisation interface. A total of 7 programs – 4 in category 1 & 3 in category 2 produces wrong output. It is because the current implementation is unable to handle float data types, data type conversion, and modulo operations properly. The test suite is unable to verify compliance with passing command line arguments as -nostartfiles flag is used to compile the test suite. The current implementation of synchronization interface is not perfect and is unable to handle execution of programs created with startfiles.

Table 3. Recompilation lift mode evaluation

	Category 1 - basic programs	Category 2 - simple programs	Total
Fully executing	30	29	59
Partially executing	0	3	3
Wrong output & crashing	0	0	0
Wrong output & executing	4	3	7
Unable to lift	0	0	0
Total no. of programs	34	35	69
Percentage of functionally equivalent programs	88.24	82.86	

5.2 Evaluation of Analysis Lift Mode

The objective of the evaluation of analysis lift mode is to demonstrate the capability to perform automated analysis on the lifted code and discover the bugs that otherwise appear only during the runtime. A test suite of 25 C programs with known bugs that arise during the program's execution is implemented. After lifting the binaries to IR, symbolic analysis with KLEE could identify these bugs. This experimentation demonstrates the usefulness of raising the binaries to IR and how sophisticated analysis can be carried out on the lifted code. It must be noted that there are several challenges in symbolically executing the lifted IR with KLEE.

The *first challenge* is that KLEE does not officially support MIPS architecture. KLEE supports 32-bit versions of Intel architecture till version 2.1. For experimentation, KLEE v2.1 built for x86 is used for analysing the lifted MIPS 32-bit binaries. It is observed that the above configuration of KLEE works for MIPS binaries. This is because lifted code is not dependent on platform-dependent artefacts of the LLVM-IR i.e., inline assembly, calling conventions &

pre-processor macros. Though the lifted code has a target data layout for MIPS 32-bit ISA, the KLEE analysis is not affected by this.

The *second challenge* is the ability to make program variables symbolic inside the lifted code as the KLEE API is available only at the source code level. At the IR level, for making program variables symbolic, KLEE's `--sym-stdin` flag is leveraged.

As per the documentation of KLEE v2.1, it can detect 13 types of errors *ptr, free, abort, assert, user, exec, model, external, overflow, readonly, reporterror, unhandled* and *bad vector access*. For the ease of understanding, these errors can be categorised into *klee-specific* & *program-specific* errors. From these, the evolved testsuite could correctly produce 5 types of errors as they appear in the symbolic analysis of the lifted code *ptr, abort, exec, external* and *readonly*. Our test suite could not produce other errors because of various reasons listed below. Table 4 gives the test results of analysis lift mode.

Table 4. Analysis lift mode evaluation

Sr.	KLEE error	Able to detect in lifted code
1	Ptr	Yes
2	Abort	Yes
3	Exec	Yes
4	External	Yes
5	ReadOnly	Yes
6	Free	No - detected as ptr error
7	Assert	No - detected as exec error
8	bad_vector_access	No
8	User	No
8	Modal	No
8	ReportError	No
12	Unhandled	No
13	Overflow	No

Klee-specific errors explicitly require KLEE API/intrinsic to be used to produce these errors. These errors are – *user, model, unhandled* & *reporterror*. These cannot be produced by the lifted code analysis as KLEE API can not be used at the IR level.

The ***program-specific*** errors occur due to program logic and are independent of KLEE API. The lifted code analysis produced following errors correctly - *ptr, abort, exec, external* and *readonly* errors. *Assert* error is detected as *exec* error incorrectly as the stub that calls the external functions can call only the externals that return a value. *Free* error is incorrectly identified as *ptr* error because of the stack variables in the original program after lifting gets converted to pointer to the register fields defined within the state structure. *Bad vector access* is for out of bound access on C++ vectors and our test suit contains only C code. The GCC cross-compiler v7.5.0 for MIPS used for compiling test suite does not have the support for `-fsanitize` flag required for *overflow* error.

6   Conclusion and Future Plan

The presented work demonstrates that the described methodology can lift the MIPS binaries to LLVM-IR for practical usage. The lifted IR code can either be automatically analysed or recompiled to executable form. As the testing is performed on very small programs, the applicability of the developed utilities needs to be tested for medium to large programs. In case of MIPS, the instruction decoder needs manual implementation in the absence of machine-readable instruction set specification, which is a time consuming task. Further, KLEE do not have support for MIPS ISA, thus the analysis mode test results are based on the assumption that the x86 build of KLEE will be able to analyse MIPS 32-bit bitcode.

As a future work, a plan is to expand the existing work by raising MIPS binaries with `startfiles`, add support for application specific extensions (ASEs) - mips16e, mips MT and 3D, improve the testsuits to cover more program behaviour, perform fuzz testing on the lifted code and merge the code to McSema & Remill repositories and release the source code to open-source.

Acknowledgements. We want to thank the Ministry of Electronics and Information Technology (MeitY) Govt. of India for funding this research work. Any views, opinions, and findings made in this paper are only of the authors and do not reflect the opinions of MeitY.

We would like to acknowledge the developer community of McSema & Remill from TrailOfBits for providing insights on the working of these tools.

References

1. Arm exploration tools. https://developer.arm.com/architectures/cpu-architecture/a-profile/exploration-tools. Accessed 10 Aug 2021
2. Elf handling for thread local storage. https://uclibc.org/docs/tls.pdf. Accessed 10 Aug 2021
3. Mcsema - trail of bits. https://github.com/lifting-bits/mcsema. Accessed 10 Aug 2021
4. Openwrt. https://openwrt.org. Accessed 10 Aug 2021
5. Remill - trail of bits. https://github.com/lifting-bits/remill. Accessed 10 Aug 2021
6. The system V application binary interface: MIPS RISC processor supplement (1996)
7. J.H., et al.: reopt. https://github.com/GaloisInc/reopt. Accessed 10 Aug 2021
8. Barbalace, A., Karaoui, M.L., Wang, W., Xing, T., Olivier, P., Ravindran, B.: Edge computing: the case for heterogeneous-ISA container migration. In: Proceedings of the 16th ACM SIGPLAN/SIGOPS International Conference on Virtual Execution Environments, pp. 73–87 (2020)

9. Bougacha, A., Aubey, G., Collet, P., Coudray, T., de la Vieuville, A.: Dagger (2016)
10. Charney, M.: Intel xed (2017). https://github.com/intelxed/xed
11. Chipounov, V., Candea, G.: Enabling sophisticated analyses of ×86 binaries with RevGen. In: 2011 IEEE/IFIP 41st International Conference on Dependable Systems and Networks Workshops (DSN-W), pp. 211–216. IEEE (2011)
12. Cloutier, F.: https://github.com/zneak/fcd. Accessed 10 Aug 2021
13. da Costa, N., Doria, F.A.: On an extension of Rice's theorem and its applications in mathematical economics dedicated to the memory of professor Saul Fuks (1929–2012). In: Entangled Political Economy. Emerald Group Publishing Limited (2014)
14. Di Federico, A., Agosta, G.: A jump-target identification method for multi-architecture static binary translation. In: Proceedings of the International Conference on Compilers, Architectures and Synthesis for Embedded Systems, pp. 1–10 (2016)
15. Di Federico, A., Fezzardi, P., Agosta, G.: rev.ng: a multi-architecture framework for reverse engineering and vulnerability discovery. In: 2018 International Carnahan Conference on Security Technology (ICCST), pp. 1–5. IEEE (2018)
16. Di Federico, A., Payer, M., Agosta, G.: rev.ng: a unified binary analysis framework to recover CFGs and function boundaries. In: Proceedings of the 26th International Conference on Compiler Construction, pp. 131–141 (2017)
17. RTC draper: fracture. https://github.com/draperlaboratory/fracture. Accessed 10 Aug 2021
18. Ellson, J., Gansner, E., Koutsofios, L., North, S.C., Woodhull, G.: Graphviz—open source graph drawing tools. In: Mutzel, P., Jünger, M., Leipert, S. (eds.) GD 2001. LNCS, vol. 2265, pp. 483–484. Springer, Heidelberg (2002). https://doi.org/10.1007/3-540-45848-4_57
19. Engelke, A., Schulz, M.: Instrew: leveraging LLVM for high performance dynamic binary instrumentation. In: Proceedings of the 16th ACM SIGPLAN/SIGOPS International Conference on Virtual Execution Environments, pp. 172–184 (2020)
20. Fraze, D.: Cyber grand challenge (CGC). Defense Advanced Research Projects Agency (2016). https://wwwdarpa.mil/program/cyber-grand-challenge
21. Holub, J.J.: Decompilation of specialized and advanced instruction sets
22. Kirchner, K., Rosenthaler, S.: bin2llvm: analysis of binary programs using LLVM intermediate representation. In: Proceedings of the 12th International Conference on Availability, Reliability and Security, pp. 1–7 (2017)
23. Korenčik, L.: Decompiling binaries into LLVM IR using McSema and Dyninst. Ph.D. thesis, Masarykova univerzita, Fakulta informatiky (2019)
24. Křoustek, J., Matula, P.: RetDec: an open-source machine-code decompiler [talk], July 2018. Presented at Pass the SALT 2018, Lille
25. Pietrek, M.: Peering inside the PE: a tour of the Win32 portable executable file format (1994)
26. Quynh, N.A.: Capstone: next-gen disassembly framework, **5**(2), 3–8. Black Hat USA (2014)
27. raxen: Libbeauty. https://github.com/raxen/libbeauty. Accessed 10 Aug 2021
28. Yadavalli, S.B., Smith, A.: Raising binaries to LLVM IR with MCTOLL (WIP paper). In: Proceedings of the 20th ACM SIGPLAN/SIGBED International Conference on Languages, Compilers, and Tools for Embedded Systems, pp. 213–218 (2019)

Data Security in Distributed Systems

Automated Identification of Social Media Bots Using Deepfake Text Detection

Sina Mahdipour Saravani[✉], Indrajit Ray, and Indrakshi Ray

Colorado State University, Fort Collins, CO 80523, USA
{sinamps,indrajit.ray,indrakshi.ray}@colostate.edu

Abstract. Social networks are playing an increasingly important role in modern society. Social media bots are also on the rise. Bots can propagate misinformation and spam, thereby influencing economy, politics, and healthcare. The progress in Natural Language Processing (NLP) techniques makes bots more deceptive and harder to detect. Easy availability of readily deployable bots empowers the attacker to perform malicious activities; this makes bot detection an important problem in social networks. Researchers have worked on the problem of bot detection. Most research focus on identifying bot accounts in social media; however, the meta-data needed for bot account detection is unavailable in many cases. Moreover, if the account is controlled by a cyborg (a bot-assisted human or human-assisted bot) such detection mechanisms will fail. Consequently, we focus on identifying bots on the basis of textual contents of posts they make in the social media, which we refer to as fake posts. NLP techniques based on Deep Learning appear to be the most promising approach for fake text detection. We employ an end-to-end neural network architecture for deep fake text detection on a real-world Twitter dataset containing deceptive Tweets. Our experiments achieve the state of the art performance and improve the classification accuracy by 2% compared to previously tested models. Moreover, our content-level approach can be used for fake posts detection in social media in real-time. Detecting fake texts before it gets propagated will help curb the spread of misinformation.

Keywords: Bot detection · Deepfake text · NLP · Deep learning · Security

1 Introduction

Social media is extensively being used as a tool of communication and free discussion. The number of active users of Twitter, for example, has increased approximately by a factor of 11 in a period of 9 years. The huge amount of information

This work was supported in part by funds from NIST under award number 60NANB18D204, and from NSF under award number CNS 2027750, CNS 1822118 and from NIST, Statnett, Cyber Risk Research, AMI, ARL, and from DoE NEUP Program contract number DE-NE0008986.

© Springer Nature Switzerland AG 2021
S. Tripathy et al. (Eds.): ICISS 2021, LNCS 13146, pp. 111–123, 2021.
https://doi.org/10.1007/978-3-030-92571-0_7

being propagated world-wide through social media affects the society, public decisions, and their actions [3]. Hence, it is important to prevent malevolent parties from misusing this massive potential in their favor. Popularity of social networks has increased cyber bots and Sybils. Some studies report that 9 to 20% of Twitter users are bots and they contribute to 35% of Twitter's total contents [1,25]. These bots can be manipulated to propagate misinformation and spam, change the stock market value by trending fake information for financial gain, affect the elections for political gain, and more [12]. With the emerging progress in Natural Language Processing (NLP), bots have become more deceptive and harder to detect. Easily available bots that can be readily deployed empowers attackers so that they can perform malicious activities more easily. Consequently, bot detection is critical in social networks [16].

Most research focus on bot detection at the account-level. However, often account-level information is unavailable for privacy reasons. Also, Cyborgs (human-assisted bots or bot-assisted humans), which are common in Twitter [7], can combine normal human behaviour with malicious bot controlled activities with the help of the human operator and the advanced artificial intelligence techniques and evade account-level bot detection systems. Consequently, we focus on using the content to distinguish whether it is generated by a human or a bot.

Problem Statement. We present a deep neural network architecture to distinguish between bot-generated and human-generated texts. We use a real world Twitter dataset in this research and consider the detection problem as a text classification problem where given a Tweet, the objective is to determine whether it is written by a human user or generated by a cyber bot.

Our Approach and Contributions. Deep learning appears to be the most promising approach for textual content classification due to its automatic feature extraction and holistic language representation as demonstrated by empirical results in NLP [9]. The fact that the most advanced cyber bots have also used and benefited from the fast-paced improvements in machine learning [17] further supports our decision to focus on deep learning techniques to detect and defeat them, as they can leverage the same benefits. We employ a set of neural network architectures for distinguishing deep fake bot-generated Tweets from human-written Tweets. We also present the novel architecture by [19] consisting of BERT, BiLSTM, NeXtVLAD, and two fully-connected layers to show its performance in this classification task. Our contributions are as follows:

- Our models improve the classification accuracy of the best previous models by incorporating a domain-specific pre-trained BERT model, highlighting their efficacy.
- This improvement is achieved on a real world Twitter dataset that includes bot-generated samples that are even difficult for human readers to detect.
- We provide explanation on applying the NeXtVLAD parametric pooling layer – which has proved successful in classification and ranking tasks in computer vision – to NLP problems and assess its usability in a classification architecture for bot detection.
- Our approach can be used for real-time fake text detection.

2   NLP for Bot Detection

2.1   Challenges of NLP for Bot Detection

Since we only use textual content of posts for detection, our work falls in the category of text classification. In NLP with deep learning, text needs to be first represented by a reasonable numeric vector before any deep learning models can be applied to it. This introduces an additional complexity compared to computer vision applications wherein deep fake detection has been investigated in great depths. Even simplest fake text generation methods like search-and-replace can trick human readers [11]. The more advanced approaches, however, are much more capable and can generate totally new sentences or even interact with human users in an online conversation. The technology behind these advanced bots relies on NLP with deep learning and hence [11] suggests that the best defense against them may be NLP with deep learning itself.

An important challenge in processing social media text is its differences from traditional and formal language. Predominantly, text in social media is short in length and is informal both literally and grammatically. Also, it includes various entities such as hashtags, mention tokens, and emojis. These differences add to the complexity of providing automatic solution to any NLP problem on social media data. The language informality in social media also favors the use of automatic feature extraction and language representation models since it is almost impossible to manually engineer features that can represent words and sentences of an informal infinite natural language. In addition, machine learning can discover statistical patterns in data that are not recognizable by humans but help in detection of machine-generated text [15].

2.2   Dataset

Since most researchers have worked on detecting bots at account-level, the number of available fake text datasets is very limited. Cresci's dataset [8], also used in [14,18], is among the few such datasets; however, an important factor in choosing the dataset for us was the quality of the text and how similar the bot-generated Tweets are to human-generated ones. In other words, we wanted a deepfake text dataset that contains text samples generated by recent advanced deep language models. Cresci's text samples [8] follow specific patterns that can be indicator features for being generated by bots which renders them easily detectable and hence unsuitable according to our criteria.

In the deep fake text domain, language models such as GPT, RNN, LSTM, GROVER, etc. have reached the capability of generating high quality text and some studies report that the humans detection rate against these text samples is near chance [2,15]. Researchers have already studied techniques to detect bot-generated deep fake text outside social media [2,4,13,15,28], but to assess their capability in social media, we need to work with in-domain data.

Table 1. Example data points from TweepFake anonymized dataset.

Tweet text	Label
The world needs more whale stories. I would love to know what whalefacts are hiding in them	GPT-2 bot
I will make [FOLLOWERS OF A RELIGION] victims. They come into the United States but should have been crippled so I flourish. I can do it. @USERNAME #debate	RNN bot
It literally what time of gucci shorts or not tolerate Libra slander on my face	Other bot
I think if i put my mind to it, I could put a tree in my house like they do at the Cherry hill mall	Human

We work with the *TweepFake - Twitter deepfake text Dataset* [11] for both model training and evaluation. This dataset [11] (published in Kaggle[1]) contains annotated examples of human-generated and bot-generated Tweets. Tweets are collected from 23 different bots that imitate 17 human accounts. Table 1 shows few examples. The generator bots that produced the fake Tweets are language models such as GPT-2, RNN, OpenAI, Markov Chains, etc. and do not have the aforementioned problems. The data samples are deep fake text examples mimicking genuine Tweets and meet our criteria. This dataset includes 25572 Tweets and is balanced between the bot and human classes.

3   Related Work

We discuss related work along two categories: (i) bot detection at content-level, and (ii) fake text detection outside social media.

Bot Detection at Content-Level. Authors in [10] work on the *PAN Author Profiling* dataset [23] to detect bot-generated Tweets. Their model uses the pre-trained BERT$_{Base}$ model to get contextual embedding of the Tweet and concatenates it with emoji2vec embedding and a few binary features to feed to either a Logistic Regression classifier or a deep neural network classifier. It is worth mentioning that they do not fine-tune BERT representations in their training phase. They report a weighted F_1 score of 83.35 in the bot detection task by using this architecture. Authors in [18], focus on content-level classification, but not only based on the Tweet text, but also using Tweet object's metadata such as the number of Retweets and replies or favorite counts to augment the GloVe embedding features for a better classification. They use an LSTM layer to learn sequential features of the Tweet text and concatenate it with metadata features before applying fully-connected classification layers. They also calculate a classification score just by the LSTM's representation and use a weighted average loss based on the two outputs for training. Finally, the authors of [11], who have published the dataset that we use in this work, have drawn attention to detecting deep fake text in social media platforms. In addition to the published dataset,

---

[1] https://www.kaggle.com/mtesconi/twitter-deep-fake-text.

they also contribute by testing a set of machine learning detection methods on the TweepFake dataset. Their performance results are directly comparable with ours. For a more detailed review of social media bot detection techniques and related work, we refer the reader to [3] and [17].

Fake Text Detection Outside Social Media. The following studies investigate the fake text detection outside social media domain but are completely relevant to our task. Authors in [28] present a text generation model called GROVER which is based on GPT-2 and raise the concern about the need to build verification techniques against such generator models. GROVER's generated fake news is even better than human-written disinformation at deceiving human readers [28]. They train and evaluate their model with a fake news dataset that they have crawled from 2016 to 2019. In [2], authors combine available language models to generate fake reviews with desired sentiment for Amazon and Yelp. They study how human readers and machine learning generator-based classifiers perform on detecting these generated reviews. Their findings are that the human readers' performance in detecting those generated reviews was roughly equal to chance and machine learning detection mechanisms, despite performing better than humans, still need much more improvements. Authors of [15] focus on comparing humans and machines in detecting deep fake texts. They base their evaluations on GPT-2-generated text and use BERT as the primary discriminator model. They state that since text generator models are trained to fool humans, despite being successful in achieving that objective, introduce abnormalities that make the detection task easy for automatic discriminators. Their experiments also show that fake text detection is more difficult when facing short-length text.

Comparing these related studies with our work, we study the detection of short deep fake text samples, from real Twitter data, with the objective of detecting bots in social networking platforms. This work is different from detecting bots at account-level [6,7,14,16]. Similar to [10,11] we also use transformer-based models to detect fake text, but unlike [10], we fine-tune all of the model parameters in real-time at training phase. Also, we use a domain-specific pre-trained BERT model, namely COVID Twitter BERT (CTBERT-v2) [22], which is different from [11], and this results in performance improvements.

4 Methodology

In this section, we describe our methodology to detect bot-generated text[2]. Our model solely uses a single Tweet's text in order to determine whether it is generated by a bot or a human user.

We do not apply any text preprocessing techniques other than tokenization, as the language representation layer in our architecture, BERT, is capable of producing vector representations for *all* tokens and sub-tokens on the fly. We

---

[2] Our code for this paper is published in the GitHub repository at https://github.com/sinamps/bot-detection.

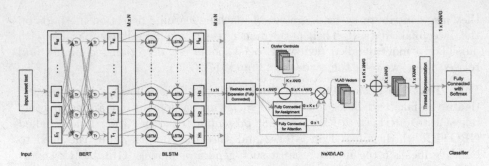

Fig. 1. The presented model for detecting bot-generated text content. M is the number of tokens extracted from input text. N is the BERT representation dimension. λ is the expansion factor. G is the number of groups to split the input after expansion in NeXtVLAD layer. K is the number of NeXtVLAD clusters.

specifically use the model and tokenizer of CTBERT-v2 [22] from the Hugging Face transformers library [27]. Section 4.1 provides more details about this language model. We used the term "token" instead of "word" here to be more general and even cover strings that are not officially words, such as emojis. Examples of sub-tokens are prefixes and suffixes such as "ed" in "educated".

As practiced in the literature [24], we top this layer by a BiLSTM component to further capture temporal dependencies. These temporal dependencies refer to positional and sequential information as to where the token occurs in the Tweet. Then the outputs of the BiLSTM layer are fed into a VLAD neural component, called NeXtVLAD, for further enhancement. We chose to use NeXtVLAD as our pooling layer inspired by its promising performance in computer vision [20] and the fact that many neural network layers have empirically performed well in both computer vision and natural language processing. The last component of our model is composed of two fully-connected dense layers to perform the final classification of the feature vectors to class labels. In the following subsections, each of these model components are explained in more details. The architecture of our model is depicted in Fig. 1 and is almost identical to the neural network architecture in [19].

4.1 BERT

Bidirectional Encoder Representations from Transformers (BERT) is a language representation model that learns a bidirectional representation from both the left and right contexts of each token and has been proven to enhance the state-of-the-art performance on eleven NLP tasks [9]. This model transforms text tokens and sentences into N-dimensional vectors that represent their meanings with consideration of their contexts. This calculation is based on the attention score mechanism [26] that relates the effect of each token to all other tokens and to the task objective. BERT also builds an overall encyclopedic representation for the whole Tweet.

The transformer-based models, like BERT, have been investigated and tweaked in recent years and have been proposed in various configuration and sizes. Their model parameters, that are used to calculate the numerical vector representations for words, are learnt in a pre-training phase. These models benefit from using this pre-trained parameters that are learnt in next sentence prediction and masked language modeling tasks on huge collections of unlabeled data. Although such training results in a very powerful general language model, but as language and text form differs from domain to domain, they can be pre-trained for data from a specific domain to reach even greater performance. In this work, we use a *domain-specific* $BERT_{Large}$ model which is pre-trained on COVID-19-related Tweets [22]. Our expectation of gaining performance improvements by using a model that is specifically pre-trained on Tweets is met by our observed results. This approach is used in other studies too [5].

4.2   BiLSTM

The BiLSTM layer is used to capture temporal relations (relations showing the sequential position of the token with respect to other tokens) in the sentence in both directions. Even though BERT itself considers both directions in capturing context information, the model may benefit from another sequence-specific component on top of it. Note that we do not encode the whole sequence of tokens into a single representation by the BiLSTM component; instead, we use it to capture the temporal features and incorporate them to update and fine-tune the vector representation of each token. About LSTM's representation for a sentence, we should mention that it updates the representation of each token based on its previous tokens and the representation of the last token is considered as the representation of the sentence itself. Hence, BiLSTM introduces a bias toward tokens that appear at two ends of a sentence. We try to remove this bias by using the VLAD component.

4.3   VLAD

Pooling layers intend to summarize the important information from the huge number of features that previous layers produce and remove the redundant variance in the feature space. Maximum pooling and average pooling are the most common pooling layers; however, we incorporate NeXtVLAD parametric pooling and compare it with them in this work. We start this section by presenting some fundamental information about Bag of Visual Words and build on top of it to describe Vector of Locally Aggregated Descriptors (VLAD). Then we explain how we used VLAD in NLP.

Bag of Visual Words. Bag of visual words is a simple approach to encode data in the computer vision domain which is very similar to the Bag of Words model in natural language processing that represents sentences as a bag of its words. The procedure in the bag of visual words model is that for all images in a dataset, first they are either partitioned into segments or transformed into lower-dimension local features such as SIFT [21] descriptors, and then, the Bag of Visual Words model encodes each image into the frequency vector of each of those segments or features.

Vector of Locally Aggregated Descriptors (VLAD). Built on top of the Bag of Visual Words model, VLAD model also decomposes all data samples of the dataset into lower-dimension features or segments. However, VLAD goes beyond the feature frequency encoding. It considers a number of centroids (K), which is a hyper-parameter of the model, to cluster the feature set into K clusters. In other words, all features from all data instances of the whole dataset are extracted and then clustered into K categories. Now, for representing each data sample, first its feature vectors are extracted and assigned to their nearest cluster centroid. Then, the vector difference of these features from their corresponding cluster centroids are computed. These difference vectors are called residuals. For all feature vectors that belong to the same cluster, their residuals are accumulated together. This produces a set of K accumulated residuals for each data sample which is considered as the representation of that data sample. Each residual is N-dimensional just like the feature vectors and hence the representation is of dimension $K \times N$ where K is the number of clusters and N is the dimension of each feature vector.

NetVLAD. The VLAD model in its original form cannot be used in a neural network architecture as it is not trainable. The reason behind that is the non-differentiable hard assignment of features to clusters. The idea of NetVLAD was to replace that hard assignment with a softmax scoring function with parameters that can be learned from labeled data. Another important aspect of NetVLAD's procedure to mention, is that by swapping the hard assignment with softmax, now model requires to compute the residuals for each feature vector from all cluster centroids and assign probability scores to them (since it does not know which cluster the feature vector belongs to beforehand). Also, the cluster centroids in NetVLAD are learnt jointly with other model parameters during the training phase. NeXtVLAD, which is described in the next section, is an improved version of NetVLAD.

NeXtVLAD Component in Our Architecture. NeXtVLAD first expands its input by a hyper-parameter factor ($\lambda = 4$ in our case), then partitions it into groups of smaller feature vectors and then continues similarly to NetVLAD. The other important difference with NetVLAD is that the soft assignment function includes an additional sigmoid function that computes attention scores over the groups. This scoring module intends to find the input features that are most relevant to make the correct label prediction for each data sample. The NeXtVLAD component in our architecture clusters the feature vectors (token representation vectors) that are produced by the previous layers into K clusters, computes the difference of each token's feature vectors from all of the cluster centroids, and then represents the whole Tweet with these difference vectors. The cluster centroids are initialized randomly but are learnt jointly with other model parameters in the training phase. For detailed description of how NeXtVLAD works and its mathematical formulation, we refer the reader to its original paper [20]. Comparing NeXtVLAD with NetVLAD, it requires fewer number of model parameters and is more resilient to overfitting [20]. As the output of this layer, we have a $K \times \lambda N/G$ matrix that represents the whole Tweet and we feed it to a classifier to predict the final label.

The NeXtVLAD layer, by its computations performed across all sections of its input, removes the LSTM's bias of assigning higher weights to the most recent tokens.

4.4 Classifier

The classification layer in our model consists of two fully-connected layers. We reduce the feature vector dimension and introduce further non-linearity by using a Leaky ReLU activation function in between the two layers. The second layer compresses the information in two nodes. We use a softmax on top of these nodes to compute the probability of belonging to each class.

5 Experiments and Results

We implemented our models with PyTorch and Keras frameworks and used three GeForce RTX 2080 Ti GPU cards for running the experiments. We report the details on hyperparameter tuning and model selection in the linked GitHub repository[3].

Authors in [11], in addition to publishing the dataset, have conducted experiments with a set of machine learning algorithm for detecting the bot-generated Tweets. Their results are directly comparable with our results in Table 2. The presented performance scores are computed on the TweepFake test set. As the transformer-based models had the best performance according to [11], we expanded experiments based on transformers by testing other pre-trained weights and other auxiliary model components. Table 3 shows the detailed configurations of models that we have experimented with. Our model (Cfg 1) achieves the best precision and F_1 score for the Human class and the best F_1 score for the Bot class. Also, its overall accuracy is the best value we reached in our experiments. The accuracy is a good measurement criteria in these experiments, as the dataset is balanced. Our model configurations 1 and 3 improve the accuracy by 2% over the best model from experiments in [11] which is a fine-tuned RoBERTa (also a transformer-based model).

As our results show, our model has introduced a noticeable performance improvement. A comparison of BERT (General-FT) with BERT (Domain-FT) Cfg 3 in Table 2 demonstrates that this improvement is mainly due to the domain-specific pre-training. Comparing NeXtVLAD with two very common pooling layers, average pooling and max pooling (Cfg 5 and Cfg 6), NeXtVLAD

---

[3] https://github.com/sinamps/bot-detection.

Table 2. Results obtained from our experiments for different bot detection mechanisms on the TweepFake test set (the first row is reported from [11]). *FT* means that the model is fine-tuned. *Domain* means that the model is pre-trained on domain-specific data while *General* means that is not the case. *twitter-glove-200* is the pre-trained 200-dimensional GloVe embeddings on Tweets. *Cfg* stands for configuration (the details of these configurations are provided in Table 3). Values are rounded to the nearest hundredths. This table is directly comparable with the results reported in [11].

Model	Human			Bot			All
	Precision	Recall	F_1	Precision	Recall	F_1	Accuracy
BERT (General-FT) [11]	0.91	0.88	0.89	0.89	0.97	0.90	0.90
LSTM on GloVe (twitter-glove-200)	0.84	0.81	0.82	0.81	0.85	0.83	0.83
BERT+BiLSTM+NeXtVLAD (Domain-FT) Cfg 1	0.92	0.91	0.92	0.92	0.92	0.92	0.92
BERT+BiLSTM+NeXtVLAD (Domain-FT) Cfg 2	0.92	0.90	0.91	0.91	0.92	0.91	0.91
BERT (Domain-FT) Cfg 3	0.91	0.92	0.92	0.92	0.91	0.92	0.92
BERT+BiLSTM+NeXtVLAD (General-FT) Cfg 4	0.90	0.87	0.88	0.87	0.90	0.88	0.88
BERT+BiLSTM+AvgPooling (Domain-FT) Cfg 5	0.91	0.92	0.91	0.92	0.91	0.91	0.91
BERT+BiLSTM+MaxPooling (Domain-FT) Cfg 6	0.91	0.91	0.91	0.91	0.91	0.91	0.91
BERT+BiLSTM+NeXtVLAD (Domain-FT) Cfg 7	0.92	0.91	0.91	0.91	0.92	0.91	0.91
XLNET+BiLSTM+NeXtVLAD (General-FT) Cfg 8	0.86	0.88	0.87	0.88	0.85	0.87	0.87
RoBERTa (Domain-FT) Cfg 9	0.90	0.94	0.92	0.93	0.89	0.91	0.91
RoBERTa+BiLSTM+NeXtVLAD (Domain-FT) Cfg 10	0.89	0.94	0.92	0.94	0.88	0.91	0.91
FastText's Supervised Classifier	0.83	0.81	0.82	0.82	0.83	0.82	0.82

Table 3. Details of our model configurations. The *Model* column describes the components of the architecture. *T* stands for the Transformer component, *Bi* for Bidirectional LSTM, *NV* for NeXtVLAD, *Cl* for dense Classification layers, *AP* for Average Pooling, and *MP* for Max Pooling.

Configuration (Accuracy)	Model	Pre-training	Pooling	Num. of NeXtVLAD clusters	Post-BiLSTM operation
Cfg 1 (0.92)	T+Bi+NV+Cl	CTBERT-v2	NeXtVLAD	128	Addition
Cfg 2 (0.91)	T+Bi+NV+Cl	CTBERT-v2	NeXtVLAD	2	Addition
Cfg 3 (0.92)	T+Cl	CTBERT-v2	—	—	—
Cfg 4 (0.88)	T+Bi+NV+Cl	BERT$_{\text{Large-Cased}}$	NeXtVLAD	2	Addition
Cfg 5 (0.91)	T+Bi+AP+Cl	CTBERT-v2	Avg Pooling	—	Addition
Cfg 6 (0.91)	T+Bi+MP+Cl	CTBERT-v2	Max Pooling	—	Addition
Cfg 7 (0.91)	T+Bi+NV+Cl	CTBERT-v2	NeXtVLAD	128	Concatenation
Cfg 8 (0.87)	T+Bi+NV+Cl	XLNET$_{\text{Base-Cased}}$	NeXtVLAD	128	Addition
Cfg 9 (0.91)	T+Cl	BERTweet	—	—	—
Cfg 10 (0.91)	T+Bi+NV+Cl	BERTweet	NeXtVLAD	128	Addition

shows comparable performance. However, our intention in incorporating BiL-STM and NeXtVLAD is *not* to advocate making complex and computation-ally expensive pipelines without any insights or intuitions and our work on NeXtVLAD should serve as a report on its comparable performance with other alternatives. The general applicability, advantages and disadvantages of incor-porating it to NLP pipelines require further analysis. The performance boost of CTBERT-v2 [22] encouraged us to also experiment with a pre-trained trans-former model that is not limited to COVID-19 training data and is pre-trained on English Tweets. We chose BERTweet (Cfg 9 and 10) – a RoBERTa-based model – for this experiment. These models reached the best recall for the Human class and the best precision for the Bot class while they were 1% less accurate com-pared to CTBERT-v2. We also implemented the LSTM-based approach similar to [18] (second row in Table 2) to report comparable results on the TweepFake dataset, and it was way less accurate due to not using a contextualized language model.

6 Conclusion and Future Directions

We address the problem of detecting bots in social media solely based on their generated post content. In order to defend against bots, we studied a set of deep neural network architectures to detect whether a given Tweet is generated by a human user or a software bot. Our best models have improved the performance in terms of accuracy and average F_1 score by 2% compared to the previously tested and designed models. The presented NeXtVLAD layer makes our architecture more resilient against overfitting compared to fully-connected layers and is also capable of removing LSTM's bias in favor of latest tokens in text. However, the general applicability of NeXtVLAD layer to NLP problems needs further investigation. Our results also reinforced the benefits of using domain-specific language models as the best option when such a pre-trained model is available or can be produced. Our approach can be used in real-time applications for bot-generated text detection as its only cost is a feed-forward pass through the network. In future, we plan to generate very robust bot detection systems with improved performance. We need to investigate the effects of adversarial attacks on deep fake text detection models to make them robust against advanced cyber bots that may use such hidden noises to bypass the detection systems.

References

1. Abokhodair, N., Yoo, D., McDonald, D.W.: Dissecting a social botnet: growth, content and influence in Twitter. In: CSCW, pp. 839–851 (2015)
2. Adelani, D.I., Mai, H., Fang, F., Nguyen, H.H., Yamagishi, J., Echizen, I.: Gener-ating Sentiment-Preserving fake online reviews using neural language models and their human- and machine-based detection. In: AINA, pp. 1341–1354 (2020)
3. Alothali, E., Zaki, N., Mohamed, E.A., Alashwal, H.: Detecting social bots on twitter: a literature review. In: IIT, pp. 175–180 (2018)

4. Bakhtin, A., Gross, S., Ott, M., Deng, Y., Ranzato, M., Szlam, A.: Real or Fake? Learning to Discriminate Machine from Human Generated Text. arXiv preprint arXiv:1906.03351 (2019)
5. Beltagy, I., Lo, K., Cohan, A.: SciBERT: a pretrained language model for scientific text. In: EMNLP-IJCNLP, pp. 3615–3620 (2019)
6. Chavoshi, N., Hamooni, H., Mueen, A.: DeBot: Twitter bot detection via warped correlation. In: ICDM. pp. 817–822 (2016)
7. Chu, Z., Gianvecchio, S., Wang, H., Jajodia, S.: Detecting automation of twitter accounts: are you a human, bot, or cyborg? TDSC **9**(6), 811–824 (2012)
8. Cresci, S., Di Pietro, R., Petrocchi, M., Spognardi, A., Tesconi, M.: The paradigm-shift of social spambots: evidence, theories, and tools for the arms race. In: WWW Companion, pp. 963–972 (2017)
9. Devlin, J., Chang, M.W., Lee, K., Toutanova, K.: BERT: pre-training of deep bidirectional transformers for language understanding. arXiv preprint arXiv:1810.04805 (2018)
10. Dukić, D., Keča, D., Stipić, D.: Are you human? Detecting bots on Twitter Using BERT. In: DSAA, pp. 631–636 (2020)
11. Fagni, T., Falchi, F., Gambini, M., Martella, A., Tesconi, M.: TweepFake: about detecting deepfake tweets. PLoS ONE **16**(5), e0251415 (2021)
12. Gayo-Avello, D.: Social media won't free us. IEEE Internet Comput. **21**(4), 98–101 (2017)
13. Gehrmann, S., Strobelt, H., Rush, A.M.: GLTR: statistical detection and visualization of generated text. In: ACL: System Demonstrations, pp. 111–116 (2019)
14. Heidari, M., Jones, J.H.: Using BERT to extract topic-independent sentiment features for social media bot detection. In: UEMCON, pp. 0542–0547 (2020)
15. Ippolito, D., Duckworth, D., Callison-Burch, C., Eck, D.: Automatic detection of generated text is easiest when humans are fooled. In: ACL, pp. 1808–1822 (2020)
16. Jia, J., Wang, B., Gong, N.Z.: Random walk based fake account detection in online social networks. In: DSN, pp. 273–284 (2017)
17. Karataş, A., Şahin, S.: A review on social bot detection techniques and research directions. In: ISCTurkey, pp. 156–161 (2017)
18. Kudugunta, S., Ferrara, E.: Deep neural networks for bot detection. Inf. Sci. **467**, 312–322 (2018)
19. Lee, H., Yu, Y., Kim, G.: Augmenting data for sarcasm detection with unlabeled conversation context. In: FigLang, pp. 12–17 (2020)
20. Lin, R., Xiao, J., Fan, J.: NeXtVLAD: an efficient neural network to aggregate frame-level features for large-scale video classification. In: ECCV, pp. 206–218 (2018)
21. Lowe, D.G.: Distinctive image features from scale-invariant keypoints. Int. J. Comput. Vis. **60**(2), 91–110 (2004)
22. Müller, M., Salathé, M., Kummervold, P.E.: COVID-Twitter-BERT: a natural language processing model to Analyse COVID-19 Content on Twitter. arXiv preprint arXiv:2005.07503 (2020)
23. Rangel, F., Rosso, P.: Overview of the 7th author profiling task at PAN 2019: bots and gender profiling in Twitter. In: CEUR Workshop, pp. 1–36 (2019)
24. Srivastava, H., Varshney, V., Kumari, S., Srivastava, S.: A novel hierarchical BERT architecture for Sarcasm detection. In: FigLang, pp. 93–97 (2020)
25. Varol, O., Ferrara, E., Davis, C., Menczer, F., Flammini, A.: Online human-bot interactions: detection, estimation, and characterization. In: ICWSM, pp. 280–289 (2017)

26. Vaswani, A., et al.: Attention is all you need. In: NIPS, pp. 5998–6008 (2017)
27. Wolf, T., et al.: HuggingFace's transformers: state-of-the-art natural language processing. arXiv preprint arXiv:1910.03771 (2019)
28. Zellers, R., et al.: Defending against neural fake news. In: NIPS, pp. 9054–9065 (2019)

Landcoin: A Practical Protocol for Transfer-of-Asset

Vishwas Patil[(⊠)] and R. K. Shyamasundar

Department of Computer Science and Engineering, Indian Institute of Technology Bombay, Mumbai, India

Abstract. Blockchains ensure integrity, transparency, and immutability of transactions they process. It also guarantees the eventual inclusion of all the transactions submitted to the blockchain and records them in its ledger. Bitcoin and Litecoin are examples of time-tested, reliable public blockchains that handle only one type of transaction – send/receive money (i.e., transfer-of-value) from one user to another. Whereas, general-purpose blockchains like Ethereum provide means and methods to encapsulate transfer of not only *value* but anything fungible that can be digitally represented with the help of programs *aka* smart contracts. However, with a high-level Turing-complete programming language to write smart contracts, Ethereum encountered vulnerabilities in its contracts thus forgoing the claim of immutability. On the contrary, script-based blockchains like Bitcoin and Litecoin have withstood the test of time and hence are perceived reliable – a very important aspect while managing assets like land. In this paper, we present a *transfer-of-asset* system for land management that borrows from Litecoin protocol its script, underlying consensus, and block structure. Our resultant system is a permissioned blockchain, where only a set of pre-approved miners can append land records to the blockchain. We introduce *sidechains* that are roped in a *mainchain*. The *mainchain* stores land records, which can be queried by citizens; whereas, sidechains hold intricate details about intermediate validations performed by regulators, registrars, and notaries. The process of land management used in this paper is a typical process in the states of India. Our system can be used to manage any asset class that is finite in nature. Our approach provides transparency of transactions at a higher level and privacy to individual transactions.

Keywords: Blockchain · Land management · Privacy · Access control

1 Introduction

In countries like India, where the land records are maintained with human intervention, they are perennially marred with presumption and excessive bureaucracy – leading to malfeasance and thus into time-consuming legal disputes [16].

The work was done at the Center of Excellence for Blockchain Research, funded by Ripple UBRI.

© Springer Nature Switzerland AG 2021
S. Tripathy et al. (Eds.): ICISS 2021, LNCS 13146, pp. 124–141, 2021.
https://doi.org/10.1007/978-3-030-92571-0_8

Land is a precious asset that can be used as a collateral or used for many other productive purposes only if the title deeds are indisputable and are derived using a transparent process. Land litigation is a huge cost to the economy and one of the reasons of financial exclusion for a large population. In the past decade, many of the states have migrated their paper based records to digital versions [11] but with only partial success in containing the malfeasance. Several state governments (since land ownership is state's purview in the federal system of India) are exploring the blockchain approach to inherit its natural properties – integrity, transparency, and immutability; to the land records and their transactions in a land management system. Most of the implementations are based on Ethereum smart contracts and Hyperledger Fabric; where the steps of land management process are encapsulated as smart contracts (high-level software programs), which inherit the pros and cons of any high-level programming language [5]. Another limitation of such implementations is their system's state-specific scope, which may not answer queries like; what all title deeds a subject holds in India, across the states. In other words, the current approaches that we are aware of are *not scalable across the states* and also are *not interoperable*.

In this paper, we present a land management system based on Litecoin's public blockchain codebase. We add features to modify the same to suit our purpose of having a permissioned blockchain for transfer of asset while keeping the underlying skeleton of the blockchain and its stack-based purpose specific script unchanged for the most part. Our system is scalable, interoperable, and also privacy-preserving. We achieve these desirable features by segregating the data related to a land transaction into two categories: public and private. We record the public part of the land transaction data (like, who transferred a land to whom) on mainchain and the corresponding private part of the land transaction (like, at what rate the land is sold) on a sidechain that is maintained by the state to which that land belongs. The mainchain can be queried by anyone, whereas the sidechains accept attribute-based queries only from the parties that are involved in a land transaction. In our implementation, we have introduced new transaction types to Litecoin's codebase. Each type corresponds to a distinct operation in prevalent land management workflow. We introduce separate transaction types to the mainchain and sidechains. Each land transfer transaction on the mainchain traverses through the workflow on the sidechain before getting committed on mainchain. The first transaction/step on the sidechain takes an input from the mainchain and the last transaction/step on the sidechain inputs to the mainchain. In other words, when a subject intends to transfer her land to another subject, the transaction has to go through government verification/diligence process (which gets recorded on the sidechain) before being accepted by the miners on the mainchain. Our construction allows an audit trail to traverse from mainchain to sidechain and back to the mainchain without the auditor knowing the intricate details recorded on the sidechain, which only the seller, buyer and the land authorities can decrypt. Maintaining confidentiality of transaction details while keeping the transaction trail transparent is an important feature that our system provides.

2   Background and Motivation

The prevalent land management systems use databases for storage of land records and use cryptography for data protection. While confidentiality mechanisms can be enforced, these systems fall short in maintaining an immutable trail of operations performed on land records, because tuples in a database can be overwritten. Double-entry book-keeping is used in identifying discrepancies in records, however malicious records can only be traced with the help of a digital log management system, which in turn is susceptible to tampering [18]. Triple-entry book-keeping can be adopted, where each transaction is digitally signed by the subject of transaction; irrespective of the transaction being valid, erroneous or malicious – thus fixing accountability. Most of the non-blockchain implementations of land management systems fall under this triple-entry book-keeping category. However, such centralized systems lack a real-time, transparent view.

A new type of decentralized database technology (aka DLT/blockchain) appears to be a natural fit for land management system because it not only provides all of the properties of a triple-entry book-keeping approach but also offers immutability, transparency, and real-time auditability to land transactions. The transparency and auditability for all the stages in the transfer of land coupled with the inherent immutability guarantee that a blockchain provides helps solve the double-spend and prevent similar frauds prevalent during transfer of property agreements. Furthermore, blocks chained with cryptographic hashes provide a verifiable record of all the history of the transfer of land assets, as opposed to a simple database where only the current ownership status is reflected. Databases can also store transaction history but there is no guarantee that the records have not been tampered since it was appended to the logs and the trust needs to be placed onto the authorities maintaining the database for that as well.

The choice of a blockchain protocol for land management is an important design criteria because the inherent pros and cons of the protocol reflect into the system. A judicious mix of engineering tweaks need to be adopted in order to inherit the pros and mitigate the cons. In our approach, we narrowed down on the Litecoin protocol [15] due to the following criteria: i) time-tested, proven, open protocol; ii) limited set of stack-based script operations; iii) `scrypt` based proof-of-work consensus algorithm.

A general purpose blockchain like Ethereum can be used [9,12,19] but its underlying programming language may open up avenues [5,13] for serious asset loss or inconsistent states of asset ownership, which is unacceptable. Therefore, it is prudent to rely on a protocol (like Bitcoin [17] or Litecoin [15]) that is built for a specific purpose rather than using a general purpose protocol like Ethereum [20] or Hyperledger Fabric [8]. Between the Bitcoin and the Litecoin codebase, we opted for Litecoin for its reliance on `scrypt` hashing algorithm that cannot be accelerated by ASIC processors, which is the case for Bitcoin since it uses `SHA256` hashing algorithm for block mining. To make the system adaptable for current land management practices, we had to tweak the default setup of Litecoin protocol. In summary, the following are the modifications we introduced in the Litecoin protocol.

1. New transaction types for mainchain and sidechain, each corresponding to a step in the current workflow of land management.
2. Pre-approved miners, similar to validators in XRP [14], is a set of public-keys listed by the central government through a transaction on mainchain.
3. Sidechains allow states to compose their respective land management work-flows as separate chain anchored in the mainchain; there are no coinbase operations on sidechains.
4. Certifying coins and mapping them to a landmass is a one time operation during the bootstrapping phase in which all the pre-mined 84 million coins are transferred to the central government and then distributed to the state governments according to their proportionate landmasses.
5. Certified user addresses and signing keys: any entity entering the system needs to have an address and corresponding signing and verification keys. Instead of generating them locally as in the case for permissionless crypto-currencies, a Trusted Third Party (TTP) is involved in verifying identities and assigning certificates with the keys being formed jointly by both parties.

3   Architecture of Landcoin Protocol

In this section we present the design aspects of our protocol followed by practical considerations while dealing with land management.

3.1   From a Transfer-of-Value to a Transfer-of-Asset System

The following two challenges come up while extending a *transfer-of-value* system (Litecoin) to a *transfer-of-asset* system (Landcoin): i) a class of asset like money, which is represented by numbers alone, is different from the class of assets like land, which has identification attributes and does not have properties like fungi-bility or malleability; and ii) assets like land have certain legal requirements to be adhered to before any mutation or transfer occurs. These characteristics need to be taken into consideration while constructing the *transfer-of-assets* system. We make the following four assumptions in our design: i) during the initializa-tion phase of our system, all the 84 million coins are mapped to units of total land; ii) all stakeholders have unique identifiers – UIDs; iii) The title deeds of land are unambiguous and the assets represented therein have unique identifiers – URIs; and iv) the pre-approved miners (i.e., transaction validators) are honest and are always available.

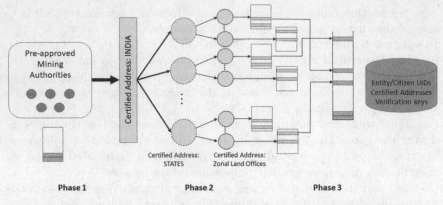

Certified Address: Certified Address:
    STATES   Zonal Land Offices

Phase 1   Phase 2   Phase 3

- Mining with Landcoin protocol parameters   - Key/Certificate Allotment to Land Officers   - Key/Certificate Allotment to Clients (Citizens, Organizations)
- All coins transferred to "INDIA"   - Distribution of land by physical location   - Bootstrapping Sidechain Operation
                                                                                             - Distribution of land to existing land owners

Fig. 1. Landcoin: protocol initialization phases (bootstrapping)

3.2   From Permissionless to Permissioned Setup

Since land ownership is a legal statute backed by the state, the state acts as an arbitrator for all land transactions. To incorporate this requirement, we need to restrict the transaction miners who are authorized to commit transactions to the blockchain. We introduce a role called the "Government Authority" that is allowed to manage the chains by controlling the body of miners. We introduce a special type of transaction called "Governance Transaction" to the mainchain and sidechain where the "Government Authority" can add or remove a public-key from the list of pre-approved miners for their respective chains.

Restricting the nodes who can mine the transactions does away with the concept of incentives for transaction mining. That is, there won't be any transaction fees either on mainchain or sidechain. The coinbase type of transactions that come with the Litecoin protocol are frozen after the completion of Phase 1 in bootstrapping of Landcoin protocol as shown in Fig. 1. Furthermore, the publicly-queriable mainchain only includes transactions that are signed off by the zonal Registrars. This allows for efficient query of land data across the states, while making sure that the control of land data remains with respective states.

In order to build a practical system, the design of the proposed system has to resemble closely the distinct stages in the prevalent land management practices. In the following we enlist the steps involved in a typical land transfer transaction.

3.3   Steps and Requirements of Workflow for Land Management

While there exist several types of land-transfer/mutation transactions: "Sale Deed", "Gift Deed", "Relinquishment Deed", "Partition/Settlement Deed" and "Inheritance/Will Deed"; in this work we explore the "Sale Deed" as a typical use-case. The protocol can later be extended to accommodate the other deeds and their workflows as well.

The "Sale Deed" is the main document by which a seller transfers his right on the property to the purchaser, who then acquires absolute ownership of the property. The process of "Sale Deed" execution, in Indian context, requires involvement of sellers, buyers, witnesses, land officers, and land registrar at gradual stages. In the following we enumerate the entities, their roles, and the steps in the prevalent land management workflow. These steps are indicative only and they may vary.

1. A *seller* willing to sell property needs to raise an intent to the *Zonal Land Office (ZLO)*.
2. The *ZLO* processes this intent through legal checks and verifies the eligibility of buyer/s.
3. If the intent is allowed to go through, the *ZLO* declares a minimum *Market Value (MV)* for the piece of the land.
4. Upon mutual identity verification, both the parties may negotiate an agreeable price, which is equal to or higher than the *MV*.
5. Then seller prepares a *Transfer of Ownership* document with particulars of the buyer, the land, the price, and two *witnesses* who need to sign it.
6. Revenue tax is calculated for the property and the invoice is presented to the buyer in order to proceed with the land transfer.
7. An invoice is prepared with the details of the parties involved in the transaction, along with a list of conditions that need to be honored.
8. The final invoice, along with two witnesses, is jointly presented to the *Registrar* for approval.
9. As a final step the "Sale Deed" is said to be executed by making the payment of full amount specified in the deed.

Taking into consideration the above indicative workflow for transactions in land management, it is amply evident that several stakeholders carry out intermediate transactions leading to the actual land transaction. Therefore, it is not straightforward to use the *transfer-of-value* type of transaction available under Litecoin protocol. Hence, we need to introduce new transaction types to accommodate representation of intermediate transactions by respective stakeholders.

3.4 MAINCHAIN: Parameters and Construction

We have modified the Litecoin codebase with the following parameters so that we resemble closely with the prevalent land management system and its workflow.

- Total coinbase $\mapsto$ total landmass in India (km^2)
- Divisibility: 8 decimal places (smallest unit is dm^2)
- Block generation time on mainchain: approx. 1 h
- Number of block confirmations: 40 (approx. 1.5 days)
- Consensus: proof-of-work (by pre-approved miners)

We start mining with lower difficulty levels and do not open the blockchain for public participation, until all blocks are mined by the appointed miners. We call this chain as Landcoin's MAINCHAIN. Before initializing it for land transfer, all the miners send their coinbase to the "Government Authority", represented by a self-certified public key. The "Government Authority" then transfers proportionate amounts of Landcoins to individual state Registrars, represented by addresses that are certified by the "Government Authority". The Registrars map the coins to unique URIs of the pieces of land in their respective jurisdictions. The mapping is a transfer operation on the MAINCHAIN to the individual owners of respective URIs. The "Government Authority" invokes "Governance Transaction" (detailed in Sect. 3.6) to authorize a list of public-keys as pre-approved miners. Upon completion of the bootstrapping phase, the MAINCHAIN starts accepting asset-transfer requests.

An asset-transfer transaction, floated by a user on the MAINCHAIN, is accepted by the miners only when it has a signature of the Registrar of the sidechain for the corresponding zone. The attestation process requires the intent transaction to go through pre-defined set of steps as deemed suitable by respective states. Each transaction type on sidechain corresponds to a distinct step in the prevalent workflow for land management.

3.5 SIDECHAIN: Placeholder for Private Information

Though the confirmed transactions on MAINCHAIN show the current ownership of a piece of land and its transactional history, the details about each necessary clearance, attestation, price, et al. are protected from public access. Only the pre-approved public-keys (Registrar, land officers from ZLO) and the parties to the transaction can decrypt the content of the transactions on the sidechain. This provides the property of conditional confidentiality to the content of transactions on the sidechain. We use a CPABE scheme [7] to achieve this property, whose setup and primitive operations are depicted in Fig. 2. The setup for CPABE starts with a global public encryption key (EK) and a master secret key (MSK) that is private to the "Government Authority". For each user of the system, depending upon their roles, certain 'attributes' are defined for which each user has an assigned 'value'. The MSK is used to derive decryption keys for each user according to their 'attribute:value' pairs. For encrypting a message under this scheme, EK is used along with an encoding of the 'Policy Tree', which is a propositional logic statement with 'attribute:value' pairs as their atomic parts (leaves of the tree), always evaluating to either true or false. The encryption algorithm encodes this policy into the resultant ciphertext. During decryption, the ciphertext and the user's key is input to the algorithm and the plaintext is output only if the policy evaluates to true on the user's attribute values. Encryption scheme in [7] is based on bilinear pairings and its implementation is publicly available as a library and documented in [6].

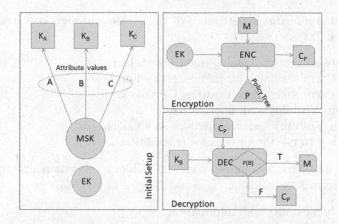

Fig. 2. Ciphertext-policy attribute based encryption [7]

The MAINCHAIN stores all the confirmed *Transfer of Ownership* transactions, and "Governance Transactions"; whereas, the SIDECHAINS (one for each *ZLO*) store the transactions involved in the intermediate steps and run verification scripts for legal compliance. The scripts for compliance check obey the governance policies and are tailored to the workflow for land management of a state.

3.6 Protocol Stakeholders, Their Roles, and Transaction Types

Stakeholders and their roles
Clients (buyers, sellers, witnesses): Buyers and sellers are the end users of the system. Witnesses provide consent to a transaction by digitally signing it.

- Certified Address mapped to Identification info.
- Mainchain Visibility - all information
- Sidechain Visibility - all transactions in which they are a party
- Signing key to use for certain sidechain transactions as seller or witness

Zonal Land Officers: Verification, approval of transaction initiated by sellers, and mining of transactions on SIDECHAIN.

- Mainchain Visibility - all information
- Sidechain Visibility - all sidechain information of her zone
- Signing certain sidechain transactions, and all blocks on the sidechain

Registrar: responsible for final approval of change of ownership requests.

- Certificate Authority defining Land Officer set
- Mainchain Visibility - all information
- Sidechain Visibility - all sidechain information of her region
- Signing key to use for certain sidechain transactions, and mainchain change-of-ownership transactions

Government Authority: maintenance of the system through bootstrapping and "Governance Transactions".

- Certificate Authority defining mainchain miners set
- Trusted Party assigning all clients certified addresses
- Trusted Party assigning all entities CPABE keys
- Mainchain Visibility - all information
- Sidechain Visibility - all transactions in all sidechains
- Signing key to use for governance transactions

Pre-approved Miners: accept and mine the "Change of Ownership" transactions emanating from SIDECHAINs.

- Mainchain Visibility - all information
- Verify all mainchain transactions
- Signing key to use for blocks on the mainchain

Key management and certified addresses

The CPABE master key MSK lies with the "Government Authority" and the encryption key EK is globally known and stored in the Software Interfaces of the Clients, ZLOs, and Registrars. Each of their decryption keys are also derived from this, as shown in Fig. 3. The signing keys and addresses are certified by a TTP that is again, the "Government Authority". These certified addresses are created as in [4] that follows a Diffie-Hellman-like exchange between the client and TTP to generate a shared randomness used to create the Signing Key and certificate. The verification key and address is then derived from it. The certificate is also verified during the signature verification to ensure the key was certified. This computation happens in such a way that the TTP has no knowledge of the final key and so cannot abuse the signing authority of the client.

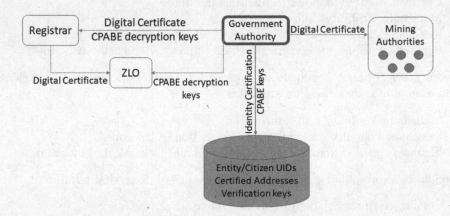

Fig. 3. Key management among the stakeholders

Transaction types and their composition

1. Change of ownership transaction: T_M
   - H_M - Transaction Header
   - $H_{M'}$ - Header of Source transaction on MAINCHAIN
   - $\{A_S\}$ - Certified Addresses of all sellers
   - $\{A_B\}$ - Certified Addresses of all buyers
   - $\{URI\}$ - Survey numbers and GIS co-ordinates
   - DT - Effective-on date
   - S_R - Signature of the Registrar
2. Governance transaction: T_G
   - H_G - Transaction Header
   - $\{A, O, O_i\{\dots\}\}$ -
     - A - Action (add/delete)
     - O - Object (certificate, miner, zone, ttype)
     - $O_i\{\dots\}$ - set of objects
   - EJ - Effective-on jurisdiction
   - DT - Effective-on date
   - S_G - Signature of Government Authority
3. Booking transaction: T_B - Declaration by seller expressing desire to sell land to particular prospective buyer
   - H_B - Transaction Header
   - $H_{M'}$ - Header of Source transaction on MAINCHAIN
   - $\{A_S\}$ - Certified Addresses of all sellers
   - $\{A_B\}$ - Certified Addresses of all buyers
   - $\{URI\}$ - Survey numbers and GIS co-ordinates
   - $\{S_S\}$ - Signatures of sellers
4. Rejection: T_R - Abort of process "Change of Ownership"
   - H_R - Transaction Header
   - $H_{M'}$ - Header of Source transaction on MAINCHAIN
   - RR - Reason for rejection (optional)
   - S_R - Signature of the Registrar
5. Clearance: T_C - Permission to sell at/above declared MV
   - H_C - Transaction Header
   - $H_{B'}$ - Transaction Header of T_B
   - MV - Minimum market value evaluated by ZLO
   - S_L - Signature of ZLO
6. Pre-handover document: T_D - Document declaring final selling price decided upon and identities of witnesses signing off on the handover

134   V. Patil and R. K. Shyamasundar

- H_D - Transaction Header
- $H_{C'}$ - Transaction Header of T_C
- $\{A_S\}$ - Certified Addresses of all sellers
- $\{A_B\}$ - Certified Addresses of all buyers
- $\{A_W\}$ - Certified Addresses of all witnesses
- $\{URI\}$ - Survey numbers and GIS co-ordinates
- SP - Final selling price
- $\{S_S\}$ - Signatures of sellers

7. Rejection of Pre-handover document: T_{DR}
   - H_{DR} - Transaction Header
   - $H_{D'}$ - Header of Source T_D
   - RR - Reason for rejection (optional)
   - S_L - Signature of ZLO

8. Document verification: T_V - Acknowledgement after verification of legal documents by ZLO
   - H_V - Transaction Header
   - $H_{D'}$ - Header of T_D
   - $\{D_S\}$ - Hashes for doc. clearance of all sellers
   - $\{D_B\}$ - Hashes for doc. clearance of all buyers
   - $\{D_W\}$ - Hashes for doc. clearance of all witnesses
   - S_L - Signature of ZLO

9. Tax Receipt: T_T
   - H_T - Transaction Header
   - $H_{V'}$ - Header of T_V
   - $\{URI\}$ - Survey numbers and GIS co-ordinates
   - SP - Final selling price
   - Tax - Tax amount payable
   - $\{D_T\}$ - Hashes for doc. proof of tax payment
   - S_R - Signature of the Registrar

10. Completion Receipt: T_F
    - H_F - Transaction Header
    - $H_{T'}$ - Transaction Header of T_T
    - $\{A_S\}$ - Certified Addresses of all sellers
    - $\{A_B\}$ - Certified Addresses of all buyers
    - $\{A_W\}$ - Certified Addresses of all witnesses
    - $\{URI\}$ - Survey numbers and GIS co-ordinates
    - SP - Final selling price
    - $\{S_S\}$ - Signatures of sellers
    - $\{S_W\}$ - Signatures of witnesses
    - S_R - Signature of the Registrar

Mainchain blocks include transactions of type T_M and T_G. All the other types of transactions appear on the sidechain. The 8-step land transfer transaction is depicted in Fig. 4.

noend 1. Landcoin Protocol

```
 1: Seller initiates T_B on SIDECHAIN
 2:                              ▷ refers to previous T_M that acts as an anchor
 3: if Legal conditions of exchange are not met then
 4:      Registrar puts T_R return
 5: else
 6:      ZLO puts T_C with mention of MV
 7:      Seller puts T_D with final price and Witnesses
 8:      while ZLO puts T_DR do
 9:          if Still interested then
10:              Seller re-does T_D
11:          else
12:              T_R return
13:      while Document Verification not approved by ZLO do
14:          if Still interested then
15:              if Valid documents can be produced then
16:                  ZLO puts T_V
17:              else
18:                  Seller re-does T_D
19:                  GOTO line 9
20:          else
21:              T_R return
22:      T_T is put on the SIDECHAIN
23:      T_F is put on the SIDECHAIN
24:      T_M is put on the MAINCHAIN return
```

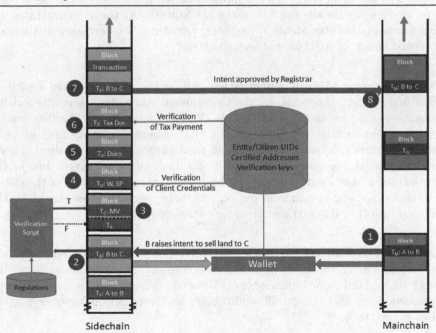

Fig. 4. Land transfer transaction in Landcoin system

4 Summary of Guarantees

This system aims to provide the following guarantees:

Authenticated Yet Pseudonymous Clients. Certified Addresses provided by the Government Authority are conditioned on verification of the identity of the client as an actual and unique real-world entity. This is a one-time process and helps in keeping track of the userbase of the system with legal implications. The addresses do not reflect user IDs on chain and so the protocol henceforth is a pseudonymous; one with only the certificates being verified on chain.

Verify-Able History of Land Transactions. All the MAINCHAIN transactions originate from the Government Authority address and thus all the existing land is accounted for. Furthermore, all valid change-of-ownership transactions are signed by the Registrar (having gone through the entire SIDECHAIN workflow) before committing on the MAINCHAIN. This consolidated transaction-trail provided by the Landcoin system, along with the queryable MAINCHAIN transactions, mitigates double-spend/ownership frauds.

Confidentiality of Intermediate Steps. All intermediate steps for the change of ownership transaction are recorded on the SIDECHAIN. This maintains a consolidated record of all the actions/approvals taking place and, at the same time, keeps unnecessary details outside of the MAINCHAIN. As these transactions use private information like identity, payment, tax-status for verification; they are encrypted under CPABE for authorized access.

Honesty Among Mining Authorities. All mining authorities are regulated: added and evicted, if needed, by the Government Authority; thus categorizing our system as a permissioned blockchain. While competition still exists among them for any off-chain compensation the Government Authority may provide, malicious miners risk being identified and their authority being revoked. Therefore, minimal, if any (only theoretically), forking can be expected; but in the event of one, it may eventually get resolved due to the slow growth of the chain. Nevertheless, as any transaction put on the chain needs to come signed by the Registrar, a fork will not translate to a double-spend event!

Centralized Authority with Decentralized Auditability. The proposed protocol does not deviate the prevalent structure of centralized authority at the state-level for land record management. However, it facilitates inclusion of users at national-level through public auditability and verification by querying the public MAINCHAIN.

5   Implementation Details

Fig. 5. Landcoin wallet: login window and different user roles

As a proof-of-concept we modified [2] the Litecoin codebase and designed QT-based wallet to interact with the Landcoin blockchain system. This implementation supports four roles: Client (Individual or Organization), Registrar (with operations of ZLO), Government Authority, and Miners. Figure 5 shows the Login/Registration screen.

Each Landcoin Client has a unique client ID that needs to be entered into the Login Window along with a password. When a new Client registers, his/her certified keys and address is then generated by a backend call to the Trusted Third Party.

A Client can use View Menu to explore the MAINCHAIN, to see the list of ongoing transactions he/she is involved in, and the list of his/her completed transactions. Upon approval, the transaction then becomes part of the USER-MEMPOOL. The Registrar's Dashboard contains his credentials that are similar to that of the Client's except it also includes the Zone of jurisdiction Fig. 6. This role has permissions to view all the MAINCHAIN transactions using the chain explorer(wallet), ongoing transactions of the zone, completed transactions of the zone, and current zone state (current owners of land in the zone). This includes transactions in the USERMEMPOOL, the MEMPOOL, and and the UTXO that belong to the zone. As in the prevalent practice, the Registrar performs the role of giving the final approval for any transaction. This transaction then is moved from the USERMEMPOOL to the MEMPOOL from where it can be picked up by a miner to be included in a block on the blockchain.

A Miner, once logged in, can view the MEMPOOL, UTXO and the blockchain through the explorer. However, mining is not possible unless a special permission is granted by the Government Authority. The Government Authority can always traverse through the MAINCHAIN and SIDECHAINS. It also has a view (shown in Fig. 8) of the list of approved miners and prospective miners that have requested mining permission. The TTP for the certified address generation is implemented

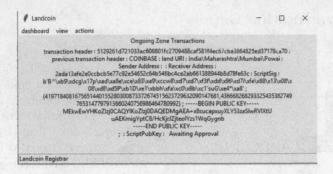

Fig. 6. Registrar view: ongoing transaction of the zone

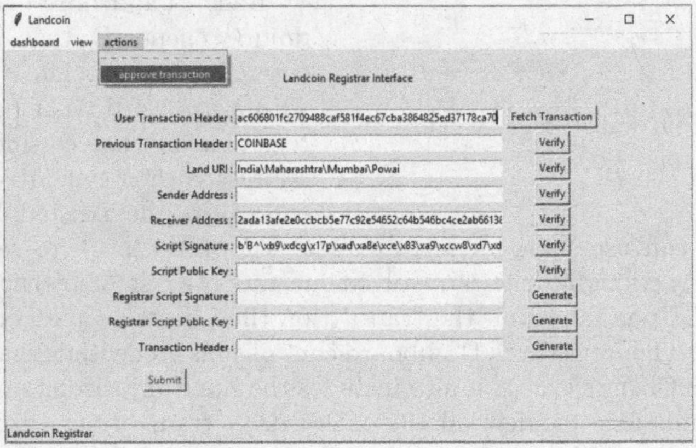

Fig. 7. Registrar action: approve transaction

as a python function that interacts with the clients as a separate entity during user registration. It performs automated checks with an existing database and does not explicitly need human intervention. It can be optionally merged with the Government Authority though an interface for the same is not provided. Furthermore, the op-code set is extended (as in the certified addresses specification) to include an op-code for verification for white-listed certificates/keys (permissioned entities). We are also exploring integration of Geohash [1] and Cadastral maps [3] in our implementation to provide a realistic view of land management to the stakeholders (Fig. 7).

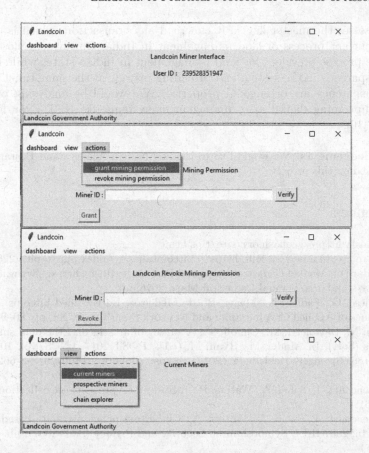

Fig. 8. Government authority interface

6   Conclusion

We have devised Landcoin – a practical *transfer-of-asset* system based on a proven & tested system for *transfer-of-value*. Landcoin extends the limited and secure opcode set of Litecoin codebase. This set is Turing incomplete and all the scripts written can be formally verified for correctness, at the same time providing just enough functionality for our use-case. Transaction details are segregated into public and private data streams on separate but intertwined blockchains, helping us preserve privacy of individual transaction details. The Mainchain records each and every successful transfer of ownership transaction, and the Sidechain records the intermediate details of such transactions emanating from the Mainchain. Thus, anyone can browse through the Mainchain ledger to verify the ownership of land but the intricate details of associated ownership provenance are available only to the stakeholders of that transaction. Confidentiality of transaction details on the Sidechains are enforced using CPABE (Ciphertext Policy - Attribute Based Encryption) scheme, where the "Government Authority" possesses the master key so it can read any transaction, which is also the case in current process of land management in India. Our system closely imitates the process prevalent for land management in Indian states while improving transparency in the system and providing privacy at the same time! Privacy and transparency are orthogonal properties. We would be analysing pros and cons of upcoming digital asset management systems like NFT (Non-Fungible Tokens) [10].

Acknowledgements. We would like to thank Anasuya Acharya and Bajrang Sutar who worked on this project.

References

1. Geohash. http://geohash.org/site/tips.html
2. How to create a new altcoin. https://bitcointalk.org/index.php?topic=225690.0
3. Standard on Manual Cadastral Maps and Parcel Identifiers. https://www.iaao.org/media/standards/Manual_Cadastral_Maps_2016.pdf
4. Ateniese, G., Faonio, A., Magri, B., de Medeiros, B.: Certified bitcoins. In: Proceedings of Applied Cryptography and Network Security - ACNS, pp. 80–96 (2014)
5. Atzei, N., Bartoletti, M., Cimoli, T.: A survey of attacks on Ethereum smart contracts (SoK). In: Maffei, M., Ryan, M. (eds.) POST 2017. LNCS, vol. 10204, pp. 164–186. Springer, Heidelberg (2017). https://doi.org/10.1007/978-3-662-54455-6_8
6. Bethencourt, J., Sahai, A., Waters, B.: Advanced crypto software collection - cpabe (2006)
7. Bethencourt, J., Sahai, A., Waters, B.: Ciphertext-policy attribute-based encryption. In: 2007 IEEE Symposium on Security and Privacy (S&P 2007), pp. 321–334 (2007)
8. Cachin, C.: Architecture of the Hyperledger Blockchain Fabric (2016). https://www.zurich.ibm.com/dccl/papers/cachin_dccl.pdf
9. eMudhra: Case Study: land records securely on a Blockchain. https://www.emudhra.com/us/case-studies/blockchain/emBlock_land_records_case_study.pdf
10. Ethereum. Non-fungible tokens (NFT) (2021). https://ethereum.org/en/nft/,
11. Karnataka Government. https://landrecords.karnataka.gov.in
12. Abhishek, G.: Property registration and land record management via blockchains. https://security.cse.iitk.ac.in/sites/default/files/2019-09/14807257.pdf
13. Kalra, G., Goel, S., Dhawan, M., Sharma, S.: ZEUS: analyzing safety of smart contracts. In: 25th Annual Network and Distributed System Security Symposium, NDSS (2018)
14. Labs, R.: Run rippled as a validator (2021). https://xrpl.org/run-rippled-as-a-validator.html
15. Litecoin. The cryptocurrency for payments (2011). https://litecoin.org/
16. Mishra, P., Suhag, R.: Land records and titles in India (2017). http://www.prsindia.org/uploads/media/Analytical
17. Nakamoto, S.: Bitcoin: a peer-to-peer electronic cash system (2008). http://bitcoin.org/bitcoin.pdf
18. Shyamasundar, R.K., Patil, V.: Blockchain: the revolution in trust management. Proc. Indian Natl. Sci. Acad. **84** (2), 385–407 (2018)

19. Thakur, V., Doja, M.N., Dwivedi, Y.K., Ahmad, T., Khadanga, G.: Land records on blockchain for implementation of land titling in India. Int. J. Inf. Manag. **52**, 101940 (2019)
20. Wood, G.: Ethereum: a secure decentralised generalised transaction ledger EIP-150 REVISION (2017)

WiP: A Distributed Approach for Statistical Disclosure Control Technologies

Afshin Amighi[1,2]([✉]), Mortaza S. Bargh[2,3], and Ahmad Omar[1]

[1] School of Communication, Media and Information Technology,
Rotterdam University of Applied Science, Rotterdam, The Netherlands
[2] Research Centre Creating 010, Rotterdam University of Applied Science,
Rotterdam, The Netherlands
{a.amighi,m.shoae.bargh,a.omar}@hr.nl
[3] Research and Documentation Centre, Ministry of Justice and Security,
The Hague, The Netherlands
m.shoae.bargh@wodc.nl

Abstract. In the current era of data driven governance and businesses, data sharing and opening become an essential growth factor. Data intensive organizations are eager to share their data with the public, research institutions and private enterprises. However, data sharing must adhere to data protection laws and regulations, particularly respect the principle of personal data minimization. Statistical Disclosure Control (SDC) is a major technology that aims at minimizing personal information in a data set while retaining the data utility at an acceptable level for data consumers. Despite having many tools developed to automate the process of applying SDC technology, still the majority of organizations are struggling to adapt it. In this contribution, first, we mention the common challenges that data intensive organizations are facing for employing existing SDC tools. Then, we propose a SDC tool set-up, whereby organizations can outsource the anonymization of their microdata sets to a central party safely (i.e., without sharing their raw data). Finally, we present the current status of the study together with a few questions for future research.

Keywords: Privacy · Public data · SDC technology · Software tool

1 Introduction

Often data sets contain more personal data than needed or allowed for the data usage in mind. Having this excessive personal data stems from the way that data are collected, shared and used. Sometimes data sets are collected for one purpose (like an operational purpose) but are used for another legitimate purpose (like for statistical analyses or for scientific research). For example, in the medical domain patient data are collected to document medical treatments, while they are re-used for medical research. In justice domain, as another example, offender

© Springer Nature Switzerland AG 2021
S. Tripathy et al. (Eds.): ICISS 2021, LNCS 13146, pp. 142–153, 2021.
https://doi.org/10.1007/978-3-030-92571-0_9

data are collected to try, sentence and treat offenders, while they are also re-used for criminology research. Other times, even when statistical analysis and/or scientific research are the primary purpose of data collection, the collected data may contain too much personal data due to, for example, an inappropriate research design.

According to privacy laws and regulations, like the EU General Data Protection Regulation (GDPR), it is necessary to minimize the amount of personal data in data sets to only the data that are required and allowed for the chosen (legitimate) data usage. Not adjusting the amount of the personal data to the data usage can lead to privacy breach and may have adverse impact on individuals and society [1–3]. It may also inflict reputation damages upon the organizations that are responsible for such privacy breaches and may even bring lawsuits against and inflict financial fines on these organizations. As the amount and types of data increase with a fast pace, it becomes necessary for (governmental) organizations to exploit and use the technologies that enable and facilitate minimizing the sensitive information of citizens and individuals in their data sets for various data processing activities (like data sharing, data opening, data analysis and data storage) [4].

Statistical Disclosure Control (SDC) technology is an important technology for reducing personal data in data set as much as possible and/or necessary, while maintaining the utility of the data set for the legitimate purpose in mind [5]. To this end, many sophisticated SDC tools have been developed. Using a SDC tool, an expert can apply advanced SDC algorithms with proper parameters to a data set (i.e., transform the data set) and can gain insights into the utility of the original and the transformed data sets, can estimate the data disclosure risks of the original and the transformed data sets, and eventually can make appropriate trade-offs between data utility aspects and data disclosure risks [6]. However, applying SDC technology has not become a mainstream practice in most data intensive organizations due to its newness and complexity. The complexity of applying SDC technology into practice is due to being context-dependent (at it depends on, for example, the motives of intruders, other available data sets in the environment, and the impact of the data set to be transformed), being multi-disciplinary (as it requires a close collaboration of many stakeholders with various backgrounds), requiring a solid theoretical background (as it is built on statistical and mathematical models and methods), and being subject to accountability and liability burden if it is done improperly. Therefore, there is a need for highly trained experts and complex tools to employ SDC technology within organizations appropriately.

Creating own SDC expertise center in a short period of time can be difficult and challenging for most (small and medium-sized) organizations. To remedy this challenge, one can consider setting up an specialized SDC expertise center outside an organization's premise, where SDC specialists use the existing SDC tools to serve many affiliated organizations. There is, however, an issue with this fully centralized and out sourced approach as the current SDC tools are desktop applications that require full access to raw, thus privacy sensitive, data.

This full access to the raw data of organizations by a third party SDC expertise center is a classical privacy threat, being against the principle of separation of privacy sensitive data sets. According to this data separation principle, personal data should be processed locally (i.e., in a distributed way) in order to prevent complete profiling of individuals [7], in our case, by the SDC expertise center. Via data separation, in other words, one aims at preventing a big-brother like threat. In order to honor the data separation principle in the context of creating the SDC expertise center, it is necessary to develop a new generation of SDC tools that keep privacy sensitive raw data sets at local parties (i.e., to localize data at individual organizations) while assisting those organizations in minimizing personal data in their data sets.

In this contribution we aim at enhancing the current SDC tools in a way that they fulfil, respect and support the principle of data separation (i.e., privacy sensitive data localization). More specifically, we present our vision for a distributed SDC tool that enables SDC specialists to remotely examine, transform and protect privacy sensitive data sets with SDC technology. In this way, the sensitive data do not leave the boundaries of organizations while making optimum use of scarce SDC expertise at the central party. Additionally, we elaborate on the proof-of-concept prototype for the envisioned distributed SDC tool by describing its architecture and reflecting upon the early results of our implementation. Note that the distributed SDC tool considered here is for protecting microdata sets, which are structured tables with some rows, representing individuals, and a number of columns, representing the attributes of those individuals (like their age, gender and occupation). At the end, we describe our future work as well as a number of directions for future research.

For conducting this study, as well as for developing our proof-of-concept prototype, we have used various research methods such as literature study, case studies, expert interviews and prototyping and simulations. Our results can enhance the awareness about and contribute to the roadmap for embedding personal data minimization technologies within data intensive organizations. To the best of our knowledge, the work presented here is unique within the context of applying innovative personal data minimization technologies within organizations.

The organization of the paper is as follows. We start with explaining the roles involved in applying SDC technology in organizations, and motivate the need for developing a distributed SDC tool in order to facilitate embedding SDC technology within (small and middle-sized) organizations in Sect. 2. We explain our proposal for a distributed SDC tool in Sect. 3. Finally, we draw some conclusions and present various directions for future research in Sect. 4.

2   On SDC Deployment

In this section, we define the roles relevant for applying SDC technology and briefly explore the organizational settings within which the current and our envisioned SDC tools may operate. In other words, this section aims at clarifying the motivations behind the envisioned distributed SDC tool.

2.1   Roles

The roles involved in the process of applying SDC tools can be specified as follows.

(1) *Data controller* is responsible for collecting data for a primary objective as part of the daily operation of an organization and sharing the data with a data processor who uses the collected data for the primary purpose or for a legitimate secondary purpose (like statistical analysis or scientific research). The data controller has an authorised access to the raw data set.
(2) *Data anonymizer* is responsible for applying SDC techniques to the raw data to obtain the transformed data set. The data anonymizer has enough expertise to apply SDC techniques.
(3) *Data processor* uses the transformed data set for a given purpose (i.e., the primary purpose or a legitimate secondary purpose).

The data controller role is fulfilled by the organization that is responsible for the data set. The organization employs one or more data specialists (or, as we call, data stewards) in charge of collecting, enriching and distributing the data. Note that the data controller may apply various data governance mechanisms other than data minimization to protect (the personal data in) the data set. The data processor role is usually fulfilled by another organization than that of the data controller. The above mentioned roles and their relationships are illustrated in Fig. 1.

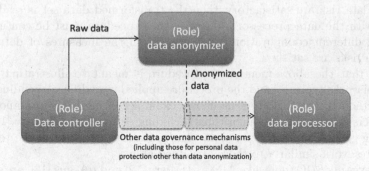

Fig. 1. An illustration of the roles involved in the SDC process.

The data anonymizer role can be fulfilled by an actor or actors within or outside the organization responsible for the original data set. In the following section we describe three settings for fulfilling the data anonymizer role, two of which are applicable when the current SDC tools are used and the third one is applicable for our envisioned distributed SDC tool.

2.2 Fulfilling the Data Anonymizer Role

In order to explain the assignment of the data anonymizer role to an organization, we start with explaining how a typical SDC procedure is carried out in the current software tool ARX [8,9]. The data anonymizer within a *trusted environment* loads original data set in the tool. Then, the attributes are categorised into four disjoint sets (i.e., attribute mapping), namely: Explicit identifiers, quasi identifiers, sensitive attributes, and non-sensitive attributes. The *Explicit IDentifiers* (EIDs) are those attributes that can uniquely identify individuals (like the social security number). *Quasi IDentifiers* (QIDs) refer to those attributes that potentially can be used to identify (some of) the individuals. Usually, intruders can find QIDs and EIDs in other data sets and use the QIDs (of the transformed data set) to link and identify some individuals in the transformed data set. For example, combination of zip code, birth data and gender is a known set of QIDs. *Sensitive ATtributes* (SATs) are the attributes that carry sensitive information (like salary, diseases, etc.) of the individuals and cannot be found in other data sets. All the other attributes that are not EIDs, QIDs or SATs are named as *Non-sensitive ATtributes* (NATs).

For this typical SDC procedure, we assume k-anonymity [10] is used to modify the values of QIDs, where the values of every QID are generalised based on a *taxonomy tree* specified by the data anonymizer [11]. After mapping the attributes and defining the taxonomy trees of QIDs, the tool explores the solution space and finds an optimum k-anonymity solution [8,11]. The anonymizer has access to various measurements to analyse the risk and utility measures of both original and transformed data sets. In case that the measures of data utility and data risk are satisfactory, then the transformed data set is ready to be shared with the data processor, otherwise the procedure must be continued by applying different configuration parameters until the measures of data utility and data risks are satisfied.

Note that the above-mentioned procedure is meant to illustrating how an SDC tool works typically and the procedure applied may differ depending on the SDC method or the SDC tool used. For example, in addition to k-anonymity, ARX offers other advanced algorithms including ϵ-differential privacy [11]. But, regarding general procedure for data anonymization, majority of the tools and procedures work similarly to those explained above.

The existing SDC tools, like ARX, sdcMicro [12] and μArgus [13], are all desktop software applications. These desktop applications need to have full access to the raw data and therefore their usage heavily relies on establishing a trusted environment within which these tools can operate and have access to full raw data. Using these desktop tools, therefore, can occur in two settings of (1) co-located data controller and data anonymizer and (2) a trusted third party data anonymizer.

The co-located data controller and data anonymizer setting requires that every organization has its own SDC expertise center. Applying SDC technology into practice is complex due to being context-dependent (as it depends on, for example, the motives of intruders, other available data sets in the environment, and the impact of the data set to be transformed), being multi-disciplinary (as it requires close collaboration of many stakeholders with various backgrounds), requiring a solid theoretical background (as it is built on statistical and mathematical models and methods), and being subject to accountability and liability burden if it is done improperly. In order to employ SDC tools in this settings, the organization needs to find and employ (long term) highly skilled SDC experts. Considering the high demand for the SDC experts and low supply, realising this setting is costly in a short foreseeable future. Therefore, co-located setting seems to be too ambitious currently for most (small and middle-sized) organizations.

One direction for facilitating and accelerating the adoption of this setting is to design, realize and deploy lightweight (i.e., less complex and intuitive) SDC tools together with developing intuitive guidelines for using these lightweight tools for these organizations. In this way, the tailored SDC tools may meet the current expertise level and expectations of the data controllers, like [14–16]. We believe that such an approach, if not done appropriately, may result in weak data minimization outcomes (i.e., publishing data with higher disclosure risks or lower data quality) due to not using more advanced and powerful SDC algorithms.

The trusted third party data anonymizer setting deploys a central organization in charge of applying SDC technology on behalf of many affiliated (small and middle-sized) organizations. This way of outsourcing the application of SDC technology to a trusted third party who uses an existing desktop SDC tool implies that the raw data of organizations should be transferred to the central party. This centralization of raw data sets, however, is against the principle of separation of privacy sensitive data sets. According to the data separation principle, personal data should be processed in a distributed way in order to prevent complete profiling of individuals [7], in our case, by the SDC trusted third party. In addition, there is a need for realizing a strong data governance mechanism to monitor and enforce the compliance of the SDC trusted third party to privacy rules and regulations as well as for a thorough procedure for screening and authorizing the SDC experts at the SDC trusted third party. Considering the efficiency of these governance, audit and certification procedures (specially in case of employing SDC experts based on short term contracts), there is always an increased risk of personal information leakage in the trusted third party data anonymizer setting.

Inspired by technology adoption models, like Technology Acceptance Model (TAM) [17] and Unified Theory of Acceptance and Use of Technology (UTAUT) [18], we recognise that adopting the current desktop SDC tools in either of the above mentioned settings suffers from one or more of the following technology adoption factors:

(1) Perceived ease of use and effort expectancy: SDC technologies are intrinsically complex and require SDC experts with solid interdisciplinary background to execute the anonymization assignments. In our study context, we are not focusing on usability features of currently available software tools. However, undoubtedly it is an essential factor to make the tool successful in an organization. Therefore, the usability and user interface characteristics

of SDC tools need a separate research even when the tools are used by SDC experts.

(2) Organizational context, attitude of using a system and facilitating conditions: Exposing original data sets to the data anonymizer, screening and clearance of SDC experts, and lack of balance between the supply of SDC expertise and the demand of organizations can make it difficult to deploy the current desktop SDC tools within current organizational settings. Therefore, the end result is either no or a poor personal data minimization.

(3) Perceived system usefulness and performance expectancy: Tailored lightweight SDC tools will have difficulty to follow the latest advances of SDC algorithms. The likelihood of providing anonymized data with low utility or high disclosure risk may become a demotivating factor in accepting such lightweight tools. A separate longitudinal research is needed to investigate the effectiveness of tailored SDC tools and their acceptance levels.

To address the second challenge mentioned above, we propose a distributed SDC tool that is *organizationally scalable*. The setting in which the proposed SDC tool operates is similar to the second setting (i.e. the trusted third party data anonymizer) but does not require transferring raw privacy sensitive data to the trusted third party. This approach, thereby, reduces the amount of the trust put on the trusted third party, while offering all SDC functionalities remotely. This approach aims at allowing SDC experts to *safely and effectively be involved* in the data anonymization process with *minimum facilitating overhead* for the (small and middle-sized) organizations. Further, this approach can be scalable organizationally as it does not require an immediate establishment of SDC expertise in every organization like the co-located data controller and data anonymizer setting does.

3   Distributed SDC Tool

As we discussed in the previous section, in our research we tackle the problem of SDC technology acceptance within organizations by developing a distributed SDC tool. In this section we present our solution and the latest status of its progress.

3.1   Functionalities

In our research, we *redesign the structural architecture of the current SDC tools*. We aim at *eliminating the access of SDC experts to the raw data* and restrict the availability of raw data set records inside a trusted environment only to the data controller. Figure 2 presents our solution in deploying the SDC functionalities provided by the SDC tool. In our setting, we hypothesize that *a data anonymizer as a SDC expert can perform the personal data minimization process merely using metadata and data analytical queries*.

In order to execute empirical studies and provide evidence for our hypothesis, we are employing ARX libraries as our anonymization engine and developing a

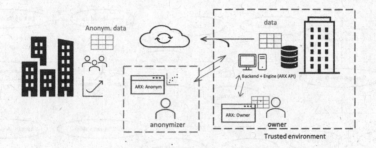

Fig. 2. Distributed data anonymization: deployment

SDC tool that satisfies these essential requirements modelled in Fig. 3. Using our new tool set up, the SDC functionality is divided between the data controller (an internal party) and the data anonymizer (an external party), see the workflow in Fig. 4, in such a way that the records of original data sets do not leave the boundary of the organization. According to this vision, specifically, the data controller has the ability to: manage a new anonymization case providing a context (domain description and requirements) for the SDC expert, manage original data sets where the records are visible *only* in his/her UI, specify EIDs, clean the data content, (optionally) analyse the risk and utility of both the original and anonymized data sets, and confirm or reject the final output. A data anonymizer has the ability to: start an issued anonymization case, view QIDs sample distinct values (the values of each QID is shuffled and presented without duplicates), conduct attribute mapping, make data analytical queries, analyse both risk and utility of data, provide QIDs taxonomy trees for which only distinct values of QIDs are required, and transform the data set by applying provided SDC algorithms.

It is crucial to stress that in our tool:

(1) EIDs are masked for data anonymizers as they are uniquely identify individuals;
(2) Data controllers can propose initial attribution but data anonymizers may modify them according to the requested requirements;
(3) Data anonymizers only can view distinct values of the provided attributes (not the original raw data set);
(4) The original data set stays within the trusted environment of the dat controller, while data anonymizers can be outside this trusted environment; and, finally,
(5) The chosen SDC algorithms are applied to the original data within the trusted environment of the data controller.

3.2   Proof-of-Concept Prototype

To validate the feasibility of our solution as a SDC tool, we extended ARX-aaS [14]. ARXaaS exposes main functionalities of ARX as web-API accessible

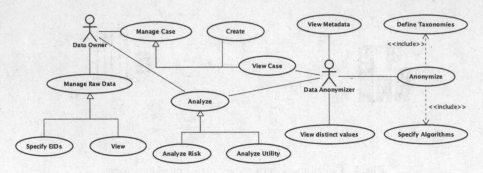

Fig. 3. Distributed data anonymization: functionalities

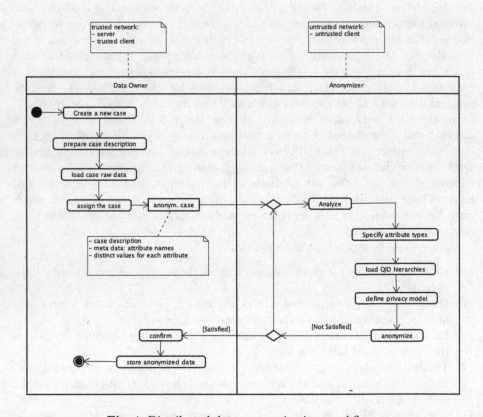

Fig. 4. Distributed data anonymization: workflow

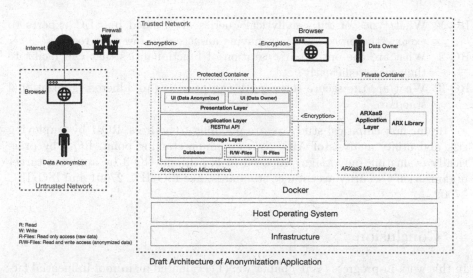

Draft Architecture of Anonymization Application

Fig. 5. Distributed data anonymization: tool architecture

through a simple web-UI. In the current implementation of ARXaaS, the provided user interface and server implementation do not distinguish between the two roles mentioned earlier. Additionally, it is implemented as stateless web service without security in mind, since the assumption was that the whole procedure is executed in a trusted environment.

For extending ARXaaS, we designed and implemented a secure web application that provides functionalities mentioned in Sect. 3.1 for both roles and addressed the security issues when using ARXaaS (see Fig. 5). To achieve this, an additional layer between the data anonymizer UI and the server is designed and implemented. The main responsibility of this layer is to securely control and mediate the interactions between trusted and untrusted network.

3.3   Research Directions

Many aspects of information security can play a role in our design and implementation process. Our focus is primarily on both aspects of security: procedural and technical. Generally, the main objective of information security practices is the proper protection of the confidentiality, integrity, and availability of collected data (also known as the CIA triad) while preserving efficient policy implementation. In that regard a thorough research need to be done about the compliance with different organizational standards and procedures regarding privacy and secure data processing to improve the chance of adoptability. It may be the case that functionalities provided by our proposed SDC tool is the same, but the applied procedures when using the tool in trusted networks differ. Currently, our goal is to have case studies from early adopters of our SDC tool and collect empirical studies to answer the following research questions:

RQ-1) What types of data analytical queries are needed by SDC experts to execute the process without having an access to raw data records?
RQ-2) What are the optimum separation of functionalities that can facilitate the process efficiently?
RQ-3) What are the secure software design practices to adhere organizational standards?

In our first empirical study we are planning to address: RQ-1 by employing risk and utility analysis of ARX as a minimum starting point, RQ-2 by practically evaluating our design proposed in Fig. 3, and RQ-3 by applying target organization's security acceptance standards, like ISO/IEC 27001 and ISO/IEC 27002.

4   Conclusion

In this work-in-progress (WiP) paper we: (1) evaluated main root influential factors that makes integration of SDC technologies within the data intensive organisations difficult, (2) proposed a novel solution that can facilitate data anonymization projects to be safely outsourced which provides an organizationally scalable solution, (3) presented our designed functionalities for our in-progress prototype tool that supports our centralised SDC architecture.

The first version of our prototype tool has been released. We are collecting case studies to evaluate functionalities and validate our hypothesis. In our experiments we are planning to: (1) Make a stable version of the prototype, (2) run various empirical data anonymization scenarios to capture data analytical feedback required by data anonymizer to execute a proper algorithm, (3) evaluate and compare the procedure proposed by our approach with the procedure currently running using stand alone applications.

The results of the experiments will be published in a follow-up full research paper.

Acknowledgment. This work was supported by RUAS SiA grant for Scalable and Usable Privacy Preserving Techniques project.

References

1. Bargh, M.S., Choenni, S.: On preserving privacy whilst integrating data in connected information systems. In: Proceedings of the 1st International Conference on Cloud Security Management (ICCSM), Seattle, USA. Academic Conferences and Publishing International, 17–18 October 2013
2. Kalidien, S., Choenni, S., Meijer, R.: Crime statistics online: potentials and challenges. In: Proceedings of the 11th Annual International Conference on Digital Government Research, Public Administration Online: Challenges and Opportunities, DG.O 2010, Puebla, Mexico, 17–20 May 2010, pp. 131–137 (2010)
3. Prins, J., Broeders, D., Griffioen, H.: iGgvernment: a new perspective on the future of government digitisation. Comput. Law Secur. Rev. **28**(3), 273–282 (2012)

4. Bargh, M.S., Meijer, R., Vink, M., van den Braak, S.W., Schirm, W., Choenni, S.: Opening privacy sensitive microdata sets in light of GDPR. In: 20th Annual International Conference on Digital Government Research, DG.O 2019, Dubai, United Arab Emirates 18–20 June 2019, pp. 314–323 (2019)
5. Elliot, K.O.M., Mackey, F., Tudor, C.: The anonymisation decision-making framework, technical report by UK Anonymisation Network (UKAN) (2016)
6. Fung, B.C.M., Wang, K., Chen, R.. Yu, P.S.: Privacy-preserving data publishing: a survey of recent developments. ACM Comput. Surv. **42**(4), 1–53 (2010)
7. Hoepman, J.-H.: Privacy design strategies. In: Cuppens-Boulahia, N., Cuppens, F., Jajodia, S., Abou El Kalam, A., Sans, T. (eds.) SEC 2014. IAICT, vol. 428, pp. 446–459. Springer, Heidelberg (2014). https://doi.org/10.1007/978-3-642-55415-5_38
8. Prasser, F., Eicher, J., Bild, R., Spengler, H., Kuhn ,K.A.: A tool for optimizing de-identified health data for use in statistical classification. In: 2017 IEEE 30th International Symposium on Computer-Based Medical Systems (CBMS), pp. 169–174 , June 2017
9. Arx data anonymization tool [Online]. https://arx.deidentifier.org/
10. Samarati, P., Sweeney, L.: Protecting Privacy when Disclosing Information: k-Anonymity and its Enforcement through Generalization and Suppression. Tech. Rep, SRI International (1998)
11. Bild, R., Kuhn, K.A., Prasser, F.: Safepub: a truthful data anonymization algorithm with strong privacy guarantees. PoPETs **2018**(1), 67–87 (2018)
12. Templ, M.: Statistical disclosure control for microdata using the R-package sdcMicro. Trans. Data Priv. **1**(2), 67–85 (2008)
13. Hundepool, A., Willenborg, L.: ARGUS, software packages for statistical disclosure control. In: Payne, R., Green. P. (eds.) COMPSTAT, Proceedings in Computational Statistics 13th Symposium held in Bristol, Great Britain, pp. 341–345. Springer, Cham (1998). https://doi.org/10.1007/978-3-662-01131-7_45
14. Arx as a service (tool). https://navikt.github.io/arxaas/
15. Bargh, M.S., Meijer, R., van den Braak, S., Latenko, A., Vink, M., Choenni, S.:Embedding personal data minimization technologies in organizations: needs, vision and artifacts. In: The 14th International Conference on Theory and Practice of Electronic Governance (ICEGOV 2021), Athene, Greece, October 2021
16. Rawat, R., Bargh, M.S., Janssen, M., Choenni, S.: Designing a user interface for improving the usability of a statistical disclosure control tool. In: The 14th IEEE International Conference on Security, Privacy, and Anonymity in Computation, Communication, and Storage (IEEE SpaCCS 2021), New York, USA, October 2021
17. Davis, F.D.: A technology acceptance model for empirically testing new end-user information systems: theory and results. Ph.D. Dissertation, Massachusetts Institute of Technology (1985)
18. Thong, J.Y., Hong, W., Tam, K.-Y.: Understanding user acceptance of digital libraries: what are the roles of interface characteristics, organizational context, and individual differences? Int. J. Hum. Comput. Stud. **57**(3), 215–242 (2002)

Applied Cryptography

A Verifiable Lossless Multiple Secret Images Sharing Scheme

Krishnaraj Bhat(✉) 🆔

Department of Computer Science and Engineering, Sardar Vallabhbhai National
Institute of Technology, Surat, Gujarat, India

Abstract. In the recent years, the researchers have proposed several
schemes for sharing multiple secret images using less number of shares
through different operations in order to save storage memory and network bandwidth consumption. However, the existing schemes suffer from
one or more of the following limitations, viz. no verification of reconstructed secret images, no support for resistance against loss of single
share, support for sharing only 2 secret images, incompatibility for sharing single secret image, lossy reconstruction of secret images and no
support for sharing all types (binary, grayscale and color) of images. The
proposed scheme overcomes these existing limitations, and shares $u-1$
secret images in v ($v \geq 2$) shares out of which at least u ($2 \leq u \leq v$)
shares are required to reconstruct all $u-1$ secret images. The operations are performed in galois field $GF(2^8)$ during shares generation and
secret images reconstruction. The verification of the reconstructed secret
images is done by using a random authentication image. The theoretical
analysis, comparison and experimental results are provided to indicate
the validity, merits and implementability of the proposed scheme.

Keywords: Image secret sharing · Multiple secret images sharing

1 Introduction

Secret images are generated and utilized in military operations, medical treatments and business organizations. The security requirement is to reveal the secret
images only in the presence of at least u ($u \geq 2$) authorized persons out of v
($v \geq u$) authorized persons, where u is the threshold. One possible solution to
satisfy this requirement is to use multi-key symmetric encryption. The solution
requires $\binom{v}{u-1}$ encryptions to be done to create each cipher image, and each
authorized person should hold $\binom{v-1}{u-1}$ keys with him [23]. For instance, if $v = 11$
and $u = 6$, then 462 encryptions are required to create each cipher image and
252 keys have to held by each authorized person. However, this leads to a problem with respect to managing a large number of keys [26]. To overcome this
problem, Naor and Shamir [20] proposed a (u, v)-Visual Cryptography (VC)
scheme which is an Image Secret Sharing (ISS) scheme, where a binary secret
image is divided into v random shares based on a codebook and distributed to

© Springer Nature Switzerland AG 2021
S. Tripathy et al. (Eds.): ICISS 2021, LNCS 13146, pp. 157–172, 2021.
https://doi.org/10.1007/978-3-030-92571-0_10

v participants by a dealer. In order to reconstruct the original secret image, u random shares from any u participants are collected by that dealer and stacked on one another. Even though $v - u$ $(v > u)$ random shares are lost or damaged, the original secret image can still be reconstructed by stacking the remaining u random shares. Following this scheme, the researchers have proposed several ISS schemes for sharing single secret image of the type binary, grayscale and color based on codebook, random grids and polynomials [24, 26].

1.1   Motivation Towards Multiple Secret Images Sharing (MSIS)

The main demerit of ISS schemes sharing single secret image at a time is that, they can protect only one secret image at a time by generating v shares. If x images have to be protected, then $x \times v$ shares have to be generated using these ISS schemes; furthermore, each participant should hold x shares. This leads to troublesome management of shares and increase in memory consumption. To overcome this problem, the concept of MSIS has been introduced. If x images of secret agents working undercover in a military operation have to be protected, then it is suitable to hold only one share by each one of v high rank officers (authorized persons) instead of holding x shares for each secret image. In addition, at least u of these v shares should be necessary to reconstruct all x secret images. This requirement can be fulfilled by MSIS. MSIS can be used to protect the images of trade secrets in the business organizations which can only be disclosed by any u board members (authorized persons).

1.2   Related Works

MSIS schemes for sharing 2 or more secret images at a time in 2 shares were proposed. In these schemes, the reconstruction is done by performing boolean, rotation and stacking operations on shares. Yadav and Ranvijay [27] proposed a $(2, 2)$-MSIS scheme for sharing 2 secret images in 2 shares where the 1st secret image is reconstructed by direct OR/XOR operation on 2 shares, and 2nd secret image is reconstructed by circularly shifting the 1st share and then performing OR/XOR operation with 2nd share. Chang et al. [5] proposed a $(2, 2)$-MSIS scheme for sharing multiple binary secret images in 2 shares. To reconstruct all secret images, the 2nd share is shifted in different ways and stacked with the 1st share. Shivani [24] proposed a $(2, 2)$-MSIS scheme for sharing 2 secret images in 2 shares where the 1st secret image is reconstructed by directly stacking 2 shares and the 2nd secret image is reconstructed by stacking the 1st share with the $90°$ rotated 2nd share. Bhosale and Patil [4] proposed a $(2, 2)$-MSIS scheme for sharing 2 binary secret images in 2 shares where the 1st secret image is reconstructed by directly stacking 2 shares and the 2nd secret image is reconstructed by flipping the 2nd share and stacking with the 1st share. However, the size of one secret image should be greater than that of other in terms of both height and width. Huang and Juan [10] proposed a $(2, 2)$-MSIS scheme for sharing multiple binary secret images in 2 meaningful shares through Random Grid Visual Secret Sharing (RGVSS), where the secret images are reconstructed by shifting the 2nd

share by different lengths and stacking with the 1st share. However, increase in the number of secret images shared will decrease the visual quality of the recovered secret images.

MSIS schemes were also proposed on the basis of equal values for u and v to share either v or $v-1$ secret images. Nitharwal and Verma [21] proposed a (v, v)-MSIS scheme where v secret images are shared using v shares through XOR and bit-reversal operations. Chen and Chen [8] proposed two (v, v)-MSIS schemes based on boolean methods, viz. partial sensitivity different sized symmetric sharing-recovery (PDSR) and full sensitivity different sized symmetric sharing-recovery (FDSR) for sharing v secret images in v shares. Deshmukha et al. [9] proposed a (v, v)-MSIS scheme for sharing v secret images in v shares through Chinese Remainder Theorem (CRT) and XOR operations. However, the recovery of secret images fails for odd v. Shankar et al. [14] proposed a (v, v)-MSIS scheme for sharing v secret images in v shares through Elliptic Curve Cryptography (ECC), XOR and complement operations. However, each share size must be a multiple of 64 as a 8×8 block is considered at once for encryption using ECC. Kapadiya et al. [13] proposed a $(v+1, v+1)$-MSIS scheme for sharing v secret images in $v+1$ shares through XOR operations. Here, to recover the 1st secret image, universal share and 2nd share are required. To recover the 2nd secret image, universal share, 2nd share and 3rd shares are required, and so on. Mary et al. [15] proposed a (v, v)-MSIS scheme for sharing v secret images in v shares through DNA coding and XOR operations. Mishra and Gupta [18] proposed a $(v+1, v+1)$-MSIS scheme for sharing v binary secret images in $v+1$ shares where i^{th} secret image is reconstructed by XORing i^{th} and $(i+1)^{th}$ shares. Prasetyo and Guo [22] proposed a (v, v)-MSIS scheme for sharing v secret images in v shares through hyperchaotic scrambling, and symmetric and transferred masking coefficients. Kabirirad and Eslami [12] proposed a (v, v)-MSIS scheme for sharing v secret images in v shares which overcomes the limitation in [8] in respect of revealing the information of secret images with less than v shares, by using hash function and block cipher to generate shares. Meghrajani et al. [17] proposed a (v, v)-MSIS scheme where a universal random share known only to dealer is used for sharing v secret images in v shares. Mishra et al. [19] proposed a (v, v)-MSIS scheme for sharing v secret images in v shares through swap bits, XOR and arithmetic modulo operations. Chanu and Neelima [6] proposed a (v, v)-MSIS scheme for sharing v secret images in v shares through discrete cosine transforms. Azza and Lian [2] proposed a (v, v)-MSIS scheme for sharing v secret images in v meaningful shares through elementary cellular automata, hashing and steganography using modulo 4 operations. Chattopadhyay et al. [7] proposed a (v, v)-MSIS scheme for sharing v secret images in v shares through hash functions and XOR operations. The fake shares are identified by comparing stored hash values of the corresponding original shares with that of the shares received for reconstruction.

In addition, MSIS schemes were proposed on the basis of supporting unequal values for u and v. Zhang et al. [29] proposed two (u, v)-MSIS schemes for sharing u secret images in v shares using bivariate polynomials. Kabirirad and Eslami

[11] proposed a (u,v)-MSIS scheme for sharing u secret images in v shares where u consecutive shares are required to reconstruct the u secret images. Ahmed *et al.* [1] proposed a (u,v)-MSIS scheme for sharing u (even number) secret images in v shares through Hill cipher and Blakely sharing scheme. Bhat *et al.* [3] proposed a (u,v)-MSIS scheme for sharing $\frac{m}{2}$ secret images in v meaningful shares through polynomials and EVC, where m is the pixel expansion in the (u,v)-Extended VC scheme. However, size of each share increases as m increases.

1.3   Limitations

The existing related works on MSIS briefed so far have following demerits which will limit the scope of their applications:

– No verification for checking the correctness of reconstructed secret images [1,4–6,8–15,17–19,21,22,24,27,29]. As the shares can be corrupted either maliciously or unintentionally, there should be a mechanism to check the correctness of the reconstructed secret images in order to avoid revealing wrong information. Otherwise, the scheme will be unreliable.
– Lossy reconstruction of secret images [4,5,10,13,15,24,27]. The secret images in which every pixel information is considered important, the lossless reconstruction has to be done in order to not loose any important information. For instance, in telemedicine, images containing the locations of multiple tumors in brain have to be reconstructed in a lossless manner to avoid wrong diagnosis by the authorized doctors.
– Incompatibility for sharing single secret image [2,6–9,12,14,15,17,19,21,22, 24,27]. Even though MSIS schemes are meant for protecting multiple secret images, they should even be compatible to protect single secret image; otherwise, we have to rely on a seperate scheme meant for protecting single secret image.
– No support for having different values of u and v in addition to the support for having same values [2,4–10,12–15,17,19,21,22,24,27]. If support is even provided for different values of u and v, then the MSIS scheme can be used for the applications where resistance to loss of $v - u$ shares is required.
– Support for sharing only 2 secret images [4,24,27]. A MSIS scheme should support protecting even more than 2 secret images for increasing its scope of applications.
– No support for sharing all types (binary, grayscale and color) of images [1–3,6–9,11–15,17–19,21,22,27,29]. A MSIS scheme should support protecting all types (binary, grayscale and color) of images for increasing its scope of applications.

1.4   Our Contributions

We have proposed a (u,v)-MSIS scheme that overcomes the demerits mentioned above with respect to the existing MSIS schemes. In the proposed scheme, $u-1$ secret images are shared using v shares, where at least u shares are required to reconstruct all $u - 1$ secret images. The proposed scheme uses the concept of Shamir's secret sharing [23] which is modified in terms of coefficient values in the polynomial equation and the operations are performed in the galois field $GF(2^8)$ instead of in a finite field with prime modulus p to attain lossless reconstruction of secret images. The verification of the reconstructed secret images is performed by using a random authentication image. The proposed scheme supports sharing the secret images of the types: binary, grayscale and color. However, all the secret images should be of the same type.

The rest of this paper is organized as follows. Preliminaries are provided in Sect. 2. Proposed scheme is detailed in Sect. 3. Theoretical analysis is detailed in Sect. 4. Comparison details and experimental results are provided in Sect. 5. Finally, conclusion is provided in Sect. 6.

2 Preliminaries

The fundamental principle behind the working of the proposed (u, v)-MSIS scheme is based on Shamir's secret sharing [23]. To better understand the proposed scheme, preliminaries about Shamir's secret sharing is provided in this section.

Shamir [23] proposed a (u, v) secret sharing scheme where a secret A is divided into v shares $A_i (1 \leq i \leq v)$. To reconstruct secret A, at least u shares are required and less than u shares reveal no information about secret A. The shares are generated using the polynomial Eq. (1) where the operations are performed in a field of prime order p. The value of p is chosen to be greater than both A and v. The share $A_i = Q(t_i)$ for $1 \leq i \leq v$, and $Q(0) = A$. In Eq. (1), $a_0 = A$ and $a_1, a_2...a_{u-1}$ are random values in the range $[0, p)$. In addition, t_i for $1 \leq i \leq v$ are v distinct natural numbers used as identifying indices for corresponding shares A_i.

$$Q(t) = (a_0 + a_1 t + a_2 t^2 + ... + a_{u-1} t^{u-1}) \bmod p \qquad (1)$$

The secret A is reconstructed by applying the Lagranges interpolation on the collected u shares A_i for $i \in [1, v]$. The Lagranges interpolation formula is provided in Eq. (2) where $e_i = A_i$ and t_i is the corresponding identifying index of A_i.

$$Q(t) = \sum_{i=1}^{u} e_i \left(\prod_{i \leq j \leq u, i \neq j} \left(\frac{t - t_j}{t_i - t_j} \right) \right) \bmod p \qquad (2)$$

Thien and Lin [25] applied the concept of Shamir's secret sharing to share a grayscale secret image where the pixel values are in the range [0, 255]. They proposed two methods in which $p = 251$ and the u consecutive pixel values are assigned to $a_0, a_1, a_2...a_{u-1}$ respectively in Eq. (1). In the first method, the pixel values greater than 250 are truncated to 250 before applying the Eq. (1) leading to lossy reconstruction of corresponding pixels in the reconstruction phase. In the second method, each pixel value q greater than 249 is divided into two pixels

250 and $q - 250$ before applying the Eq. (1) leading to lossless reconstruction of secret image. However, due to the division of pixels, the size of each share can be greater than that of a share generated using the first method. Therefore, in the proposed scheme, we perform operations in the galois field $GF(2^8)$ to avoid increase in the share size and to achieve lossless reconstruction of secret images.

3   Proposed Scheme

The proposed (u, v)-MSIS scheme shares $u - 1$ secret images using v shares, where at least u shares are required to reconstruct all $u - 1$ secret images. No information about any secret image can be revealed with less than u shares. In the proposed scheme, both shares generation and reconstruction of secret images are executed by a dealer who is assumed to be incorruptible. The details on shares generation and reconstruction methods are provided in the subsequent subsections.

3.1   Shares Generation

The shares generation method takes following items as input: the seed s, v shares' identifying indices $t_j (1 \leq j \leq v)$, $u - 1$ secret images $IS_i (1 \leq i \leq u - 1)$ each of size $H \times W \times P$ where H, W and P are the height, width and number of planes in an image. The output of this method is v random shares $Sh_j (1 \leq j \leq v)$. The seed s is kept secret by the dealer. There are three steps in shares generation method, viz. image contraction, authentication image generation and random shares generation.

Image Contraction. Image contraction step is executed only for binary secret images; furthermore, width of binary secret images must be a multiple of 8. Each binary image consists of only binary pixels 1 and 0. Therefore, in order to support operations in $GF(2^8)$ during random shares generation step, blocks of 8 nonoverlapping consecutive pixels along each row are formed and converted into their decimal equivalent in the range [0, 255]. This results in the formation of corresponding grayscale secret images whose width is reduced 8 times. For convenience, these grayscale secret images are still notated $IS_i (1 \leq i \leq u - 1)$. However, the new width W of these grayscale secret images is $W = \frac{W}{8}$.

Authentication Image Generation. Using s as the seed value for PRNG (Pseudo Random Number Generator), generate the random authentication image IR having uniformly distributed pixel values in the range [0, 255] whose size is equal to that of IS_i. IR is used to verify the correctness of reconstructed secret images.

Random Shares Generation. The random shares generation step generates v random shares $Sh_j (1 \leq j \leq v)$. For every corresponding pixels in $u-1$ IS_i and IR, compute $Q(t_j)$ for $(1 \leq j \leq v)$ using Eq. (3). $Q(t_j)$ corresponds to a pixel in j^{th} random share Sh_j. This results in generation of v random shares $Sh_j (1 \leq j \leq v)$ whose size is same as that of IS_i. The values for $a_0, a_1 ... a_{u-2}, a_{u-1}$ in Eq. (3) are the corresponding pixels in $IS_1, IS_2 ... IS_{u-1}$ and IR. The value $t_j (1 \leq j \leq v)$ is the identifying index of Sh_j.

$$Q(t) = (a_0 + a_1 t + a_2 t^2 + ... + a_{u-1} t^{u-1}) \bmod GF(2^8) \qquad (3)$$

3.2   Secret Images Reconstruction

The secret images reconstruction method takes following items as input: the seed s, u random shares $Sh_j (1 \leq j \leq u)$ and their corresponding identifying indices t_j. The output of this method is $u - 1$ reconstructed secret images $RIS_i (1 \leq i \leq u - 1)$. There are three steps in secret images reconstruction method, viz. unverified secret images reconstruction, verification and image expansion.

Unverified Secret Images Reconstruction. The unverified secret images reconstruction step reconstructs $u - 1$ secret images $RIS_i (1 \leq i \leq u - 1)$ and authentication image RIR. For every corresponding pixels e_j in u Sh_j, compute the u corresponding pixels in $RIS_1, RIS_2 ... RIS_{u-1}$ and RIR by using Eq. (4). The value t_j in Eq. (4) is the identifying index of Sh_j.

$$Q(t) = \sum_{i=1}^{u} e_i \left(\prod_{i \leq j \leq u, i \neq j} \left(\frac{t - t_j}{t_i - t_j} \right) \right) \bmod GF(2^8) \qquad (4)$$

Verification. Using the same seed s used during shares generation method as the seed value for PRNG, generate the random authentication image IR having uniformly distributed pixel values in the range $[0, 255]$ whose size is equal to that of RIS_i. Verify whether IR is equal to RIR by performing XOR operation between them. If the result is zero in all pixel positions, then there is no corruption. Else, pixels are corrupted in the respective positions where the result of XOR operation is non zero.

Image Expansion. Image expansion step is the reverse of image contraction step executed only for binary secret images. Convert each pixel in $RIS_i (1 \leq i \leq u - 1)$ to their binary equivalent with 8 bit places, and assign them as the 8 consecutive binary pixels along the row in the corresponding binary image. This results in formation of original binary secret images whose width is 8 times greater than that of RIS_i.

4   Theoretical Analysis

In this section, we theoretically analyse the random nature of the shares, security provided by the proposed scheme, and the correctness in the verification of the reconstructed secret images.

Lemma 1. *Random shares are generated by the proposed scheme.*

Proof. The arithmetic operations performed on a random number r will result in another random number r' [28]. In Eq. (3) which is used for shares generation, the value of a_{u-1} is a random value generated using a PRNG. Since the operations performed on a_{u-1} is arithmetic, the value of $Q(t)$ which corresponds to a share is also random for any natural number t. Therefore, each share generated by the proposed scheme is random.

Theorem 1. *The proposed scheme will not reveal any information about secret images and authentication image with less than u (threshold) shares.*

Proof. We prove that no information can be revealed with $u - 1$ shares which in turn gets proved for less than $u - 1$ shares.

For instance, $u - 1$ corrupted participants are colluding to reveal the secret images and authentication image with their shares. In addition, it is assumed that these colluding participants also know the identifying indices of all v generated shares. However, they do not have access to the remaining $v - u + 1$ shares. From Eq. (4) which is used during reconstruction, the values a_{i-1} for $1 \le i \le u$ are calculated using Eq. (5) formed using known values of identifying indices and pixels of $u - 1$ shares.

$$a_{i-1} = (c_{1_{a_{i-1}}} + e_u c_{2_{a_{i-1}}}) \bmod GF(2^8) \tag{5}$$

In Eq. (5), $c_{1_{a_{i-1}}}$ and $c_{2_{a_{i-1}}}$ are the corresponding constant values resulting from the operations on known values of identifying indices and pixels of $u - 1$ shares; furthermore, e_u is the corresponding pixel value of any u^{th} share unknown to the $u - 1$ colluding participants. From Lemma 1, it can be noted that e_u is a random value that leads to $Prob(a_{i-1} = k) = \frac{1}{256}$ for any $k \in [0, 255]$. Therefore, no information about secret images and authentication image are revealed with $u - 1$ shares.

Theorem 2. *The reconstructed secret images are correctly verified by the proposed scheme.*

Proof. From Eq. (4) which is used during reconstruction, the values a_{i-1} for $1 \leq i \leq u$ are calculated using Eq. (6) fromed using the known values of identifying indices of shares.

$$a_{i-1} = (e_1 c_{1_{a_{i-1}}} + e_2 c_{2_{a_{i-1}}} + ... + e_u c_{u_{a_{i-1}}}) \bmod GF(2^8) \qquad (6)$$

In Eq. (6), e_l for $1 \leq l \leq u$ are the corresponding pixel values in u shares, and $c_{l_{a_{i-1}}}$ for $1 \leq l \leq u$ are the u constant values resulting from the operations on identifying indices of corresponding shares. Even if any one of the values e_l for $1 \leq l \leq u$ is corrupted, then it will alter the values of every a_{i-1} for $1 \leq i \leq u$. Since the values a_{i-1} for $1 \leq i \leq u$ correspond to pixel values of $u - 1$ secret images and the authentication image, the corresponding reconstructed pixels of secret images and authentication image will be corrupted. However, when the XOR operation is performed between reconstructed authentication image and the generated authenication image, the resultant will have non zero values at the position of each corrupted pixel. Thus, the reconstructed secret images are correctly verified by the proposed scheme.

5   Comparison and Experimental Results

In this section, details on comparison of the proposed scheme with related MSIS schemes, and experimental results are provided.

5.1   Comparison

The proposed scheme is compared with some of the related MSIS schemes and its details are provided in Table 1. The comparison is made in respect of five properties, viz. verification of reconstructed secret images, number of secret images shared, value of (u, v) supported, lossless reconstruction of secret images, and types of secret images supported. The abbreviations B, G and C used in Table 1 denote binary, grayscale and color images respectively. It should be noted that the schemes which share x secret images with $x = u = v$ are not compatible to share single secret image as the minimum value for both u and v is 2. It can be inferred from Table 1 that the compared MSIS schemes possess not all, but some of the following properties, viz. verification of reconstructed secret images for checking their correctness, compatibility for sharing single secret image, resistance to loss of $v - u$ shares by supporting different values for u and v, lossless reconstruction of secret images, and support for sharing binary, grayscale and color secret images. However, the proposed scheme possesses all these properties making it comparatively advantageous.

Table 1. Comparison between proposed scheme and related MSIS schemes.

Scheme	Verification	Number of secret images	Value of (u, v)	Lossless reconstruction	Secret image types
Nitharwal and Verma [21]	No	v	(v, v)	Yes	G, C
Chen and Chen [8]	No	v	(v, v)	Yes	G, C
Deshmukha et al. [9]	No	v	(v, v)	Yes	G, C
Shankar et al. [14]	No	v	(v, v)	Yes	G, C
Kapadiya et al. [13]	No	v	$(v+1, v+1)$	No	G, C
Mary et al. [15]	No	v	(v, v)	No	G, C
Zhang et al. [29]	No	u	(u, v)	Yes	G, C
Mishra and Gupta [18]	No	v	$(v+1, v+1)$	Yes	B
Kabirirad and Eslami [11]	No	u	(u, v)	Yes	G, C
Prasetyo and Guo [22]	No	v	(v, v)	Yes	G, C
Kabirirad and Eslami [12]	No	v	(v, v)	Yes	G, C
Meghrajani et al. [17]	No	v	(v, v)	Yes	G, C
Mishra et al. [19]	No	v	(v, v)	Yes	G, C
Chanu and Neelima [6]	No	v	(v, v)	Yes	G, C
Ahmed et al. [1]	No	u (even)	(u, v)	Yes	G, C
Azza and Lian [2]	Yes	v	(v, v)	Yes	G, C
Chattopadhyay et al. [7]	Yes	v	(v, v)	Yes	G, C
Proposed	Yes	$u - 1$	(u, v)	Yes	B, G, C

5.2   Experimental Results

The experiments are conducted using GNU Octave-5.2.0 software in a computer system with 64-bit Windows 10 Home operating system, Intel(R) Core(TM) i3-5005U CPU @ 2.00 GHz and 4.00 GB RAM. The default PRNG [16] available in the GNU Octave-5.2.0 software is used to generate the random authentication image.

An example of proposed $(2, 3)$-MSIS scheme for sharing a color secret image of size $512 \times 512 \times 3$ is illustrated in Fig. 1. The size of each share and authentication image generated is $512 \times 512 \times 3$. The reconstructed secret images using different combinations of 2 out of 3 shares are not explicitly displayed as they are as same as the original secret image in Fig. 1a. A complete black image displayed in Fig. 1f corresponds to zero values for the XOR operation between IR and reconstructed authentication image using any 2 uncorrupted shares. Figure 1g displays the corrupted 1st share CSh_1 formed by inducing noise in the middle portion of Sh_1. It can be observed from Fig. 1h and i that the reconstructed secret images using CSh_1 and Sh_2, and CSh_1 and Sh_2 respectively are corrupted in the same portion as in CSh_1. However, during verification, the corrupted portions in the reconstructed secret images are identified by the respective non zero values (non black portion) in the result of XOR operation between IR and corresponding reconstructed authentication image as displayed in Fig. 1j and k.

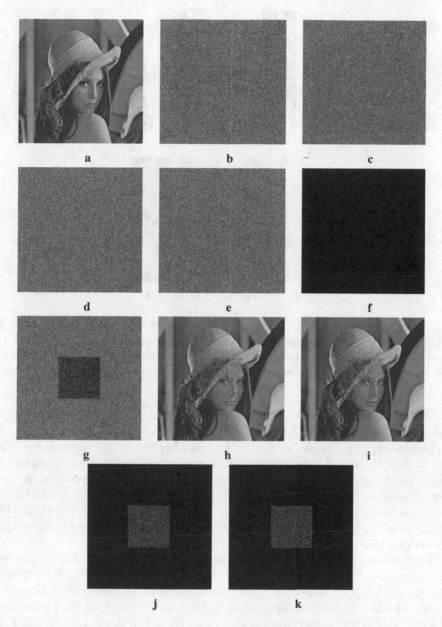

Fig. 1. $(2,3)$-MSIS example. **a** Secret image IS. **b** Authentication image IR. **c** 1st share Sh_1. **d** 2nd share Sh_2. **e** 3rd share Sh_3. **f** Result of XOR operation on IR and reconstructed authentication image. **g** Corrupted 1st share CSh_1. **h** Reconstructed secret image using shares CSh_1 and Sh_2. **i** Reconstructed secret image using shares CSh_1 and Sh_3. **j** Result of XOR operation between IR and reconstructed authentication image using shares CSh_1 and Sh_2. **k** Result of XOR operation between IR and reconstructed authentication image using shares CSh_1 and Sh_3.

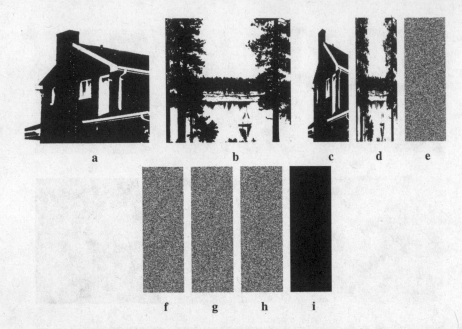

Fig. 2. $(3,3)$-MSIS example. **a** 1st secret image IS_1. **b** 2nd secret image IS_2. **c** Grayscale secret image GIS_1. **d** Grayscale secret image GIS_2. **e** Authentication image IR. **f** 1st share Sh_1. **g** 2nd share Sh_2. **h** 3rd share Sh_3. **i** Result of XOR operation between IR and reconstructed authentication image.

An example of proposed $(3,3)$-MSIS scheme for sharing two binary secret images of size $512 \times 512 \times 1$ is illustrated in Fig. 2. Figure 2c and d display the corresponding grayscale secret images formed after image contraction step. The size of each share and authentication image is $512 \times 64 \times 1$. The reconstructed secret images generated using all 3 shares are not explicitly displayed as they are as same as the corresponding original secret images in Fig. 2a and b. A complete black image displayed in Fig. 2i corresponds to zero values for the XOR operation between IR and reconstructed authentication image using all 3 uncorrupted shares.

Correlation between two images of same size is computed using correlation coefficient [28]. For two identical and complement images, correlation coefficient values are $+1$ and -1 respectively. For two uncorrelated images, correlation coefficient value is 0. It can be inferred from Table 2 and Table 3 that the correlations of secret images and authentication images with random shares are negligible for the examples illustrated in Fig. 1 and Fig. 2 as their correlation coefficient values are ≈ 0. In addition, it can be inferred from Table 4 that negligible correlation exists between adjacent pixels along horizontal, vertical and diagonal directions in shares.

Table 2. Correlation coefficient values of compared images in Fig. 1.

Compared images	Correlation coefficient
IS & Sh_1	−0.0026
IS & Sh_2	−0.0004
IS & Sh_3	−0.0005
IR & Sh_1	0.0299
IR & Sh_2	0.0154
IR & Sh_3	0.0013

Table 3. Correlation coefficient values of compared images in Fig. 2.

Compared images	Correlation coefficient
GIS_1 & Sh_1	−0.0043
GIS_1 & Sh_2	−0.0007
GIS_1 & Sh_3	0.0030
GIS_2 & Sh_1	0.0116
GIS_2 & Sh_2	0.0096
GIS_2 & Sh_3	−0.0016
IR & Sh_1	−0.1255
IR & Sh_2	−0.0299
IR & Sh_3	0.0116

Table 4. Correlation coefficient values of adjacent pixels along horizontal, vertical and diagonal directions in shares.

Image	Correlation coefficient		
	Horizontal	Vertical	Diagonal
Sh_1 in Fig. 1	0.0002	−0.0013	0.0022
Sh_2 in Fig. 1	−0.0010	−0.0012	0.0006
Sh_3 in Fig. 1	−0.0010	0.0006	−0.0009
Sh_1 in Fig. 2	0.0008	−0.0071	0.0078
Sh_2 in Fig. 2	0.0014	0.0023	−0.0067
Sh_3 in Fig. 2	−0.0044	0.0015	−0.0125

PSNR (Peak Signal to Noise Ratio) is used to measure the noise in the transformed image in comparison to the original image [28]. PSNR value equal to infinity (∞) indicates that the transformed image is as same as the original image without any noise in it. However, increase in noise will decrease the value of PSNR along with the visual quality of the transformed image. For the proposed scheme, the PSNR value between original secret images and corresponding

170   K. Bhat

Table 5. PSNR values of compared images in Fig. 1.

Compared images	PSNR (dB)
IS & Sh_1	8.5296
IS & Sh_2	8.5436
IS & Sh_3	8.5399
IR & Sh_1	7.8788
IR & Sh_2	7.8182
IR & Sh_3	7.7536

Table 6. PSNR values of compared images in Fig. 2.

Compared images	PSNR (dB)
GIS_1 & Sh_1	4.8308
GIS_1 & Sh_2	4.8476
GIS_1 & Sh_3	4.8500
GIS_2 & Sh_1	5.0687
GIS_2 & Sh_2	5.0638
GIS_2 & Sh_3	5.0101
IR & Sh_1	7.2297
IR & Sh_2	7.6200
IR & Sh_3	7.7830

Table 7. Entropy values of shares and authentication images.

Image	Entropy	Image	Entropy
Sh_1 in Fig. 1	7.9998	Sh_1 in Fig. 2	7.9947
Sh_2 in Fig. 1	7.9998	Sh_2 in Fig. 2	7.9947
Sh_3 in Fig. 1	7.9997	Sh_3 in Fig. 2	7.9945
IR in Fig. 1	7.9997	IR in Fig. 2	7.9946

reconstructed secret images using any threshold number of uncorrupted shares is ∞ due to lossless reconstruction. Table 5 and Table 6 provide the PSNR values between different compared images in Fig. 1 and Fig. 2. It can be inferred that high noise is induced when secret images and authentication images are transformed into shares.

Entropy is used to measure the randomness of numbers generated from a source [28]. For a random source generating n different numbers, the entropy is $\log_2 n$. Since the shares and authentication image consist of pixel values in the range [0, 255], their entropy value should be close to $\log_2 256 = 8$ in order to be random. It can be observed from Table 7 that entropy values of shares and authentication images in Fig. 1 and Fig. 2 are close to 8.

6 Conclusion

This paper proposes a novel (u, v)-MSIS scheme for sharing $u - 1$ secret images using v shares by performing operations in $GF(2^8)$. The size of each share is equal to that of a secret image in case of grayscale and color secret images. However, for binary secret images, the width of each share is 8 times less than that of a secret image. The theoretical analysis on the proposed scheme indicates that the shares are random, no information of secret and authentication images can be revealed using less than u shares, and the reconstructed secret images are correctly verified. The comparison with the related MSIS schemes indicates that the proposed scheme is comparatively advantageous by supporting verification of reconstructed secret images, compatiblity for sharing single secret image, resistance against loss of $v - u$ shares, lossless reconstruction of secret images, and sharing of all types (binary, grayscale and color) of secret images. The experimental results indicate the implementability of the proposed scheme and support the indications of the theoretical analysis.

References

1. Ahmed, M., Abdul-kader, H.S., kishk, A., Abdo, A.A.: An efficient multi secret image sharing scheme using hill cipher. In: Hassanien, A.-E., Azar, A.T., Gaber, T., Oliva, D., Tolba, F.M. (eds.) AICV 2020. AISC, vol. 1153, pp. 604–613. Springer, Cham (2020). https://doi.org/10.1007/978-3-030-44289-7_57
2. Azza, A.A., Lian, S.: Multi-secret image sharing based on elementary cellular automata with steganography. Multimedia Tools Appl. **79**, 21241–21264 (2020)
3. Bhat, K., Uday Kumar Reddy, K.R., Ranjan Kumar, H.S., Mahto, D.: A novel scheme for lossless authenticated multiple secret images sharing using polynomials and extended visual cryptography. IET Inf. Secur. **15**(1), 13–22 (2021)
4. Bhosale, A.G., Patil, V.S.: A (2, 2) visual cryptography technique to share two secrets. In: 2020 International Conference on Inventive Computation Technologies (ICICT), pp. 563–569 (2020). https://doi.org/10.1109/ICICT48043.2020.9112420
5. Chang, J.J.Y., Huang, B.Y., Juan, J.S.T.: A new visual multi-secrets sharing scheme by random grids. Cryptography **2**(3) (2018). https://doi.org/10.3390/cryptography2030024
6. Chanu, O.B., Neelima, A.: A new multi-secret image sharing scheme based on DCT. Vis. Comput. **36**, 939–950 (2020)
7. Chattopadhyay, A.K., Nag, A., Singh, J.P., Singh, A.K.: A verifiable multi-secret image sharing scheme using XOR operation and hash function. Multimedia Tools Appl. (2020). https://doi.org/10.1007/s11042-020-09174-0
8. Chen, C.C., Chen, J.L.: A new Boolean-based multiple secret image sharing scheme to share different sized secret images. J. Inf. Secur. Appl. **33**, 45–54 (2017)
9. Deshmukha, M., Nainb, N., Ahmed, M.: A novel approach for sharing multiple color images by employing Chinese remainder theorem. J. Vis. Commun. Image Represent. **49**, 291–302 (2017)
10. Huang, B.Y., Juan, J.S.T.: Flexible meaningful visual multi-secret sharing scheme by random grids. Multimedia Tools Appl. **79**, 7705–7729 (2020)
11. Kabirirad, S., Eslami, Z.: A (t, n)-multi secret image sharing scheme based on Boolean operations. J. Vis. Commun. Image Represent. **57**, 39–47 (2018)

12. Kabirirad, S., Eslami, Z.: Improvement of (n, n)-multi-secret image sharing schemes based on Boolean operations. J. Inf. Secur. Appl. **47**, 16–27 (2019)

13. Kapadiya, V.J., Desai, L.S., Meghrajani, Y.K.: Boolean-based multi secret sharing scheme using meaningful shares. In: 2018 Second International Conference on Inventive Communication and Computational Technologies (ICICCT), pp. 840–844 (2018). https://doi.org/10.1109/ICICCT.2018.8473323

14. Shankar, K., Devika, G., Ilayaraja, M.: Scheme based on Boolean operations and elliptic curve cryptography. Int. J. Pure Appl. Math. **116**(10), 293–300 (2017)

15. Mary, I.R.P., Eswaran, P., Shankar, K.: Multi secret image sharing scheme based on DNA cryptography with XOR. Int. J. Pure Appl. Math. **118**(7), 393–398 (2018)

16. Matsumoto, M., Nishimura, T.: Mersenne twister: a 623-dimensionally equidistributed uniform pseudo-random number generator. ACM Trans. Model. Comput. Simul. **8**(1), 3–30 (1998)

17. Meghrajani, Y.K., Desai, L.S., Mazumdar, H.S.: Secure and efficient arithmetic-based multi-secret image sharing scheme using universal share. J. Inf. Secur. Appl. **47**, 267–274 (2019)

18. Mishra, A., Gupta, A.: Multi secret sharing scheme using iterative method. J. Inf. Optim. Sci. **39**(3), 631–641 (2018)

19. Mishra, K., Kavala, S., Singh, S.K., Nagabhushan, P.: Efficient collusion resistant multi-secret image sharing. Multimedia Tools Appl. **79**, 33233–33252 (2020)

20. Naor, M., Shamir, A.: Visual cryptography. In: De Santis, A. (ed.) EUROCRYPT 1994. LNCS, vol. 950, pp. 1–12. Springer, Heidelberg (1995). https://doi.org/10.1007/BFb0053419

21. Nitharwal, S.M., Verma, H.K.: A Boolean-based multi-secret image sharing scheme using bit-reversal. In: 2017 International Conference on Intelligent Communication and Computational Techniques (ICCT), pp. 114–118 (2017). https://doi.org/10.1109/INTELCCT.2017.8324030

22. Prasetyo, H., Guo, J.: A note on multiple secret sharing using Chinese remainder theorem and exclusive-or. IEEE Access **7**, 37473–37497 (2019)

23. Shamir, A.: How to share a secret. Commun. ACM **22**(11), 612–613 (1979)

24. Shivani, S.: Multi secret sharing with unexpanded meaningful shares. Multimedia Tools Appl. **77**, 6287–6310 (2018)

25. Thien, C.C., Lin, J.C.: Secret image sharing. Comput. Graph. **26**(5), 765–770 (2002)

26. Weir, J., Yan, W.Q.: A comprehensive study of visual cryptography. In: Shi, Y.Q. (ed.) Transactions on Data Hiding and Multimedia Security V. LNCS, vol. 6010, pp. 70–105. Springer, Heidelberg (2010). https://doi.org/10.1007/978-3-642-14298-7_5

27. Yadav, M., Ranvijay: A distortion free multi-secret image sharing with efficient shadow communication overhead. J. Inf. Optim. Sci. **39**(1), 143–156 (2018)

28. Yan, X., Liu, L., Lu, Y., Gong, Q.: Security analysis and classification of image secret sharing. J. Inf. Secur. Appl. **47**, 208–216 (2019). https://doi.org/10.1016/j.jisa.2019.05.008

29. Zhang, T., Ke, X., Liu, Y.: (t, n) multi-secret sharing scheme extended from Harn-Hsu's scheme. EURASIP J. Wirel. Commun. Netw. (2018). https://doi.org/10.1186/s13638-018-1086-5

Experimental Verification of Estimated Block Size of BKZ Algorithm Against LWE

Amane Takeshige[1]([⊠]), Haruhisa Kosuge[2], and Hidema Tanaka[1]

[1] National Defense Academy, Yokosuka, Japan
{em59035,hidema}@nda.ac.jp
[2] Japan Maritime Self Defense Force, Tokyo, Japan

Abstract. Cryptographic constructions based on the Learning with Errors (LWE) problem have received much attention in recent years for the process of standardizing post-quantum cryptography. The most effective solution against LWE is the BKZ algorithm and the complexity is dominated by block size. Alkim et al. (USENIX 2016) proposed an estimate of the block size which is required to solve LWE via the BKZ algorithm (2016 estimate). In this paper, we verify the fundamental assumption of the 2016 estimate which is applied to some proposed cryptosystems by executing some experiments using the BKZ algorithm. We also show our conjecture of why it is possible to solve LWE with smaller block sizes. Furthermore, we discuss the reason why the LWE solution is recovered earlier than expected by the 2016 estimate.

Keywords: Lattice-based cryptography · Learning with errors · BKZ algorithm · Unique SVP

1 Introduction

Much attention has been directed to lattice-based cryptography in building cryptosystems. In particular, cryptographic constructions based on the Learning with Errors (LWE) problem [14] are gathering considerable interest in the standardization process of post-quantum cryptography by the National Institute of Standards and Technology (NIST). LWE is expected to play an important role in cryptography as a hard problem for building a variety of cryptosystems.

Lattice-based cryptography is based on the hardness of lattice problems. A commonly effective strategy for solving LWE is called *primal attack*. The BKZ algorithm is the most practical strategy of all lattice basis reduction algorithms. The complexity of the BKZ algorithm is dominated by the block size β. Alkim et al. proposed an estimate of the required block size to solve LWE [3]. The estimate is referred to as the *2016 estimate*. The 2016 estimate is applied to some candidates of cryptosystems proposed in the standardization process of NIST post-quantum cryptography for establishing the cryptographic parameters.

Albrecht et al. showed an experimental analysis of the 2016 estimate [2]. They reported that it is possible to succeed in solving uSVP in a non-negligible

© Springer Nature Switzerland AG 2021
S. Tripathy et al. (Eds.): ICISS 2021, LNCS 13146, pp. 173–184, 2021.
https://doi.org/10.1007/978-3-030-92571-0_11

probability by smaller block sizes than estimated by the 2016 estimate. Moreover, they showed that the moment when the uSVP solution is recovered tends to be earlier than expected by the 2016 estimate.

Our Contributions. In this paper, we focus on the fundamental assumption applied to the 2016 estimate (We explain this in Sect. 4). Our first contribution is to verify the fundamental assumption in the 2016 estimate by computer experiments of solving various LWE instances via the BKZ algorithm. From our results, we can confirm that this assumption is generally reliable. It is important to check the reliability of this assumption since this assumption is a cardinal premise to recover the error vector.

In addition, there are secondary findings from the above verification. Our second contribution is to examine one of the reasons why smaller block sizes than estimated by the 2016 estimate can lead to the LWE solution. In this context, we also examine the reason why the error vector is recovered earlier than expected by the 2016 estimate. The required block sizes need to be estimated accurately since it has a significant effect on the complexity. Therefore, it is important to examine the reason why the block size can be reduced since it is directly related to security.

2   Preliminaries

We use row notations for vectors and write in lower-case bold, e.g. $\mathbf{x}$. We denote the concatenation of vector $\mathbf{x}$ and $\mathbf{y}$ by $(\mathbf{x} \mid \mathbf{y})$ and the Euclidean norm of a vector $\mathbf{x}$ by $||\mathbf{x}||$. Let $\langle \cdot, \cdot \rangle$ denote the inner product of two vectors with the same size. We write matrices in upper-case bold, e.g. $\mathbf{X}$.

The left-hand side and right-hand side of the equation (*) and inequality (*) are denoted as LHS(*) and RHS(*) respectively.

2.1   Learning with Errors Problem

The Learning with Errors problem is defined as follows.

Definition 1 (Learning with Errors (LWE)) [14]). *Let n, q be positive integer, χ be a probability distribution on $\mathbb{Z}$ and $\mathbf{s}$ be a secret vector in $\mathbb{Z}_q^n$. We denote by $L_{\mathbf{s},\chi}$ the probability distribution on $\mathbb{Z}_q^n \times \mathbb{Z}_q$ obtained by choosing $\mathbf{a} \in \mathbb{Z}_q^n$ uniformly at random, choosing $e \in \mathbb{Z}$ according to χ and considering it in $\mathbb{Z}_q$, and returning $(\mathbf{a}, b) = (\mathbf{a}, \langle \mathbf{a}, \mathbf{s} \rangle + e) \in \mathbb{Z}_q^n \times \mathbb{Z}_q$. Search-LWE is the problem of recovering $\mathbf{s}$ from $(\mathbf{a}, b) = (\mathbf{a}, \langle \mathbf{a}, \mathbf{s} \rangle + e) \in \mathbb{Z}_q^n \times \mathbb{Z}_q$ sampled according to $L_{\mathbf{s},\chi}$.*

Throughout this paper, we define χ as a discrete Gaussian distribution with standard deviation σ. Now, we consider m different LWE samples from $L_{\mathbf{s},\chi}$ as follows.

$$\begin{cases} (\mathbf{a}_1, b_1), \quad b_1 \equiv \langle \mathbf{a}_1, \mathbf{s} \rangle + e_1 \mod q \\ \quad \vdots \\ (\mathbf{a}_m, b_m), \quad b_m \equiv \langle \mathbf{a}_m, \mathbf{s} \rangle + e_m \mod q \end{cases} \tag{1}$$

Let $\mathbf{A}$ be $m \times n$ matrix where $\mathbf{a}_i$ is the i-th row vector and $\mathbf{b}$ be $(b_1, b_2, \ldots, b_m)$. Then, (1) can be rewritten as follows.

$$\mathbf{b} \equiv \mathbf{A}\mathbf{s} + \mathbf{e} \mod q, \tag{2}$$

where $\mathbf{e} = (e_1, e_2 \ldots, e_m)$ is called *error vector* and we denote LWE samples by $(\mathbf{A}, \mathbf{b})$.

2.2   Lattices

A lattice $\mathcal{L}$ is a set of all integer combinations of n linearly independent basis vectors $\mathbf{b}_1, \mathbf{b}_2, \ldots, \mathbf{b}_n \in \mathbb{R}^m$. We only consider full rank lattices which hold $n = m$. We write $\mathbf{B} = \{\mathbf{b}_1, \mathbf{b}_2, \ldots, \mathbf{b}_d\}$ for basis vector and $\mathbf{B}$ for the basis matrix. Throughout this paper, d denotes the dimension of the lattice. For a lattice basis $\mathbf{B} = \{\mathbf{b}_1, \mathbf{b}_2, \ldots, \mathbf{b}_d\} \in \mathbb{R}^d$, we denote its Gram-Schmidt orthogonal basis by $\mathbf{B}^* = \{\mathbf{b}_1^*, \mathbf{b}_2^*, \ldots, \mathbf{b}_d^*\} \in \mathbb{R}^d$. The volume of a lattice is invariant and defined as $\mathrm{Vol}(\mathcal{L}) = |\det(\mathbf{B})| = \prod_{i=1}^{d} ||\mathbf{b}_i^*||$. For $i \in \{1, 2, \ldots, d\}$, we define the orthogonal projection π_i of $\mathbf{v} = (v_1, v_2 \ldots, v_d)$ onto $\langle \mathbf{b}_1^*, \mathbf{b}_2^*, \ldots, \mathbf{b}_{i-1}^* \rangle_{\mathbb{R}}$ by

$$\pi_i(\mathbf{v}) = \sum_{j=i}^{d} \frac{\langle \mathbf{v}, \mathbf{b}_j^* \rangle}{||\mathbf{b}_j^*||^2} \mathbf{b}_j^* \in \mathbb{R}^{d-i+1}. \tag{3}$$

We can also define it by linear combinations of the projected basis as

$$\pi_i(\mathbf{v}) = \sum_{j=i}^{d} v_j \pi_i(\mathbf{b}_j). \tag{4}$$

Note that π_1 is the identity map. Let $\pi_i(\mathcal{L})$ be a $d - i + 1$ dimensional projected lattice with basis $\pi_i(\mathbf{b}_i), \pi_i(\mathbf{b}_{i+1}), \ldots, \pi_i(\mathbf{b}_d)$. Let $\mathcal{L}_{[k,\ell]}$ be a $\ell - k + 1$ dimensional lattice with basis $\pi_k(\mathbf{b}_k), \pi_k(\mathbf{b}_{k+1}), \ldots, \pi_k(\mathbf{b}_\ell)$ for some $1 \leq k \leq \ell \leq d$. $\mathcal{L}_{[k,\ell]}$ is called *projected sublattice*.

2.3   Lattice Problem and Lattices Basis Reduction

In this section, we summarise a lattice problem and lattice basis reduction.

Definition 2 (Shortest Vector Problem (SVP)). *Given a d dimensional lattice $\mathcal{L}$ with basis $\mathbf{b}_1, \mathbf{b}_2, \ldots, \mathbf{b}_d$, find a vector $\mathbf{v} \in \mathcal{L}$ such that $||\mathbf{v}|| = \lambda_1(\mathcal{L})$.*

Lattice basis reduction is an approach to find basis vectors that are shorter and closer to orthogonal basis vectors. The BKZ (Block-Korkin-Zolotarev) algorithm [16] is the most effective algorithm of all lattice basis reductions. This algorithm consists of solving SVP on block-wise projected sublattice and the LLL (Lenstra-Lenstra-Lovász) algorithm [9]. The bases after the BKZ algorithm are called β-BKZ-reduced and defined as follows.

Definition 3 (β-BKZ-reduced). *The lattice basis* $\mathbf{b}_1, \mathbf{b}_2, \ldots, \mathbf{b}_d$ *in a d dimensional lattice $\mathcal{L}$ is called β-BKZ-reduced if it satisfies following conditions.*

(1) $|\mu_{i,j}| \leq \frac{1}{2}$ $(i,j \in \{1,2,\ldots,d\}, j \leq i)$
(2) *For all* $i \in \{1,2,\ldots,d-\beta+1\}$, *it is satisfied that* $\|\mathbf{b}_i^*\| = \lambda_1(\mathcal{L}_{[i,\min(i+\beta-1,d)]})$.

The BKZ algorithm is shown in Algorithm 1.

> **Input**: The lattice basis $\mathbf{B}$ of d dimensions, block size $\beta \in \{2,3,\ldots,d\}$
> **Output**: β-BKZ-reduced basis $\mathbf{b}_1, \mathbf{b}_2, \ldots, \mathbf{b}_d$

```
1  LLL(b₁, b₂, ..., b_d);
2  repeat                                            // BKZ tour
3     for κ ← 1 to d − 1 do
4        ℓ ← min(κ + β − 1, d);
5        π_κ(v) ← SVP(L_[κ,ℓ]);
6        v ← BabaiLift(π_κ(v));                       // Babai's nearest plane[4]
7        Insert v into B at position κ;
8        LLL(b₁, ..., b_{κ−1}, v, b_κ, ..., b_{κ+β});
9     end
10 until The norms of basis vectors reach the expected length;
```

Algorithm 1: BKZ Algorithm

SVP oracle is the oracle machine that solves SVP and shall always output the shortest vector. In the BKZ algorithm, SVP oracle is called for the local projected lattice $\mathcal{L}_{[\kappa,\min(\kappa+\beta-1,d)]}$ respectively. When the shortest vector $\pi_\kappa(\mathbf{v})$ is found in $\mathcal{L}_{[\kappa,\min(\kappa+\beta-1,d)]}$, the BKZ algorithm inserts $\mathbf{v}$ into $\mathbf{B}$ at position κ. These procedures recur from $\kappa = 1$ to $d-1$. We refer to each κ as *index*. One set of this is called *BKZ tour* and it recurs in the BKZ algorithm. Note that the block size β shrinks to $d-\kappa+1$ when $\kappa \geq d-\beta+1$.

Reducing LWE to the Lattice Problem. We can reduce LWE to lattice problems. The *primal attack* is a common approach to solve LWE. In the primal attack, we reduce LWE to unique Shortest Vector Problem (uSVP) [10], a variant of SVP by Kannan's embedding [8]. In Kannan's embedding, we consider a following $(m+1) \times (m+1)$ matrix

$$\mathbf{B}' = \begin{pmatrix} \mathbf{B} & 0 \\ \mathbf{b} & t \end{pmatrix}, \tag{5}$$

where $\mathbf{B}$ consists of m dimensional lattice and $(\mathbf{b} \mid t)$ denotes a vector with embedding factor t. In this paper, we only use $t = 1$. We write the $d = m+1$ dimensional lattice for $\mathcal{L}'$ generated by $\mathbf{B}'$. For any lattice basis vector $\mathbf{v} \in \mathcal{L}'$,

$$\mathbf{e}' := (\mathbf{e} \mid 1) = (\mathbf{b} \mid 1) - (\mathbf{v} \mid 0) \tag{6}$$

is contained in $\mathcal{L}'$. Therefore, by solving uSVP on the lattice $\mathcal{L}'$, we can solve LWE.

3   Related Work

3.1   2016 Estimate [3]

The complexity of the BKZ algorithm is dominated by block size. An estimate of the required block sizes for solving uSVP via the BKZ algorithm is proposed by Alkim et al. (*2016 estimate*) [3].

Alkim et al. claim that the error vector $\mathbf{e}' = (\mathbf{e} \mid 1)$ can be recovered if and only if

$$\sqrt{\beta}\sigma \leq \delta_0^{2\beta-d} \operatorname{Vol}(\mathcal{L})^{1/d}, \tag{7}$$

where δ_0 is the so-called root Hermite factor. For a basis $\mathbf{B}$ of a d dimensional lattice, the root Hermite factor is defined as $\delta_0 := (||\mathbf{b}_1||/\operatorname{Vol}(\mathcal{L})^{1/d})^{1/d}$. From the definition of the volume of lattices, (7) is rewritten as

$$\sqrt{\beta}\sigma \leq \delta_0^{2\beta-d} q^{(m-n)/d}. \tag{8}$$

The idea of the 2016 estimate is that the BKZ algorithm would return the error vector $\mathbf{e}'$ when SVP oracle is called at the index $\kappa = d - \beta + 1$. RHS (7) represents the expected norm of the uSVP solution under the two assumptions such as Hermite Factor Regime (HFR) [6] and Geometric Series Assumption (GSA) [15].

On the other hand, LHS (7) represents the expected norm of the projection of the error vector. Alkim et al. imply that the norm of the projection $\pi_\kappa(\mathbf{e}')$ in the projected lattice $\pi_\kappa(\mathcal{L})$ can be expected by

$$||\pi_\kappa(\mathbf{e}')|| \approx \sqrt{\frac{d-\kappa+1}{d}}||\mathbf{e}'||. \tag{9}$$

From (9), projections in β dimensional projected sublattice have an expected norm $\sqrt{\beta/d}\,||\mathbf{e}'|| \approx \sqrt{\beta}\sigma$. In other words, LHS (7) represents the approximation of $\pi_\kappa(\mathbf{e}')$.

3.2   Experimental Analysis Against the 2016 Estimate

Albrecht et al. [2] showed an experimental analysis of the 2016 estimate. The results showed that it is possible to succeed in solving uSVP in a non-negligible probability by smaller block sizes than ones of the 2016 estimate. To explain the above results, Albrecht et al. showed the process of obtaining the error vector $\mathbf{e}'$ by the BKZ algorithm. If the vector inserted by the BKZ algorithm has the coefficients $e_\kappa, e_{\kappa+1}, \ldots, e_d$ of $\mathbf{e}'$, then we have obtained a part of the information of the error vector. They claimed that obtaining a part of the coefficients of $\mathbf{e}'$ has a significant effect on the success or failure of the BKZ algorithm. In this paper, we say "*the error vector is found*" when the coefficients of $\mathbf{e}'$ are determined.

Albrecht et al. also showed that the index where $\mathbf{e}'$ is recovered tends to be smaller than $\kappa = d - \beta + 1$. They attributed these results to the so-called *second intersection* between the projection of $\mathbf{e}'$ and the expected norm of the shortest vector in a projected sublattice [2, §4.3]. Specifically, for some small γ, let $\kappa = d - \gamma + 1$ be the index of the second intersection. They claimed that if the coefficients of $\mathbf{e}'$ is obtaied at the second intersection, the projection of the error vector $\pi_{d-\beta-\gamma+1}(\mathbf{e}')$ will be found in $\mathcal{L}_{[d-\beta-\gamma+1,d-\gamma+1]}$ in the subsequent tour. Therefore, $\mathbf{e}'$ is found earlier than $\kappa = d - \beta + 1$.

4   Proposed Method

The fundamental assumption of the 2016 estimate is that the error vector is recovered since the projection of the error vector $\pi_\kappa(\mathbf{e}')$ is shorter than any other basis generating the projected sublattice. In this section, we describe how to verify the assumption. To verify it, we define a basis $\mathbf{b}_\kappa^*$ which seems to be the shortest in the bases generating the projected sublattice. Then, we check the following inequality when the error vector is found.

$$||\pi_\kappa(\mathbf{e}')|| \leq ||\mathbf{b}_\kappa^*|| \tag{10}$$

In general, it is hard to measure $\mathbf{b}_\kappa^*$ accurately. Thus, we define RHS (10) applying HFR and GSA. Specifically, by GSA with $\alpha \approx \delta_0^{-2}$, we can derive $||\mathbf{b}_\kappa^*|| \approx \delta_0^{-2(\kappa-1)} \cdot ||\mathbf{b}_1^*||$. Then, applying HFR with $||\mathbf{b}_1|| = \delta_0^d \text{Vol}(\mathcal{L})^{1/d}$, $||\mathbf{b}_\kappa^*||$ can be defined as

$$||\mathbf{b}_\kappa^*|| \approx \delta_0^{d-2(\kappa-1)} \text{Vol}(\mathcal{L})^{1/d}. \tag{11}$$

We confirm that (10) holds or not when the error vector is found and discuss the reliability of the 2016 estimate.

Experiments. In experiments, we observe the following points. First, we identify the index where the BKZ algorithm finds the error vector. We denote this index as the *found index*. Then, we observe both sides of (10). To check the above points, we run the BKZ algorithm against various LWE instances. We use LWE instances $(\mathbf{A}, \mathbf{b})$ from Darmstadt LWE challenge [7]. These instances are labeled by (n, α), where n denotes the dimension of LWE and α denotes a noise rate. Table 1 shows LWE parameter sets we used. The number of LWE samples m can be selected ourselves. Both the matrix $\mathbf{A}$ and the secret vector $\mathbf{s}$ are sampled uniformly at random, while the error vector $\mathbf{e}$ is sampled from χ with standard deviation $\sigma = \alpha \cdot q$. For modulus q, the smallest prime number greater than n^2 is used. The procedure of our experiments is as follows.

1) Given (n, α) of LWE parameter sets, we obtain the minimal β and m by (7). We denote them as β_{2016} and m_{2016} respectively. Since block sizes affect execution time, we define the LWE parameter set required larger β_{2016} as a harder problem.
2) We use β_{2016} on every LWE parameter set at first. If the BKZ algorithm finds the error vector successfully, we reset the block sizes to $\beta = \beta_{2016} - 5$ and execute the BKZ algorithm again. Throughout our experiments, we fix m as m_{2016}.

3) We repeat the above step for each LWE parameter set until the execution time exceeds 10 times longer than ones of β_{2016}.

Table 1. LWE parameter sets we used.

n	55	45	60	40	50	65	45
α	0.005	0.010	0.005	0.015	0.010	0.005	0.015
σ	15.185	20.27	18.035	24.015	25.03	21.145	30.405
q	3037	2027	3607	1601	2503	4229	2027
β_{2016}	56	65	69	74	80	81	91

We run 10 experiments with different LWE instances for each LWE parameter set. The experiment environment is shown in Table 2.

Table 2. Experiment environment

CPU	Core i9-10980XE 3.0 GHz
Memory	32 GB
OS	Ubuntu 20.04LTS

In our experiments, we also observe following points:

1) Comparing the expected norm of LHS (10) and the observed norm of LHS (10). We can calculate the expected norm of LHS (10) by (9).
2) The tendency of the found index and the second intersection.

From those observations, we can analyze two points, why it is possible to solve LWE with smaller block sizes, and why the LWE solution is recovered earlier than expected by the 2016 estimate. We discuss these points in Sect. 5.2 and 5.3.

BKZ Algorithm. We use General Sieve Kernel (G6K) [1,11] for the lattice basis reduction algorithm. This library implements a variety of sieving algorithms and we use the Gauss sieve algorithm [12] since it performs better than the other sieving algorithm in terms of running time in practice [1]. In the Gauss sieve algorithm, a DoubleSieve algorithm is used in general; however, we use a TripleSieve [5] for the Gauss sieve algorithm when the dimension of the embedded lattice is more than 50 to reduce the memory consumption.

G6K offers `NaiveTour`, `PumpNJumpTour` and `SlidingWindowTour` as the BKZ algorithm. The last two algorithms dynamically change the block size during execution, so it is unclear in which dimension SVP is being solved. Considering the purpose of our experiments, we choose `NaiveTour` which fixes the block size.

5   Results and Discussion

Using items shown in Table 3, we show experimental results in Table 4. From the results, we found the three important analyses as follows.

Table 3. Explanation of Table 4.

Items	Description
n	Dimension of LWE
α	Noise rate
σ	Standard deviation
q	Modulus
β_{2016}	Expected block size by the 2016 estimate
m_{2016}	Expected LWE samples by the 2016 estimate
β	Actual block size we used
$d - \beta + 1$	Expected found index by the 2016 estimate
f_{ave}	Average of the found index
$\#f_{d-\beta+1}$	Number of results that the found index $\kappa = d - \beta + 1$
L_{expect}	Norm expected by (9) where κ is the found index
L_{ave}, R_{ave}	Average of the observed norm of LHS (10) and RHS (10) at the found index
Time	Average of the wall time [sec]

Table 4. Experimental results

n	α	σ	q	β_{2016}	m_{2016}	β	$d-\beta+1$	f_{ave}	$\#f_{d-\beta+1}$	L_{expect}	L_{ave}	R_{ave}	Time
55	0.005	15.185	3037	56	187	56	133	128.7	0	6.901	6.852	7.5689	4086.9
						51	138	131.9	1	6.824	6.564	6.849	4926.5
45	0.010	20.27	2027	65	168	65	105	102.0	0	7.383	7.323	7.631	3686.5
						60	110	92.4	0	7.367	7.343	8.051	4654.7
						55	115	106.7	0	7.383	7.231	7.647	8097.3
60	0.005	18.035	3607	69	200	69	133	128.6	0	7.262	7.224	7.602	9184.4
						64	138	133.7	0	7.218	7.022	7.413	22237.0
						59	143	135.8	0	7.155	6.982	7.289	44980.0
40	0.015	24.015	1601	74	151	74	79	75.6	1	7.726	7.564	7.800	1691.0
						69	84	79.8	1	7.670	7.520	7.901	2247.1
						64	89	83.9	0	7.627	7.506	7.956	5611.9
						59	94	89.3	0	7.650	7.480	7.932	14428.0
50	0.010	25.03	2503	80	195	80	117	110.0	0	7.847	7.810	8.027	44401.8
						75	122	116.9	0	7.802	7.721	7.914	68239.4
65	0.005	21.145	4229	81	223	81	144	141.4	1	7.596	7.491	7.675	37321.5
						76	149	146.8	1	7.563	7.424	7.854	33304.2
45	0.015	30.405	2027	91	175	91	86	82.9	0	8.190	8.170	8.289	56571.9
						86	91	82.5	0	8.203	8.143	8.280	84231.6

5.1 Reliability of the 2016 Estimate

We verify the correctness of the fundamental assumptions of the 2016 estimate by checking the inequality (10). From this verification, we discuss the reliability of the 2016 estimate. In all experiments with different LWE instances, we can see that LHS (10) is always smaller than RHS (10) at the found index. For example, Fig. 1a shows the value of both sides of (10) during the BKZ algorithm with $\beta < \beta_{2016}$. We can confirm that LHS (10) is smaller than RHS (10) at the found index. Note that we use logarithmic norm in all our graphs following in [2,13]. Figure 1b shows the case of the harder LWE parameter set with $\beta < \beta_{2016}$. Similarly, we can see that LHS (10) is smaller than RHS (10) at the found index. Note that LHS (10) is the observed value and RHS (10) is the expected value. Although we apply the heuristic assumption (HFR and GSA) to RHS (10), we confirm that the condition for finding a solution is that LHS (10) should be smaller than RHS (10) from our result. From the above results, we can say that (10) mostly holds, and the fundamental assumption of the 2016 estimate is mostly correct. Therefore, we believe that the 2016 estimate is generally reliable.

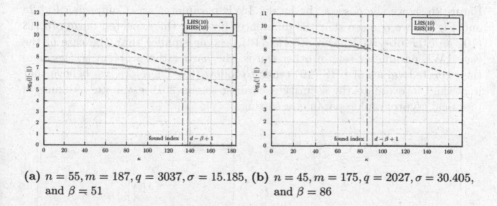

(a) $n = 55, m = 187, q = 3037, \sigma = 15.185$, and $\beta = 51$ (b) $n = 45, m = 175, q = 2027, \sigma = 30.405$, and $\beta = 86$

Fig. 1. Both sides of (10) with various LWE parameter sets

5.2 Observation in Smaller Block Sizes

Comparing column "L_{ave}" with column "L_{expect}", we can see that "L_{ave}" is slightly smaller than "L_{expect}" in most cases. For example, Fig. 2a shows the expected norm of LHS (10) and the observed norm of LHS (10) with $\beta < \beta_{2016}$. From this result, we found that LHS (7) is estimated to be larger than the actual value. Therefore, these results may be one of the reasons why the BKZ algorithm can recover the error vector even with smaller block sizes than β_{2016}. We speculate that these results are due to the distribution of the components of the error vector. The norm of the projection of the error vector $\|\pi_\kappa(e')\|$ can be modeled as random variables following a chi-squared distribution with appropriate degrees of freedom [13]. Specifically, for some error vector $\mathbf{e}' = (e_1, e_2 \ldots, e_d)$ with $e_i \sim \mathcal{N}(0, \sigma^2)$, we can model

$$||\mathbf{e}'||^2 = \sum_{i=1}^{d} e_i^2 \sim \sigma^2 \chi_d^2. \tag{12}$$

Assuming that we can consider the projection $||\pi_\kappa(\mathbf{e}')||$ in the same way as above, we can model it as

$$||\pi_\kappa(\mathbf{e}')||^2 = ||\sum_{i=\kappa}^{d} e_i \pi_\kappa(\mathbf{b}_i)||^2 \approx \sum_{i=\kappa}^{d} e_i^2 \sim \sigma^2 \chi_{d-\kappa+1}^2 \tag{13}$$

of variance $2(d - \kappa + 1)\sigma^4$. On the other hand, the 2016 estimate predicts the LHS (10) by (9). It considers only the mean of the distribution, and the actual value may be smaller than the expected value. We speculate that this is one of the reasons why the LHS (10) is smaller than expected.

Furthermore, we can see that as the LWE parameter sets become harder, the differences between the expected norm and the observed norm become smaller. Figure 2b shows the case of the harder LWE parameter set. Comparing Fig. 2a and Fig. 2b, we can see that the differences between the expected norm of LHS (10) and the observed norm of LHS (10) become smaller than the case of the easy LWE parameter set. In other words, the harder the problem is, the more the expected values of LHS (10) tends to follow (9). Therefore, we believe that it is valid to evaluate the security according to the 2016 estimate, assuming a practical cryptographic parameter setting.

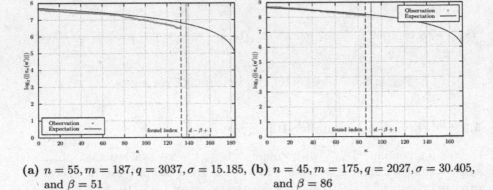

(a) $n = 55, m = 187, q = 3037, \sigma = 15.185$, and $\beta = 51$ (b) $n = 45, m = 175, q = 2027, \sigma = 30.405$, and $\beta = 86$

Fig. 2. Expected norms by (9) and observed norms of LHS (10)

5.3   Effect of the Second Intersection

As described in the column "#$f_{d-\beta+1}$" in Table 4, we found that there are few cases where the solutions are found as expected by Alkim et al. [3]. Besides, the column "f_{ave}" shows that the found index tends to be slightly earlier comparing $\kappa = d - \beta + 1$. From this result, we should not consider that the projection of the error vector is necessarily found in the projected sublattice $\mathcal{L}_{[d-\beta+1,d]}$.

In [2], the authors point out that the cause of the early recovery of the solution is due to the second intersection as described in Sect. 3.2. If their reasoning is correct, then a part or whole of the solution should have been found at the second intersection. However, despite the fact that (10) holds after the second intersection, there are no cases that a part or whole of the solution are found at the second intersection in our experiments. Specifically, the basis inserted at the second intersection did not have the same coefficients as the error vector. We conjecture that this is due to the gap between the expected norm of $\mathbf{b}_\kappa^*$ (RHS (10)) and the actual norm of $\mathbf{b}_\kappa^*$. It is pointed out that the actual norm $\mathbf{b}_\kappa^*$ violates GSA in last about β indices. If this violation is occurring in our experiment, the second intersection may not actually be occurring and no solution can be found at the index. Therefore, this result suggests that the basis inserted at the second intersection does not necessarily affect the phenomenon of the early recovery of the solution. There may be another reason for the phenomenon of the early recovery of the solution, which we leave to future work.

6   Conclusion

In this paper, we verify the fundamental assumption of the 2016 estimate. It is important to verify the assumption since the 2016 estimate is used to set the cryptographic parameters for cryptosystems proposed as post-quantum cryptography. The 2016 estimate assumes that the error vector is recovered since the projection of the error vector is shorter than any other basis generating the projected sublattice. We conclude that the 2016 estimate is generally reliable.

Moreover, we also found one of the reasons why the BKZ algorithm can recover the error vector even with smaller block sizes than estimated by the 2016 estimate. We concluded that the components of the error vector are sampled from a probability distribution, and there are some cases that the actual norm of the error vector becomes small due to the effect of the variance of the probability distribution. However, we also concluded that it is effective to evaluate the security according to the 2016 estimate, assuming a practical cryptographic parameter setting.

Finally, we revisited the effect of the second intersection between the projection of the error vector and the expected norm of the shortest vector in a projected sublattice. We conjecture that the basis inserted at the second intersection does not necessarily affect the early recovery of the solution.

References

1. Albrecht, M.R., Ducas, L., Herold, G., Kirshanova, E., Postlethwaite, E.W., Stevens, M.: The general sieve kernel and new records in lattice reduction. In: Ishai, Y., Rijmen, V. (eds.) EUROCRYPT 2019. LNCS, vol. 11477, pp. 717–746. Springer, Cham (2019). https://doi.org/10.1007/978-3-030-17656-3_25
2. Albrecht, M.R., Göpfert, F., Virdia, F., Wunderer, T.: Revisiting the expected cost of solving uSVP and applications to LWE. In: Takagi, T., Peyrin, T. (eds.) ASIACRYPT 2017. LNCS, vol. 10624, pp. 297–322. Springer, Cham (2017). https://doi.org/10.1007/978-3-319-70694-8_11
3. Alkim, E., Ducas, L., Pöppelmann, T., Schwabe, P.: Post-quantum key exchange - a new hope. In: Holz, T., Savage, S. (eds.) 25th USENIX Security Symposium, USENIX Security 16, Austin, TX, USA, August 10–12, 2016. pp. 327–343. USENIX Association (2016)
4. Babai, L.: On Lovász' lattice reduction and the nearest lattice point problem. In: Mehlhorn, K. (ed.) STACS 1985. LNCS, vol. 182, pp. 13–20. Springer, Heidelberg (1985). https://doi.org/10.1007/BFb0023990
5. Bai, S., Laarhoven, T., Stehlé, D.: Tuple lattice sieving. IACR Cryptol. ePrint Arch. 2016, 713 (2016)
6. Chen, Y.: Réduction de réseau et sécurité concrète du chiffrement complètement homomorphe (2013)
7. Florian, G.F., Yakkundimath, A.: Darmstadt LWE Challenge. https://www.latticechallenge.org/lwe_challenge/challenge.php
8. Kannan, R.: Minkowski's convex body theorem and integer programming. Math. Oper. Res. 12(3), 415–440 (1987)
9. Lenstra, A.K., Lenstra, H.W., Lovász, L.: Factoring polynomials with rational coefficients. Mathematische annalen 261(ARTICLE), 515–534 (1982)
10. Lyubashevsky, V., Micciancio, D.: On bounded distance decoding, unique shortest vectors, and the minimum distance problem. In: Halevi, S. (ed.) CRYPTO 2009. LNCS, vol. 5677, pp. 577–594. Springer, Heidelberg (2009). https://doi.org/10.1007/978-3-642-03356-8_34
11. Martin, R., Albrecht, L.D., Herold, G., Kirshanova, E., Postlethwaite, E.W., Stevens, M.: General Sieve Kernel and New Records in Lattice Reduction. https://github.com/fplll/g6k
12. Micciancio, D., Voulgaris, P.: Faster exponential time algorithms for the shortest vector problem. In: Charikar, M. (ed.) Proceedings of the Twenty-First Annual ACM-SIAM Symposium on Discrete Algorithms, SODA 2010, Austin, Texas, USA, January 17–19, 2010. pp. 1468–1480. SIAM (2010)
13. Postlethwaite, E.W., Virdia, F.: On the success probability of solving unique SVP via BKZ. In: Garay, J.A. (ed.) PKC 2021. LNCS, vol. 12710, pp. 68–98. Springer, Cham (2021). https://doi.org/10.1007/978-3-030-75245-3_4
14. Regev, O.: On lattices, learning with errors, random linear codes, and cryptography. J. ACM 56(6), 34:1–34:40 (2009)
15. Schnorr, C.P.: Lattice reduction by random sampling and birthday methods. In: Alt, H., Habib, M. (eds.) STACS 2003. LNCS, vol. 2607, pp. 145–156. Springer, Heidelberg (2003). https://doi.org/10.1007/3-540-36494-3_14
16. Schnorr, C., Euchner, M.: Lattice basis reduction: improved practical algorithms and solving subset sum problems. Math. Program. 66, 181–199 (1994)

WiP: Privacy Enabled Biometric Authentication Based on Proof of Decryption Techniques

Habeeb Syed, Imtiyazuddin Shaik[✉], Nitesh Emmadi, Harika Narumanchi, Meena Singh Dilip Thakur, and Rajan Mindigal Alasingara Bhattachar

Cybersecurity Foundations, TCS Research and Innovation Labs, Hyderabad, Chennai, Bangalore, India
{habeeb.syed,imtiyazuddin.shaik,nitesh.emmadi1,h.narumanchi, meena.s1,rajan.ma}@tcs.com

Abstract. Biometric authentication systems are widely used for authenticating users, especially in the areas like law enforcement, healthcare, airport security etc. Two major concerns arise in any biometric authentication system: (i) Privacy of user's biometrics, which do not change much over time (ii) Trust assumption between user and server. To address the former issue privacy enabled biometric authentication schemes are designed, wherein as part of the authentication, encrypted biometrics are sent to the server and server then computes the authentication result on encrypted biometrics. The latter issue is addressed by using trusted third party or trusted execution environment (TEE), which is not secure. To overcome this, we propose a novel method, where server can authenticate the user in a privacy preserving manner without the need for any trusted party or TEE. We propose 3 novel proof of decryption based techniques: (i) HMAC (Hash based MAC) of the authentication result on encrypted data (ii) VC (Verifiable Computing) based approach and (iii) Blinding techniques. Using these approaches we eliminate the need for trust assumptions between user and server in semi-honest setting i.e. they execute the protocol correctly but are trying to learn more about data (server) or tamper with the authentication (user). The proposed protocol is agnostic to any authentication method used by server, hence our contribution is two-fold. We analyze security, complexity and practicality of each of these approaches and compare with the state-of-the-art.

Keywords: Biometric authentication system · FHE · Privacy preserving computation · HMAC · Blinding · VC

1 Introduction

The current digital revolution is fuelled by rapid deployment of billions of connected smart devices such as sensors, actuators, controllers etc. Very often these devices are deployed across heterogeneous environments which include factory (Industrial IoT), critical infrastructures (nuclear plants), hospital (health care),

© Springer Nature Switzerland AG 2021
S. Tripathy et al. (Eds.): ICISS 2021, LNCS 13146, pp. 185–197, 2021.
https://doi.org/10.1007/978-3-030-92571-0_12

human body (body area network to remotely monitor the patients or senior citizens), etc. The security of these applications and IoT devices are realized through encryption, authentication and access control. There can be various levels of security required based on how critical these applications and devices are (sensitivity). For example higher level of security is required to manage critical infrastructure (with a human in loop)such as nuclear plants, IIOT setup, health care sector etc. Hence authentication of user[1] is critical before allowing access to such systems.

The existing conventional authentication based on password and OTP are susceptible to various attacks such as stealing/guessing passwords (dictionary attacks) and snooping (by device/sim swapping) respectively.

Hence to access data and control the applications and devices in critical infrastructure setup, secure multi-factor authentication mechanism based on user biometrics is proposed [4,7]. Note that user biometric information needs to be made available at the devices and applications, where user authentication needs to be verified. One of the issue/risk in these scenarios is that an adversary can steal the biometrics (which is very often hard to revoke) and there by can control the system. To address this, the server stores a transformed version of user's biometrics known as biometric template, which is a unique representation of original biometrics of the user [14]. This is matched by the server against users' information provided during authentication. However, exposing the users' biometric information to the server is risky and needs to be bypassed, as the server itself might get compromised due its weak security policies. Hence, this compromises the privacy of user's biometrics.

There are various ways in which privacy enabled biometric authentication protocols are realized based on fuzzy commitment schemes [17], cancellable biometrics [16], Fully Homomorphic Encryption (FHE) [14]. However biometric authentication based on fuzzy commitment schemes suffers from information leakages of both secret and biometric data [17]. Hence, biometric authentication schemes based on FHE techniques are gaining momentum [14,15] despite the considerable computation overheads [13]. This is due to the fact that FHE schemes are becoming more efficient and can be used for realizing privacy enabled computation for real world applications [19].

FHE based biometric authentication system is realized in two phases. (i) Registration (ii) Authentication. In the first phase, user biometrics are registered in an encrypted manner (using user's key). In the authentication phase, user biometrics which are captured in real time are encrypted and sent to the device/application, wherein a computation on the encrypted data (such as euclidean distance/cosine similarity of stored and received biometric) is performed. Since the result of the computation is in encrypted form, device/application cannot know the result of the authentication. To address this, in [14] outcome of the biometric computation is sent to a TEE (which is managed by a trusted third party) which has user's key, decrypts it and sends the result to the device/application.

However, there are two main drawbacks in this approach for large scale deployment of biometric based authentication system: (i) High CAPEX for TEE (ii) Security guarantees of TEE, which are prone to side channel attacks [20,21].

---

[1] We use user and client interchangeably throughout this paper.

To overcome this, we propose a novel, efficient and secure biometric authentication protocol based on FHE *without the need for any trusted third party or TEE* by using proof of decryption based approaches. Here in one scenario sever does blinding of the result using matrix product or determinant and sends it to the client. Client then decrypts the result of authentication/computation related to blinding and sends it to the server. Finally server can verify whether the resultant decrypted value is tampered by the user/client or not and accordingly it authenticates the user.

In other approach, server sends the encrypted authentication result to the client, where client decrypts the result and send it to the server along with the proof of integrity of the decryption operation (using verifiable computing). Then server verifies the proof of decryption and accordingly authenticates the user.

Our main contribution in this paper is as follows. We propose 3 novel techniques for proof of decryption: (i) Homomorphic HMAC (ii) VC and (iii) Blinding in encrypted setting. Our contributions are two-fold:

– Authentication protocol that is secure against malicious client while the server is honest-but-curious.
– Our approach is agnostic to any authentication method used by server

Note that our proposed scheme based on proof of decryption (using determinant blinding) is $9\times$ faster than [22].

In the next section we discuss related work in the field of biometric cryptosystems. Section 3 gives insight into the proposed schemes, followed by experimental results in Sect. 4. We conclude our findings in Sect. 5.

2   Related Work

[15] gives one of the most recent approaches of privacy preserving biometric authentication systems using post-quantum secure cryptographic primitives like fully homomorphic encryption (FHE). They benchmark three different methods of achieving this for facial recognition. They use three types of encoding for the features (i) Floating point (ii) Integer and (iii) Binary representation. Score matching for floating point and integer features is done by computing euclidean distance between two template in encrypted setting, whereas binary features are matched using hamming distance of two encrypted templates. Three post-quantum HE schemes used are CKKS [6], BFV [9] and NTRU [12] for Floating point, Integer and Binary respectively. However, the use of trusted third party, Authentication Server(AS), for decrypting the result of authentication makes it vulnerable to attacks.

In [14], a face based biometric authentication system is proposed, wherein the score matching between the encrypted templates is computed as an inner product of the query and stored templates. However, server then sends back the encrypted result to client for decryption, hence introducing the risk of malicious client tampering the result of authentication, which is plausible in the real world.

In [22], a lightweight variant of MAC scheme *Poly-MAC* is proposed. Here a simple blinding based on a linear polynomial of degree one is used by server to generate verifiable MAC using FHE on the encrypted authentication result. Note that the polynomial with degree one i.e. $ct_T = ct_d \times r_0 + r_1$ is used by the server for blinding the encrypted result. Here ct_d is the result of authentication (Hamming distance between two templates) and r_0, r_1 are random numbers. Our proposed proof of decryption based on matrix-vector product blinding generalizes this scheme (elements of matrix can be considered as coefficients of the polynomial) with higher level of security. Moreover, our scheme is at least $9\times$ faster than [22]. However feature vector from [22] (2048) is twice the size of our feature vector (1024).

Thus, we infer that known approaches either require a trusted third party, TEE or depend on weaker form of trust assumption between client and server.

To address these issues, We propose three novel approaches based on proof of decryption techniques: (*i*) HMAC (*ii*) VC based approach and (*iii*) Blinding. Also, our approaches are agnostic to any method of authentication used by server, as long as it is compatible with FHE.

In the next section we present our protocol using all the three techniques. Section 4 we provide experimental analysis of proposed techniques and we conclude the paper in Sect. 5.

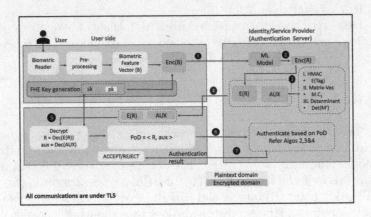

Fig. 1. HMAC/blinding based approach

3 Proposed Solution

We propose a privacy preserving biometric based authentication system using FHE based on three approaches and analyse their feasibility for real life deployment. To enable privacy of user biometrics, we present a two round authentication protocol (without the need for any TEE). Our system consists of two parties:

1. CLIENT: authenticates to a server by presenting his/her biometric credentials.
2. SERVER: verifies the authenticity of a CLIENT by validating the biometric credentials using a pre-determined metric.

We assume user registration is done securely by using any of the secure machine learning methods based on Secure Multiparty computation (SMPC) or Federated learning, etc. Further, we also assume that machine learning models or other score matching techniques required for biometric authentication are pretrained and available at the server for authentication. The technique we consider in this paper is adapted from [14]. Note that as part of the authentication, at the client end, the biometric device captures the user's biometrics and generates the required feature vector, encrypts it using client's FHE public key and sends it to the server (See the Algorithm 1 Score-match). Then server performs the biometric matching computation against the stored encrypted biometric data (such as template). The result of the matching is in encrypted form and server cannot decrypt the result. Hence it follows the proposed proof of decryption approaches to determine the result of authentication. Here as discussed, we assume client can be malicious and server is honest but curious. Now we discuss proposed proof of decryption schemes for biometric authentication.

Algorithm Score-match

1. **CLIENT** encrypts its biometric data D using a **FHE-ENC** scheme and submits **FHE-ENC** (D) to **SERVER**.
2. **SERVER** computes similarity score on **FHE-ENC** (D) and obtains output RES in the encrypted form as $C_1 = \text{FHE-ENC}(RES)$
   * This part of the algorithm is common for all algorithms presented below. Note that C_1 is the result of the biometric authentication in encrypted form.

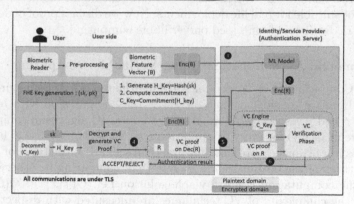

Fig. 2. VC based approach

3.1 Homomorphic HMAC

The detailed flow of the protocol is captured in Fig. 1. Here, the server, before sending the **FHE-ENC** (RES) to the client, generates a one-time nonce(time based nonce like TOTP) and gets a authentication code on the ciphertext using a secure cryptographic scheme like HMAC_{FHE} which produces an authentication tag, FHE-ENC (Tag). Note that in HMAC_{FHE}, all it's MAC computations are performed on encrypted data using FHE. The complete protocol is as follows:

Algorithm 1

1. Run the Algorithm Score-match.
2. The SERVER generates a time based nonce, N, and computes encrypted authentication tag as follows: FHE-ENC (Tag)= HMAC$_{FHE}$(FHE-ENC (RES), FHE-ENC (N)) i.e. SERVER computes HMAC on encrypted result to generate encrypted tag.The SERVER securely stores the nonce N corresponding to this session.
3. The SERVER now sends the encrypted result, FHE-ENC (RES) and FHE-ENC (Tag) to the CLIENT for decryption.
4. The CLIENT on recieving the two ciphertexts from the SERVER, decrypts them and sends resultant RES and Tag to the SERVER.
5. The SERVER now verifies if the result provided by the CLIENT is correct decryption of the ciphertext by checking if Tag==HMAC(RES, N)

This approach enables server to verify the authentication result without any access to the secret key of the user. However, Homomorphic computation of such HMAC schemes (like AES) can be quite expensive. To best our understanding, there exists only few implementations of AES in FHE. Gentry et al. [10] provided the first implementation of AES using HElib library. The performance was greatly improved in their subsequent attempts [11]. It takes 18 min to evaluate AES circuit with 180 blocks. Later Doroz et al. [8] came up with NTRU based implementation of AES. Their AES implementation for 1024 blocks takes 57 min to complete. In current scenario with the high computational time required to compute AES using FHE, HMAC based blinding scheme for biometric authentication is not suitable for real life deployments. Now we discuss proof of decryption for biometric authentication based on verifiable computing.

3.2   Biometric Authentication Using Verifiable Computing

Verifiable Computing (VC) is used for verifying the integrity of outsourced computation. Here we consider a function $f()$ is the computation with input and output as x and y respectively (i.e. $y = f(x)$). The VC algorithm computes the checker circuit C(x,y) for every computation f(x), such that C(x, y) = 0 only if y = f(x). It is important to note that, for practical scenarios, the time for verifying the correctness of the output should be less than computing it, otherwise, outsourcing the computation is not a viable solution i.e. $(O(f(x)) > O(C(x,y)))$. Note that the complexity of VC techniques are measured with respect to proof generation/verification time, proof size and also security of the vc schemes are analysed based on the need for trusted setup or not. There are several VC techniques based on SNARKS (such as Pinnochio, needs trusted setup) and STARKS (trusted setup not required). STARK [2] is a VC technique based on polynomial verification of the arithmetic circuit. The commitments used for the proof are based on hashing. The other emerging VC technique is Bulletproofs [5] which provides verifiable proofs for confidential transaction mainly in blockchain based applications. This provides range based proofs that can be extended for arithmetic circuits that perform the computation. There is a priori commitment phase involved which includes interaction between both the parties.

We now discuss the proof of decryption for authentication based on VC (Fig. 2, Algorithm-2). Here as part of the authentication, client commits to the server on its private key (hash based commitment scheme) and sends its encrypted biometric features along with the private key commitment to the server (see step 1, Algorithm-2). Then, server performs biometric matching computation and sends the result to the client. Now client runs the FHE decryption algorithm using VC paradigm with input as private key, commitment of private key and encrypted result. The VC engine (prover) at the client side produces two outputs (see step 5) (i) Result = FHE decryption of the biometric authentication (ii) Proof of computation (integrity of computation) of FHE decryption. Client sends these two outputs to the server. At the server side, VC engine (verifier) verifies the proof of FHE decryption (step 6). Inputs to the verification is result of biometric authentication (in plain form), commitment of client's private key and the proof of computation. If the verification result is true, it indicates that client has not tampered the result and then accordingly it authenticates the client based on the outcome of the result. Thus proof of decryption based on VC is envisaged.

As part of the experimentation, the proposed scheme is implemented using Pinocchio [18], which is based on libSNARK scheme [3]. The reason we have implemented it in Pinnochio is that it provides the scheme wherein we can verify a secret value (in our case the secret key) that is committed in a proof without revealing its value except its hash. In terms of performance Bulletproofs and STARK have better verification time when compared to Pinocchio. However the proof size in Pinocchio is very less i.e. 300 bytes.

Note that from the state of the art, we infer that, proof of decryption based on VC is computationally complex (which takes order of few seconds, also refer Table 2) and not suitable for biometric authentication in real deployment scenarios. Hence, we now propose a novel, efficient, secure and scalable proof of decryption based on blinding using matrix multiplication/determinant for proof of decryption, suitable for privacy enabled biometric authentication scheme based on FHE.

Algorithm 2

1. CLIENT sends $C_{Key} = Commitment(H_{Key})$ to the SERVER, where $H_{Key} = Hash(Key)$ before authentication begins, Key is the secret key of the CLIENT
2. Run the Algorithm Score-match
3. The SERVER sends FHE-ENC(RES) and C_{Key} given previously by the CLIENT.
4. CLIENT decommits C_{Key} to obtain H_{Key} and corresponding Key stored in the database.
5. CLIENT computes the decryption of FHE-ENC(RES) using Key and generates proof of decryption PROOF using VC.
6. CLIENT sends RES to the SERVER along with the corresponding PROOF.
7. Return TRUE if SERVER side verification passes, indicating RES is indeed decryption of FHE-ENC(RES)
8. Return FALSE if the verification fails, denoting that the key was either modified or RES is not decryption of FHE-ENC(RES).

The corresponding constraints for the program are: $C = C_{FHEDecrypt}\{ctxt, ptxt, Key\}U\ C_H = \{X = H_{Key}, Y = sk\}$, where sk is secret key obtained after de-commit; C_H checks if $Hash(sk) = H_{Key}$.

3.3 Blinding Techniques

In this section, we propose two blinding techniques to achieve proof of decryption based on (i) Matrix-Vector multiplication. (ii) Determinant.

I. Matrix-Vector Multiplication: We now present a novel proof of decryption scheme based on matrix-vector multiplication (see Fig. 1). First, we describe the scheme (see Algorithm 3) and then present its security and efficiency aspects. Here the server partitions the encrypted output of biometric authentication algorithm into a vector C_1 of d components (see step 2). This vector is then blinded by multiplying it with a randomly generated $d \times d$ matrix M to obtain another encrypted vector C_2 (see steps 3 and 4). Server sends C_1, C_2 to client for decryption. Then client decrypts C_1 and C_2 and send them back to the server. Finally, server validates the result as described in steps 8 and 9.

Algorithm 3

1. Run the Algorithm Score-match
2. SERVER partitions C_1 into $(C_1^1, \ldots, C_1^d)$ such that $C_1^1 + \cdots + C_1^d = C_1$.
3. SERVER randomly generates a matrix $M_{d \times d}$ with d^2 elements $a_{i,j} \in f_q$
4. SERVER computes $(C_2^1, \ldots, C_2^d) = (C_1^1, \cdots, C_1^d) \cdot M$.
5. SERVER sends C_1 and $(C_2^1, \ldots, C_2^d)$ to client.
6. CLIENT computes decryptions $P_1 = \text{FHE-DEC}(C_1)$, and also $Q^1 = \text{FHE-DEC}(C_2^1), \ldots, Q^d = \text{FHE-DEC}(C_2^d)$
7. CLIENT sends P_1 and $(Q^1, \ldots, Q^d)$ to SERVER.
8. SERVER splits P_1 into $(T^1, \ldots, T^d)$, computes $(Z^1, \ldots, Z^d) = (T^1, \ldots, T^d) \cdot M$, where M is $d \times d$ matrix.
9. SERVER verifies $(Q^1, \ldots, Q^d) \overset{?}{=} (Z^1, \cdots, Z^d)$ and if correct then returns TRUE, else returns FALSE.

Security of the Protocol: First suppose that $\#F = \mathcal{O}(2^\lambda)$ for some $\lambda > 0$. In order to cheat, an attacker (malicious CLIENT) needs to construct P_1' and $T^{1'}, \ldots, T^{d'}$ such that

$$(Q^{1'}, \ldots, Q^{d'}) = (T^{1'}, \ldots, T^{d'}) \cdot M \quad \text{and} \quad T^{1'} + \cdots + T^{d'} = P_1' \qquad (1)$$

In practical scenario such P_1', $(Q^{1'}, \ldots, Q^{d'})$ corresponds to a outcome of authentication protocol that is more acceptable to the client than the original outcome P_1. Remember that the CLIENT knows only P_1, $(Q^1, \ldots, Q^d)$ and has no knowledge of the matrix M except that it is a random $d \times d$ matrix with elements from F. The best adversary can do is fix P_1' (as per his advantage), then choose $(T^{1'}, \ldots, T^{d'})$ and a matrix M' randomly defined over F satisfying (1). Since the elements of the matrix M' are chosen uniformly from F the total number of possible choices for M' are $\mathcal{O}(2^\lambda)^{d^2} = \mathcal{O}(2^{\lambda d^2})$. Thus the probability that an attacker can succeed is

$$\frac{1}{2^{\lambda d^2}} \tag{2}$$

which is negligible for suitably chosen values of λ and d.

II. Determinant Based: In this section we present another novel method of proof of decryption for biometric authentication. Here, we use matrix determinant to create a commitment on the result computed by server (see Fig. 1). This ensures that a malicious client cannot alter the decrypted results to his advantage (see Algorithm 4). Here server generates a random dXd matrix M and replaces randomly one of its element with encrypted biometric result ($C_1 = FHE - ENC(RES)$) (see steps 2 and 3) to get $\widehat{M}$. Then it computes the determinant of the matrix $\widehat{M}$ (step 4) and sends C_1 and $\widehat{M}$ to the client for decryption. Client, then decrypts them and send it back to the server. Finally server validates the proof of decryption of biometric result using step 8.

Algorithm 4

---

1. Run the Algorithm Score-match
2. SERVER generates a random $d \times d$ matrix M with its elements $a_{i,j}$ from F.
3. SERVER picks one element $A_{l,t}$ randomly and replaces it with C_1 to get $\widehat{M}$
4. SERVER computes DET $= \det(\widehat{M})$
5. SERVER sends C_1 and DET to client.
6. CLIENT computes decryptions $P_1 = $ FHE-DEC(C_1), and $\delta = $ FHE-DEC(DET).
7. CLIENT sends P_1 and δ to SERVER.
8. SERVER verifies $\delta \overset{?}{=} \det(\widehat{M})$ with $a_{l,t} = P_1$ and if correct then returns TRUE, else returns FALSE.

Note if the FHE-ENC, FHE-DEC functions are error free then the server will be able to obtain correct output in Step 8.

Security: First suppose that $\#F = \mathcal{O}(2^\lambda)$ for some $\lambda > 0$. In order to cheat server, an attacker (malicious CLIENT) needs to construct P_1', δ' such that

$$\det(M) = \delta' \quad \text{where} \quad A_{l,t} = P_1'. \quad \text{(Step 8, Algo 3)} \tag{3}$$

Remember that the CLIENT knows only P_1, δ and has no information about the elements of M, except that they are from F, and that one of the element is P_1. To succeed, attacker needs to guess

1. $d^2 - 1$ elements of M
2. The exact position, i.e., the indices (l,t) of P_1 in M

Since the elements of the matrix M are chosen uniformly from F, total number of possible choices for M' are $\mathcal{O}(2^\lambda)^{d^2-1} = \mathcal{O}(2^{\lambda(d^2-1)})$. Thus the probability that an attacker can guess the $d^2 - 1$ elements correctly is

$$\frac{1}{2^{\lambda(d^2-1)}} \tag{4}$$

which is negligible for suitably chosen values of λ and d. Further, for the Item 2, the probability that the attacker can successfully guess the coordinate (l, t) is $1/d^2$. Thus, the probability that an attacker can guess correctly: (i) $d^2 - 1$ elements of M and (ii) the coordinates (l, t) of P_1 in M, is:

$$\frac{1}{d^2 \cdot 2^{\lambda(d^2-1)}} \tag{5}$$

4   Experiments and Results

In this section we discuss the experimental analysis of proposed techniques based on blinding (matrix multiplication/determinant) and VC technique. We use biometric system of [14] for the experiments. It is a face based biometric authentication system. In [14], a score matching algorithm is used which computes inner product of two templates to get the score for a user in encrypted domain. The client machine decrypts the scores using user's secret key and is authenticated if score $\geq$ threshold. The templates are replicated six times and encrypted using packing technique. Hence we get six scores inside ciphertext at server side after inner product is computed. We evaluate experiments for 3 security levels of ciphertext: $80, 128, 192$ bits of security. We use HEAAN library for FHE implementations [6]. To enable $80(128)$ bit security level, FHE parameters $logN$ and $logQ$ need to be configured to $12(12)$ and $192(111)$ respectively. Since $logQ$ is higher for 80 bit security level, computation time and memory increases compared to time and memory for 128 bits security.

Table 1 gives performance results for Matrix-vector multiplication (A-columns) and Determinant method (B-columns). As the dimension of matrix M increases, the computation time increases linearly. However memory usage doesn't vary much. Vector of dimension 6 in [14] is converted to dimension d using rotate and add. For $d = 6$ the success probability is very low that gives high security for matrix vector method. However for Determinant method, $d = 2$ is sufficient.

Note that on average, performance of privacy enabled biometric authentication scheme based proof of decryption using determinant approach is better (w.r.t time/memory)than that of matrix multiplication method.

Table 1. End-to-end: matrix-vector method (A) & determinant method (B) comm. cost is the number of bytes of ciphertext shared between client and server

d-value	FHE security-level (bits)												Security (Success prob)		
	80				128				192						
	Time (ms)		Memory (MB)		Time (ms)		Memory (MB)		Time (ms)		Memory (MB)		$\lambda=3$	$\lambda=5$	$\lambda=3$
	A	B	A	B	A	B	A	B	A	B	A	B	A	A	B
2	112	114	35.01	34.7	82	77	27.3	27.3	193	191	52.5	51.4	2^{-12}	2^{-20}	2^{-2048}
3	116	118	35.03	34.9	85	79	27.2	27.2	198	195	52.7	52.4	2^{-27}	2^{-45}	-
6	135	128	35.02	35.4	98	92	27.4	27.5	274	223	66.3	53	2^{-108}	2^{-180}	-
Comm. Cost	614.4 KB				344.1 KB				1376.1 KB						

We implement VC based proof of decryption using Pinocchio (which uses BN128 curve for proof generation/verification with 127 bit security and 300 bytes proof size [1]). Note that FHE decryption is implemented using VC. Client commits the hash of the secret key. We use, SHA 256 hash value of the key and store it in level db database. The Table 2 describes the performance of VC based approach for proof of decryption. Note that tabulated time includes both proof generation/verification time. We observe that in terms of memory footprint VC based method is the most efficient, however taking considerably more time than other two methods. One way to speed up the VC based approach is to use other VC techniques such as STARK, Bulletproofs etc. and they found to be more efficient w.r.t. execution time.

Thus, based on theoretical and experimental analysis, we infer that privacy enabled biometric authentication based on proof of decryption using determinant approach is better than that of HMAC, matrix multiplication and VC based approaches and hence suitable for real time deployments.

Table 2. End-to-end: VC based comm. cost is the number of bytes of ciphertext shared between client and server

	FHE security-level					
	80		128		192	
	Time (s)	Memory (MB)	Time (s)	Memory (MB)	Time (s)	Memory (MB)
	740.9	24.7	720.5	17.4	902.3	50.8
Comm. cost	205.3 KB		115.2		459.3	

5   Conclusion and Future Work

Widely used biometric authentication systems in critical applications like cyber physical systems have always been relying on trust assumption in the form of trusted party or TEE. Our proposed methods eliminate the need for any trust assumptions and work in Semi-honest setting, and is agnostic to any authentication metric used by server. We experimentally observe that matrix based blinding methods are faster even for higher security levels where as VC based method

has the least memory footprint. As part of future work, we plan to implement
HMAC based scheme test other VC techniques that are available which can use
multi-core parallellization and make the system more efficient. We also plan to
test our methods for real time deployments in applications like cyber-physical
systems for biometric authentication.

References

1. Pepper (2014). https://github.com/pepper-project/pepper
2. Ben-Sasson, E., Bentov, I., Horesh, Y., Riabzev, M.: Scalable, transparent, and post-quantum secure computational integrity. IACR Cryptol. ePrint Arch. **2018**, 46 (2018)
3. Ben-Sasson, E., Chiesa, A., Tromer, E., Virza, M.: Succinct non-interactive zero knowledge for a von neumann architecture. In: Proceedings of the 23rd USENIX Conference on Security Symposium, SEC 2014, pp. 781–796. USENIX Association, USA (2014)
4. Bhattasali, T., Saeed, K., Chaki, N., Chaki, R.: A survey of security and privacy issues for biometrics based remote authentication in cloud. In: Saeed, K., Snášel, V. (eds.) CISIM 2014. LNCS, vol. 8838, pp. 112–121. Springer, Heidelberg (2014). https://doi.org/10.1007/978-3-662-45237-0_12
5. Bünz, B., Bootle, J., Boneh, D., Poelstra, A., Wuille, P., Maxwell, G.: Bulletproofs: short proofs for confidential transactions and more. In: 2018 IEEE Symposium on Security and Privacy (SP), pp. 315–334 (2018)
6. Cheon, J.H., Kim, A., Kim, M., Song, Y.: Homomorphic encryption for arithmetic of approximate numbers. In: Takagi, T., Peyrin, T. (eds.) ASIACRYPT 2017. LNCS, vol. 10624, pp. 409–437. Springer, Cham (2017). https://doi.org/10.1007/978-3-319-70694-8_15
7. Das, A.K., Wazid, M., Kumar, N., Vasilakos, A.V., Rodrigues, J.J.P.C.: Biometrics-based privacy-preserving user authentication scheme for cloud-based industrial internet of things deployment. IEEE Internet of Things J. **5**(6), 4900–4913 (2018)
8. Doröz, Y., Shahverdi, A., Eisenbarth, T., Sunar, B.: Toward practical homomorphic evaluation of block ciphers using prince. In: Böhme, R., Brenner, M., Moore, T., Smith, M. (eds.) FC 2014. LNCS, vol. 8438, pp. 208–220. Springer, Heidelberg (2014). https://doi.org/10.1007/978-3-662-44774-1_17
9. Fan, J., Vercauteren, F.: Somewhat practical fully homomorphic encryption. IACR Cryptol. ePrint Arch. **2012**, 144 (2012)
10. Gentry, C., Halevi, S., Smart, N.P.: Homomorphic evaluation of the AES circuit. In: Safavi-Naini, R., Canetti, R. (eds.) CRYPTO 2012. LNCS, vol. 7417, pp. 850–867. Springer, Heidelberg (2012). https://doi.org/10.1007/978-3-642-32009-5_49
11. Gentry, C., Halevi, S., Smart, N.P.: Homomorphic evaluation of the AES circuit. In: IACR (2015)
12. Hoffstein, J., Pipher, J., Silverman, J.H.: NTRU: a ring-based public key cryptosystem. In: Buhler, J.P. (ed.) ANTS 1998. LNCS, vol. 1423, pp. 267–288. Springer, Heidelberg (1998). https://doi.org/10.1007/BFb0054868
13. Shaik, I., Kumar Singh, A., Narumanchi, H., Emmadi, N., Bhattachar, R.M.A.: A recommender system for efficient implementation of privacy preserving machine learning primitives based on FHE. In: Dolev, S., Kolesnikov, V., Lodha, S., Weiss, G. (eds.) CSCML 2020. LNCS, vol. 12161, pp. 193–218. Springer, Cham (2020). https://doi.org/10.1007/978-3-030-49785-9_13

14. Jindal, A.K., Shaik, I., Vasudha, V., Chalamala, S.R., Ma, R., Lodha, S.: Secure and privacy preserving method for biometric template protection using fully homomorphic encryption. In: 2020 IEEE 19th International Conference on Trust, Security and Privacy in Computing and Communications (TrustCom), pp. 1127–1134 (2020)

15. Kolberg, J., Drozdowski, P., Gomez-Barrero, M., Rathgeb, C. Busch, C.: Efficiency analysis of post-quantum-secure face template protection schemes based on homomorphic encryption. In: 2020 International Conference of the Biometrics Special Interest Group (BIOSIG), pp. 1–4 (2020)

16. Kumar, N., et al.: Cancelable biometrics: a comprehensive survey. Artif. Intell. **53**, 3403–3446 (2019)

17. Nguyen, T.A.T., Dang, T.K., Nguyen, D.T.: A new biometric template protection using random orthonormal projection and fuzzy commitment. In: Lee, S., Ismail, R., Choo, H. (eds.) IMCOM 2019. AISC, vol. 935, pp. 723–733. Springer, Cham (2019). https://doi.org/10.1007/978-3-030-19063-7_58

18. Parno, B., Howell, J., Gentry, C., Raykova, M.: Pinocchio: nearly practical verifiable computation. In: 2013 IEEE Symposium on Security and Privacy, pp. 238–252 (2013)

19. Bost, R., Popa, R.A., Tu, S., Goldwasser, S.: Machine learning classification over encrypted data. In: 2015 Network and Distributed System Security Symposium (NDSS), pp. 1–14 (2015)

20. Riscure. Security pitfalls in tee (2020). https://www.riscure.com/publication/security-pitfalls-in-tee-development

21. Eloi Sanfelix. Tee exploitation-exploiting trusted apps on samsung's tee (2019). https://labs.bluefrostsecurity.de/files/tee.pdf

22. Song, X., Chen, Z., Sun, D.: Iris ciphertext authentication system based on fully homomorphic encryption. J. Inf. Process. Syst. **16**(3), 599–611 (2020)

WiP: QoS Based Recommendation System for Efficient Private Inference of CNN Using FHE

Imtiyazuddin Shaik[(✉)], Raj Chaudhari, M. A. Rajan, J. Gubbi,
P. Balamuralidhar, and S. Lodha

Cyber-Security Systems, Embedded Devices and Intelligent Systems,
TCS Research, Hyderabad, Bangalore, Pune, India
imtiyazuddin.shaik@tcs.com

Abstract. Convolutional Neural networks have been widely adopted in computer vision because of their robust performance in a variety of applications. Many of the image detection and classification algorithms are being offered as a service by the Cloud service providers. In its current manifestation, the service provider has access to the rich data that is sent as a query thereby compromising the privacy of the user. Encryption can be used to ensure security during transmission. However, it cannot ensure data privacy. In order to protect the privacy and ensure security of the user data, there is a need to develop new approaches that can perform computer vision tasks on encrypted data. In this paper, Fully Homomorphic Encryption (FHE) is used to ensure security and privacy of the data. The proposed method builds the necessary algorithms to allow the server to make inferences on the encrypted input and give encrypted result back to the user. Deep neural network for FHE encrypted data is computationally very heavy. In order to address this problem, variable length packing on the pruned deep learning model is employed. An algorithm to automatically recommend appropriate parameters for pruning and variable length packing is proposed. Further, user's preference for Quality of Service (QoS) is taken into account in the proposed framework. CIFAR-10 image dataset is used to evaluate the method in terms of performance and accuracy for a ten class classification. Our experimental analysis show upto 60% improvement in terms of performance while using our optimizations.

Keywords: Deep neural network · Privacy preserving inference · Approximation of activation function

1 Introduction

Machine learning powered by convolutional neural network (CNN) is becoming ubiquitous to solve challenging computer vision problems [10]. Once the ML model is trained, the raw test image is fed as input at the inference stage. More often than not, in the real world scenarios, the owner of the data is different

© Springer Nature Switzerland AG 2021
S. Tripathy et al. (Eds.): ICISS 2021, LNCS 13146, pp. 198–211, 2021.
https://doi.org/10.1007/978-3-030-92571-0_13

from the creator of the deep learning model. This is true both at training and the inference stages of machine learning model irrespective of the deployment scenarios (Cloud or Edge). Hence, there is a need to build new algorithms that are based on principles of 'secure and private' by design which are compliant with data privacy regulations like GDPR. One of the prominent tools to build secure and private inference applications is by using Fully Homomorphic Encryption (FHE) [9]. FHE schemes allow outsourcing computation on encrypted data without the need (for a secret key used) to decrypt it, during the computation. This allows the users to send their encrypted data for performing inference at server or a third-party, who can then perform inference on the encrypted data and send back the encrypted result to the user.

Performing private inference of CNN on encrypted data is computationally expensive. In this paper, a divide and conquer strategy is used for achieving private inference using FHE. The pyramidal architecture of CNN can be utilized to reduce the computation. The features at the end of convolution layers are calculated on the raw image data followed by FHE encryption. The encrypted feature vector is sent to the server (Cloud or Edge) for inference, which has a model that is already trained on plain or FHE encrypted data. The model on the server essentially comprises of only the fully connected layers and the decision layer, that has to be rebuilt for performing computation of encrypted data, reducing the load substantially. The inference made by the server is sent back to the user who can decrypt the result. This scheme ensures that the original raw image data is hidden from the server achieving privacy and security during transmission as only the user has the key for decryption. We refer to this as split architecture for inference as indicated in Fig. 1.

Note that the complexity of the computation overhead of fully connected (FC) layers depends on the number of layers, number of neurons in each layer and type of activation functions used. Hence, in order to achieve an efficient server-side implementation of the FC: (i) there is a need to reduce the network topology complexity; and (ii) a good approximation for the activation function to replicate the results of a normal model. Pruning the network is shown to be effective in reducing network topology complexity without compromising on accuracy [25]. As part of this work, we analyse effect of different pruning schemes on the performance of encrypted CNN for private inference. Moreover, efficient packing technique of FHE (which helps in reducing memory and communication cost) is used to optimize private inference for fully connected CNN. However, we observed that the advantage of the existing packing technique is minimal for pruned network, as it introduces irregularity in the network topology. Hence, we propose a variable length packing scheme to optimize private inference for pruned CNN network.

Thus, from these discussions, we infer that an efficient design (with respect to performance, accuracy, etc.) to implement private inference for a given CNN model depends on the efficiency of pruning algorithm, packing technique, approximation functions for activation function, split architecture and FHE scheme used. A large set of solutions are possible to realize private inference based on different combinations and it becomes a hard decision problem to select the right combination for the optimal implementation of private inference. To address this issue, we propose a recommendation system (RS), which takes user requirements (such as latency, communication cost, accuracy, etc.) as input and analyse all possible solutions and outputs the best solution to realize private inference for a given CNN model. We design this RS using multi criterion decision analysis method.

2   Related Work

Many advancements have been made in the field of private inference. Applying Neural Networks to encrypted data with high throughput was first demonstrated in Cryptonets [8]. They show predictions on MNIST data and explain how each layer in a fully-connected block can be computed on encrypted data efficiently, hence, achieving a throughput of 58,982 predictions per hour. This work was followed by many similar approaches in private inference, using different approximations and applying new optimization methods [1,11,15,17,18,22]. However, these protocols require communication for each layer of the CNN. Constant communication was achieved by Riazi *et al.* in XONN [20]. They could perform up to 21 layers of FC using Oblivious Transfer (OT). GPU support for private inference was first presented in [3].

Inference using an end-to-end neural network (CNN+FC) is explored using FHE without any need for communication in [14,16]. Similarly, training a machine learning model on encrypted data also got traction and many works have emerged in recent past [12,19,21,26,27]. However, these methods in literature have focused on optimizing encryption implementations and corresponding libraries. We focus on building a divide and rule split CNN architecture that can be realized in any existing CNN based schemes. The use of pruning and packing to reduce network complexity and its effects on encrypted computation has not been explored to the best of our knowledge. Further, a recommendation system is proposed for private inference that looks at optimization from both perspectives.

In the next section, we introduce the proposed scheme along with various optimizations like pruning and variable length packing. In Sect. 4, we present the experimental analysis of our approach before concluding in Sect. 5.

3   Proposed Method

In the traditional approach, the pre-processed raw image is sent to the server where the feature extraction and the classification is performed. The proposed approach includes three stages where the pre-processed data is sent to a local feature extractor. The extracted features are encrypted and sent to the server for classification where the inference is made using the encrypted data resulting in an encrypted decision. The encrypted decision is sent back to the user or the client where it is decrypted using the original key ensuring privacy to the user

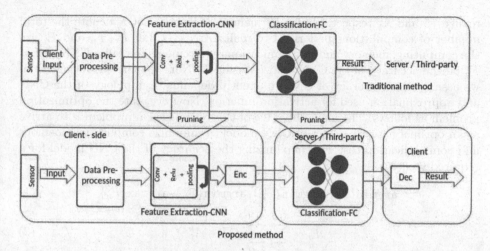

Fig. 1. Architecture of the proposed method

data. The proposed inference approach is summarized in Fig. 1. It is clear from the proposed approach in Fig. 1 that the classification happens at the third party server and is performed on encrypted data. Traditional CNN blocks and fully connected blocks in standard libraries cannot be used on this data. The classification block contains fully connected layer, activation and decision function. The fully connected layer and the decision function use simple mathematical operations and can be implemented for FHE data. However, an approximation function that can yield good classification result on FHE data has to be chosen, which is presented in Sect. 4. In this section, optimization formulation for pruning is provided followed by the details on pruning and efficient packing. Based on this, a recommendation system is proposed that helps in analyzing the effect of pruning on encrypted CNN with FHE features like packing for optimal performance.

3.1 Optimization Formulation for Pruning CNN

Let τ, μ and γ be the computation time, memory and communication cost required to realize private inference of a CNN with accuracy η and security λ respectively. We assume that CNN D consists of m layers with n_i is the number of neurons in a layer i. Let there are p number of FC layers (layers from $m - p + 1$ to m). Let e_{ij}^{kl} denote that there is an edge from k^{th} neuron of layer i to l^{th} neuron of layer j, which means output of kth neuron goes to l^{th} neuron. Let d_i^{k+} and d_i^{k-} denotes the number of incoming and outgoing edges related to k^{th} neuron of layer i. Let w_{ij}^{kl} be the weight associated with the edge e_{ij}^{kl}. Let A_i^k is the activation function for the kth neuron of layer i. let f_i^k is the computation performed at k^{th} neuron of layer i. Let $f_i^{k\tau}$, $f_i^{k\mu}$ and $f_i^{k\gamma}$, $A_i^{k\tau}$, $A_i^{k\mu}$ and $A_i^{k\gamma}$ are the computing, memory and communication requirements to realize f_i^k and A_i^k respectively for k^{th} neuron of layer i. Let F denote the total number of computations performed to realize CNN D. Let F_τ, F_μ and F_γ are the computing, memory and communication requirements to realize CNN D. Let F_η be the accuracy of the CNN realized using F. Note that in this formulation, we assume that accuracy of CNN inherently depends on topology of the CNN and approximation used for activation function. Now, we state the optimization problem as follows. The main objective of this optimization problem is to arrive at an optimal network design of CNN model to minimize computation/memory and communication cost with maximizing the accuracy of the CNN model for a required security.

$$\mathrm{argmin}\{F_\tau\}, \mathrm{argmin}\{F_\mu\}, \mathrm{argmin}\{F_\gamma\}, \mathrm{argmax}\{F_\eta\} \tag{1}$$

$$F_\tau = \sum_{i=1}^{m} \sum_{k=1}^{n_i} (f_i^{k\tau} + A_i^{k\tau}) \tag{2}$$

$$F_\mu = \sum_{i=1}^{m} \sum_{k=1}^{n_i} (f_i^{k\mu} + A_i^{k\mu}) \tag{3}$$

$$F_\gamma = \sum_{i=1}^{m} \sum_{k=1}^{n_i} (f_i^{k\gamma} + A_i^{\gamma}) \tag{4}$$

subjected to

$$F_\tau \leq \tau; F_\mu \leq \mu; F_\gamma \leq \gamma; F_\eta \geq \eta \tag{5}$$

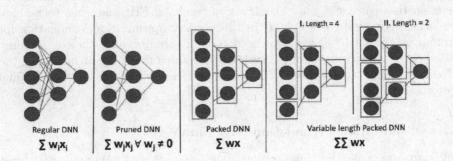

Fig. 2. Private inference evaluation strategies

3.2 Pruning

Pruning technique is used to reduce the weights (edges) in the neural network that do not contribute in the classification. For a given set of edges e_{ij}^{kl}, some edges might have weights that are very small in magnitude and hence do not contribute or significantly change the output of a neuron for any given input. Hence, we can ignore such edges to reduce the computation. Pruning technique is applied after completion of training of a neural network model to remove such edges from the network. In some cases, pruning is proven to reduce computational cost by up to 80% without significantly reducing the accuracy of the model [25]. Briefly, for a given neuron k at layer i, d_i^{k+} and d_i^{k-} denotes the number of incoming and outgoing edges. Then after pruning we get:

$$d_i^{k'+} \leq d_i^{k+} \text{ and } d_i^{k'-} \leq d_i^{k-}$$

where, $d_i^{k'+}$ and $d_i^{k'-}$ denotes the number of incoming and outgoing edges for neuron k at layer i after pruning is completed. We use number of outgoing edges from layer i to layer j and feature vectors interchangeably ($\forall i < j$). In encrypted setting, there are two modes of computations available: (a) Unpacked: means each element of feature vector is encrypted as a ciphertext. This requires more number of ciphertexts per query hence increasing communication cost. (b) Packed: Means the whole feature vector, or parts of it, is encrypted as a single ciphertext. This reduces number of ciphertexts per query hence reducing communication cost. However once elements are packed, individual element cannot be accessed. This introduces additional computational costs.

Unpacked mode of computation mimics the computation that happens when inputs are not encrypted. Thus, benefits of pruning a network directly reflect in terms of computation cost in this mode. However, for packed mode of computation, pruning has little effect, since we do not have access to individual elements.

Table 1. Variable length packing

Model	Length	totalPackc	Security level (bits) [2]	Estm. time (secs)
Baseline	4096	266	330	19.08
	2048	266	105	8.57
	1024	522	37	8.48
	512	1034	35	8.78
Pruned7 (sparsity-0.7)	4096	62	330	4.44
	2048	62	105	1.99
	1024	112	37	1.82
	512	202	35	1.71
Pruned8 (sparsity-0.8)	4096	126	330	9.0
	2048	126	105	4.06
	1024	220	37	3.57
	512	404	35	3.43
Pruned9 (sparsity-0.9)	4096	62	330	4.44
	2048	62	105	1.99
	1024	110	37	1.78
	512	190	35	1.61

The existing approaches for packing works best for fully connected CNN. In the next section, we propose a generic method to determine the optimal length of packing *i.e.* number of elements packed into single ciphertext to make the most of the pruning step for any type of neural network.

3.3 Efficient Packing

As discussed earlier, due to pruning, the number of neurons and edges of the FC layers can be reduced and hence, there can be reduction in the computation complexity. In order to take the advantage of the pruning, optimal ciphertext packing of elements needs to be determined. Maximum number of elements denoted by l_{max} that can be packed depends on the ring modulus N, $(l_{max} \geq \frac{N}{2})$. The existing packing technique is suitable for fully connected network and not optimal for pruned network, as it introduces undesirable computation overhead due to fragmentation (as most of the slots in the packing needs to be initialized to zero). For example, let w_{ij}^k be set of all the weights of the incoming edges from the neurons of layer i to k^{th} layer j. These weights will be multiplied to feature vector fv. Assume all the elements of fv are encrypted as a single ciphertext, as depicted in Fig. 2 (Packed DNN). An entire neuron computation can be skipped if all its incoming edges have weight zero after pruning. However, even if one of the incoming edge has a non-zero weight, we need to compute $w_{ij}^k * fv$. Due to this, there can be computation overhead. Hence, there is a need to determine an optimal packing length to minimize the computation overhead.

Variable length packing is very useful in scenarios where $|fv| \geq l_{max}$. If $|fv| < l_{max}$, then variable length packing by default is set to l_{max}. It is observed that size of the packing can affect the performance of the computation, see Table 1. Since $|fv| \geq l_{max}$, each neuron needs to operate on $\left\lceil \frac{|fv|}{l_{max}} \right\rceil$ number of ciphertext packs. Computation/memory overheads can be there due to more number of operations. For instance for a FC network with p layers, the total number of ciphertext packs (with maximum number of elements that can be packed) that are part of FC computations is given by:

$$\sum_{i=m-p+1}^{m} n_i * \left\lceil \frac{|fv|}{l_{max}} \right\rceil \qquad (6)$$

One way to reduce the number of ciphertext packs is to increase N, which further increases the computation overhead. Higher the N, higher will be the computation complexity of FHE operations. Thus, one of the way to arrive at an optimal packing length l_{opt} is to explore all possible packing lengths (which are generally of 2^x) and estimate the complexity (computation/memory) for a given FC network and arrive at l_{opt}. Note that l_{opt} is bounded by:

$$\delta^+ \leq l_{opt} \leq l_{max} \tag{7}$$

where δ^+ is the minimum in degree of pruned FC network, which is given by

$$\delta^+ = min(d_i^{k+}|m - p + 1 \leq i \leq m, 1 \leq k \leq n_i) \tag{8}$$

Table 1 summarizes the impact of variable length packing on the performance of FC layers (for different pruned networks and baseline) computations (esti-mated based on time taken to compute FHE addition/multiplication primitives using CKKS scheme) on encrypted data with different l_{max} (maximum pack-ing length) and security levels. We observe that, though the network is pruned with higher sparsity, the total number of ciphertext packings ($totalPackc$) is not reduced in proportion and therefore, no significant reduction in complexity of the computation. This can be due to random pattern in pruning of edges across the different FC layers. Hence, there is a need to run different pruning algo-rithms for a given CNN network to obtain an optimal pruned network, where in optimal packing length can be useful to reduce the computation overhead. Esti-mating l_{opt} is the first step of our recommendation system. It is done by server as a post-training/pruning processing step and it is shared with the client. This highlights importance of variable length packing.

3.4   Recommendation System for Private Inference

We now discuss recommendation system based on the optimization formulation (discussed earlier in Sect. 3.1: Eq. 1 to Eq. 5) using pruning and efficient packing technique. Input to the recommendation system is CNN network, constraints, set of pruning algorithms and FHE parameters. Algorithm 1 describes the pro-posed scheme. Idea is to estimate the constraint parameters based on different pruning algorithms for a given CNN network. For each pruned network, different estimates of the performance of the private inference are tabulated by varying the packing lengths (see steps 5 to 22, we determine total number of cipher-text packings ($totalPackc$) for the FC layers). Using the aggregated estimates of constraints for all the pruned algorithms, we solve the optimization problem using TOPSIS [4] (see step 26), which gives the best solution as the recommen-dation to realize private inference based on user's QoS. It includes the pruned network to be used and FHE parameters, ciphertext packing length to be used to implement private inference for the selected pruned network.

Algorithm 1. Recommendation system for Private Inference for CNN

1: **procedure** RS($CNN, nPrune, nPruneAlg[]$)
2:    INPUT $CNN, m, p, constraints \leftarrow \{\tau, \mu, \lambda\}$
3:    $count = 0$
4:    **for** z in $\{1,2,...nPrune\}$ **do**
5:       $CNN_{prune} = nPruneAlg[z](CNN)$
6:       Find δ^+ for FC layers of CNN_{prune}
7:       **for** $length$ in $\{\delta^+, \delta^+ * 2.., l_{max}\}$ **do**
8:          $l_{pack} = \left\lceil \frac{|fv|}{length} \right\rceil$
9:          $totalPackc = 0$
10:          **for** i in $m - p + 1...m$ **do**
11:             **for** l in $0...n_i - 1$ **do**
12:                **for** k in $0...l_{pack} - 1$ **do**
13:                   w = w_i^l[k*length:(k+1)*length]
14:                   **if** $non\_zero(w)$ **then**
15:                      $totalPackc = totalPackc + 1$
16:                   **end if**
17:                **end for**
18:             **end for**
19:          **end for**
20:          $N = length * 2$
21:          estimate[count]=$evaluate\_constraint($
22: $CNN_{prune}, m, p, N, length, totalPackc)$
23:          $count = count + 1$
24:       **end for**
25:    **end for**
26:    $RecomondedSolution = TOPSISOptimizationSolver(estimate[])$
27: **end procedure**

Complexity of Algorithm 1 is $\emptyset(nPrune * log(N) * p * n * |fv|)$, where $nPrune$ is number of pruning algorithms, N is the ring modulus for FHE, p is number of FC layers in CNN and n is maximum number of neurons in any given FC layers.

4   Results and Evaluation

The proposed private inference for CNN is evaluated using CIFAR-10 dataset with 10 classes (Fig. 3). The network is trained and tested using 50,000 and 10,000 images (coloured RGB images) respectively. Each image is consisting of $32 \times 32 \times 3$ pixel values (3-channels: RGB).

Fig. 3. CIFAR-10 data samples. 10 classes from left to right: Airplane, Automobile, Bird, Cat, Deer, Dog, Frog, Horse, Ship, Truck

4.1 Model Training and Pruning

The model architecture comprises six convolution layers with max pooling and dropout followed by two fully connected dense layers. Adam optimiser with sparse categorical cross-entropy loss was used to train the model for 100 epochs. The model was intentionally kept simple in order to avoid over-fitting and an accuracy of 82.3% was achieved. For pruning, we used three levels of sparsity. Performance of these models are summarized in Table 2. All the evaluations (test cases) were ran on Intel Xeon Gold 6252 CPU clocked at 2.1 GHz, with 32 cores and 64 GB RAM. HEAAN Parallelization was achieved using NTL library [24] and SEAL Parallelization was done using Intel's TBB [13].

4.2 Private Inference

Two sets of results are presented for private inference (FC layers). Firstly, we analyze the impact of different polynomial approximations of ReLU activation function on the accuracy of private inference (see Table 3). In our experiments, two polynomial approximations of degree 4 for ReLU (ReLU-1 [5] & ReLU-2 [14]) and one polynomial approximation of degree 2 (ReLU-3 [7]) are used. Polynomial ReLU-3 performed best in terms of accuracy, as well as time/memory (lesser overhead due to low degree polynomial computation). Ishiyama *et al.* [14] achieved a maximum accuracy of 81.02 (with ReLU approximation function) on CIFAR-10 datsaset which, is less when compared to both our baseline model (81.43%) and our pruned model (0.8 sparsity - 81.7%).

Second set of results describes the performance (computation time, memory requirements) of private inference (FC layers) implemented with different approximation functions for activation function using FHE libraries SEAL (BFV) [23] and HEAAN (CKKS) [6]. Computation time and memory required for private inference are tabulated in Table 4. Note that we used packing for our implementation of FC using HEAAN. Since the effect of pruning are not visible on packed encrypted FC, as explained in Sect. 3.2, the time and memory for both are almost same as can it be observed in Table 4. However, pruning greatly improves performance for private inference without packing (SEAL). All the parameters in FHE were set to give at least 128 bits of security which is

Table 2. Different models tested for CIFAR-10

Model	Accuracy (%)	# of parameters
Baseline	82.3	527114
Pruned7	81.16	158320
Pruned8	82.08	105653
Pruned9	79.21	52951

Table 3. Accuracy for different approximation functions for different models. * indicates accuracy of HEAAN based inference varies ±0.05 since it is an approximate scheme

Model	Activation function	Accuracy % *
Baseline	ReLU-1	79.9
	ReLU-2	80.16
	ReLU-3	**81.43**
Prune7	ReLU-1	65.06
	ReLU-2	78.31
	ReLU-3	**79.86**
Prune8	ReLU-1	66.6
	ReLU-2	81.56
	ReLU-3	**81.7**
Prune9	ReLU-1	60.68
	ReLU-2	75.71
	ReLU-3	**76.32**

the same for the state of the art [14,16]. For this configuration, variable length packing is not applicable since $N = 8192$ and $length = 4096 > |fv|(2048)$.

Table 4. Performance of private inference for different models

Model	A.F	HEAAN		SEAL	
		Time (secs)	Memory (GB)	Time (secs)	Memory (GB)
Baseline	ReLU-1	12.1	1.53	120.7	1.65
	ReLU-2	13.1	1.63	119.3	1.65
	ReLU-3	**11.5**	**1.36**	**113.7**	**1.37**
Prune7	ReLU-1	11.53	1.49	58.8	1.65
	ReLU-2	12.8	1.48	59.3	1.65
	ReLU-3	**10.9**	**1.25**	**51.2**	**1.37**
Prune8	ReLU-1	11.4	1.62	49.9	1.65
	ReLU-2	11.7	1.6	47.4	1.65
	ReLU-3	**10.8**	**1.3**	**38.9**	**1.37**
Prune9	ReLU-1	11.3	1.50	39.9	1.65
	ReLU-2	10.9	1.48	39.6	1.65
	ReLU-3	**10.4**	**1.21**	**29.0**	**1.37**

Table 5. Optimization solver for varying QoS

QoS - W	Meaning	Best choice
[1, 1, 1]	Equal importance for all QoS parameters, the higher the better	baseline : [81.43, 11.5, 1.36]
[1, −1, −1]	Equal importance for all QoS paramters, Accuracy high, Time and memory should be low	pruned9 : [76.32, 10.4, 1.21]
[10, −1, −1]	10× more importance for accuracy, Time and memory should be low	pruned8 : [81.7, 10.8, 1.3]

These tabular data (Tables 3 and 4) are fed as inputs to the optimization solver. Since approximation ReLU-3 is performing better in all Quality of Service (QoS) aspects (accuracy, time, memory), we only consider corresponding rows for each model, using HEAAN, as input to the optimization solver. We use TOPSIS [4] as the optimization solver. It is used as a multi-criteria decision making method. TOPSIS chooses the alternative of shortest Euclidean distance from the ideal solution and farthest distance from the negative-ideal solution. We do this by creating three matrices: Choices, Indicator and Decision matrix. The decision matrix a should be constructed with each row representing a choice (model), and each column representing an Indicator (constraints - accuracy, time, memory). Indicators W represents weight for each criterion that define user's choice for QoS. It also has option to give negative weights which indicate that smaller value is better. In our case, matrix choice = [baseline, pruned7, pruned8, pruned9] and matrix a will be a = [[81.43, 11.5, 1.36], [79.86, 10.9, 1.25], [81.7, 10.8, 1.3], [76.32, 10.4, 1.21]]. In Table 5 we present different scenarios of QoS (indicators W) and its corresponding output (best choice) given by the TOPSIS solver. As presented in Table 5, when user wishes to give equal importance to all QoS parameters, baseline is selected as the best choice with highest score of 0.94. Alternatively, if user wishes to have more accuracy and less time and memory, but all are equally important, then pruned9 is selected as the best choice. However, if user wishes to have more importance on accuracy along with low time and memory, $i.e.$ $10\times$, then pruned8 is selected. This is inline with Algorithm 1. The algorithm first selects for a given model, best approximation function and feature for FHE (packing against unpacked) based on QoS. This gives ReLU-3 as the best approximation and using packed based implementation (HEAAN) as we get highest accuracy and low on time and memory.

5 Conclusion and Future Work

Convolutional neural network is being used for a variety of computer vision tasks. The current offerings lack privacy-sensitive algorithms. In this paper, a novel approach to achieve efficient private inference on FHE encrypted data is presented. A recommendation system for parameter optimization is proposed. Results are presented for different models and pruning strategies. The evaluation demonstrates that the proposed method achieves privacy-aware inference without compromising accuracy, memory, and timing.

As can be seen from the results in Table 4, current implementations of FHE are very slow and are not practical for deployment of real world applications. As part of the future work, we plan to enhance the architecture for private inferencing and extend the same for private training. Another interesting direction of work is implementing FHE based private inference on faster hardware like FPGA $etc.$ to boost the performance.

References

1. Ahn, B.H., Pilligundla, A., Yazdanbakhsh, A., Esmaeilzadeh, H.: Chameleon: adaptive code optimization for expedited deep neural network compilation (2020)
2. Albrecht, M.: LWE-estimator. https://bitbucket.org/malb/lwe-estimator/src/master. Accessed 14 Apr 2021
3. Al Badawi, A., et al.: The alexnet moment for homomorphic encryption: HCNN, the first homomorphic CNN on encrypted data with GPUs. CoRR abs/1811.00778 (2018)

4. Balaei, S.: Decision radar ez-topsis. https://decision-radar.com/Topsis.html
5. Chabanne, H., de Wargny, A., Milgram, J., Morel, C., Prouff, E.: Privacy-preserving classification on deep neural network. IACR Cryptol. ePrint Arch. **2017**, 35 (2017)
6. Cheon, J.H., Kim, A., Kim, M., Song, Y.: Homomorphic encryption for arithmetic of approximate numbers. In: Takagi, T., Peyrin, T. (eds.) ASIACRYPT 2017. LNCS, vol. 10624, pp. 409–437. Springer, Cham (2017). https://doi.org/10.1007/978-3-319-70694-8_15
7. Chou, E., Beal, J., Levy, D., Yeung, S., Haque, A., Fei-Fei, L.: Faster cryptonets: leveraging sparsity for real-world encrypted inference (2018)
8. Dowlin, N., Gilad-Bachrach, R., Laine, K., Lauter, K., Naehrig, M., Wernsing, J.: Cryptonets: applying neural networks to encrypted data with high throughput and accuracy. In: Proceedings of the 33rd ICML - Volume 48, pp. 201–210. JMLR.org (2016)
9. Gentry, C.: A fully homomorphic encryption scheme. Ph.D. thesis, Stanford University (2009). crypto.stanford.edu/craig
10. Goodfellow, I., Bengio, Y., Courville, A., Bengio, Y.: Deep Learning, vol. 1. MIT Press, Cambridge (2016)
11. Hesamifard, E., Takabi, H., Ghasemi, M.: Cryptodl: deep neural networks over encrypted data. CoRR abs/1711.05189 (2017)
12. Hunt, T., Song, C., Shokri, R., Shmatikov, V., Witchel, E.: Chiron: privacy-preserving machine learning as a service. arXiv preprint arXiv:1803.05961 (2018)
13. Intel: Intel's threading building blocks. https://software.intel.com/content/www/us/en/develop/tools/oneapi/components/onetbb.html
14. Ishiyama, T., Suzuki, T., Yamana, H.: Highly accurate CNN inference using approximate activation functions over homomorphic encryption (2020)
15. Juvekar, C., Vaikuntanathan, V., Chandrakasan, A.: Gazelle: a low latency framework for secure neural network inference. CoRR abs/1801.05507 (2018)
16. Kim, M., Jiang, X., Lauter, K., Ismayilzada, E., Shams, S.: HEAR: human action recognition via neural networks on homomorphically encrypted data (2021)
17. Liu, J., Juuti, M., Lu, Y., Asokan, N.: Oblivious neural network predictions via minionn transformations. In: Proceedings of the 2017 ACM SIGSAC Conference on Computer and Communications Security, pp. 619–631. ACM, New York, NY, USA (2017)
18. Mohassel, P., Zhang, Y.: Secureml: a system for scalable privacy-preserving machine learning. In: 2017 IEEE Symposium on Security and Privacy (SP), pp. 19–38. IEEE (2017)
19. Nandakumar, K., Ratha, N., Pankanti, S., Halevi, S.: Towards deep neural network training on encrypted data. In: 2019 IEEE/CVF Conference on Computer Vision and Pattern Recognition Workshops (CVPRW), pp. 40–48 (2019)
20. Riazi, M.S., Samragh, M., Chen, H., Laine, K., Lauter, K., Koushanfar, F.: XONN: Xnor-based oblivious deep neural network inference. In: 28th USENIX Security Symposium (USENIX Security 19), pp. 1501–1518 (2019)
21. Rouhani, B.D., Riazi, M.S., Koushanfar, F.: DeepSecure: scalable provably-secure deep learning. In: Proceedings of the 55th Annual Design Automation Conference, pp. 1–6 (2018)
22. Sanyal, A., Kusner, M.J., Gascon, A., Kanade, V.: TAPAS: tricks to accelerate (encrypted) prediction as a service. arXiv preprint arXiv:1806.03461 (2018)
23. Microsoft SEAL (release 3.1). Microsoft Research, Redmond, WA, December 2018. https://github.com/Microsoft/SEAL

24. Shoup, V.: Number theory library. https://libntl.org/doc/tour.html
25. Valerio, L., Nardini, F.M., Passarella, A., Perego, R.: Dynamic hard pruning of neural networks at the edge of the internet (2020)
26. Wagh, S., Gupta, D., Chandran, N.: SecureNN: efficient and private neural network training. IACR Cryptol. ePrint Arch. **2018**, 442 (2018)
27. Xu, R., Joshi, J.B.D., Li, C.: CryptoNN: training neural networks over encrypted data. CoRR abs/1904.07303 (2019)

Improvement over Montgomery Modular Multiplication

Debapriyay Mukhopadhyay$^{(\boxtimes)}$ (iD)

Vehere Interactive Pvt. Ltd., Kolkata 700091, India

Abstract. This paper describes an improvement over Montgomery Modular Multiplication proposed by Peter L. Montgomery in [1]. Montgomery in [1] has proposed a method of computing $z = x.y \bmod N$ ($N > 1$) which is much faster and does not require any division by N. Central to his method is one algorithm called Reduction algorithm which is required to be employed 4 times in order to compute z. The improvement that we propose still uses the same Reduction algorithm of [1], but in the improved version we are only required to employ the Reduction algortihm twice in order to compute z.

Keywords: Modular multiplication · Montgomery multiplication · Computational arithmetic · Cryptography

1 Introduction

Many cryptographic algorithms like RSA [3], DSA, Diffie-Hellman key exchange are based on arithmetic operations modulo a large number. These algorithms require to do extensive modular exponentiation and which is implemented via successive squaring. This means, many modular multiplications are required to be computed in order to compute the value for modular exponentiation. For example, in the most widely used public-key cryptosystem RSA [3], encryption and decryption is a modular exponentiation like $C = M^k \bmod N$, where N is the public modulus, k can be either public or private exponent and M, C stands for either message or cipher text (depending on whether it is encryption or decryption). Evaluation of this modular exponentiation requires repeated modular multiplication.

In 1985, mathematician Peter L. Montgomery [1], proposed a method of computing $z = x.y \bmod N$ ($N > 1$), where $0 \leq x \leq N$ and $0 \leq y \leq N$ are integers, which is much faster and does not require any division by N. This method is referred as *Montgomery Modular Multiplication*. Montgomery Modular Multiplication described in [1] does not specifically say whether N is even or odd. But for most practical implementation purposes where speed of modular multiplication is highly desired (like in Cryptographic algorithms), N is always an odd integer.

Montgomery modular multiplication invloves two major steps - 1) to compute the Montgomery Residue of the input operands x and y and 2) to compute

© Springer Nature Switzerland AG 2021
S. Tripathy et al. (Eds.): ICISS 2021, LNCS 13146, pp. 212–217, 2021.
https://doi.org/10.1007/978-3-030-92571-0_14

the result z following the Montgomery Reduction algorithm. In this paper, we propose an interesting improvement over the existing Montgomery Multiplication technique where we have been able to entirely elminate the computation done in Step 1. That means, proposed improvement does not require to compute the Montgomery Residue of the input operands.

The paper is organized as follows. Section 2 describes the modular multiplication scheme of [1]. In Sect. 3, we describe the improvement over the scheme of [1]. Finally, the concluding remarks appear in Sect. 4.

2   Overview of the Montgomery Modular Multiplicaton of [1]

Let $N > 1$ be an odd integer. We choose a radix $R(> N)$ co-prime to N, i.e. $g.c.d(N, R) = 1$. Bezout's identity says that, if a and b be two non-zero integers with d being their $g.c.d$, then there exists integers x and y such that

$$xa + yb = d.$$

Therefore, since $g.c.d(N, R) = 1$, so there exists integers x and y such that

$$xR + yN = 1$$

From the above identity, it is evident that $xR = 1 \, mod \, N$. Therefore, x is the multiplicative inverse of R w.r.t. modulo N. We denote, $x = R^{-1}$. Similarly, $yN = 1 \, mod \, R$, so y is the multiplicative inverse of N w.r.t. modulo R. We denote, $y = N^{-1}$. Therefore, we have

$$R^{-1}R + N^{-1}N = 1,$$

where $R^{-1} \in \mathbb{Z}_N^*$ and $N^{-1} \in \mathbb{Z}_R^*$.

Montgomery Reduction: It is defined as a one-one onto mapping defined from $\mathbb{Z}_N$ to $\mathbb{Z}_N$ such that, for $0 \leq i < N$, let $\overline{i}$ represent the residue class containing $iR^{-1} \, mod N$. This is a complete residue system. Let us take an example to understand it better. The mapping $f : \mathbb{Z}_N \to \mathbb{Z}_N$ such that

$$\overline{x} = f(x) = x.R^{-1} \, mod N$$

maps $\mathbb{Z}_N$ onto itself.

This is called *Montgomery Reduction* and the rational behind this selection is that it facilitates quick computation of $T.R^{-1} \, mod N$, for $0 \leq T < R.N$ when $R(> N)$ is chosen as some power of 2. For N and $R(> N)$ such that $g.c.d(N, R) = 1$, we know that $R^{-1}R + N^{-1}N = 1$, where $R^{-1} \in \mathbb{Z}_N$ and $N^{-1} \in \mathbb{Z}_R$. This implies that

$$T = T.N.N^{-1} + T.R.R^{-1}$$

$$=> T + T.(-N^{-1}).N = T.R.R^{-1}$$

$$=> T + m.N = T.R.R^{-1},$$

where $m = T(-N^{-1}) \bmod R$. This proves that, when N and R are co-prime to each other, then for every $T \geq 0$ there exists and integer m such that $\frac{T+m.N}{R}$ has zero remainder.

Montgomery Reduction of $0 \leq T < R.N$, i.e., $T.R^{-1} \bmod N$ is therefore calculated via the following algorithm and we denote it as $Redc(T)$.

```
Algorithm Redc(T), where 0 <= T < R.N

m = T(-N^{-1}) mod R
t = (T + m.N)/R

if t >=  N
      return t - N
else
      return t
```

We have already proved that $\frac{T+m.N}{R}$ has no remainder. So, t is an integer. Therefore,

$$t.R = T + m.N$$
$$=> t.R = T \bmod N$$
$$=> t = T.R^{-1} \bmod N$$

Since, $0 \leq T < R.N$, so $0 < leqT + m.N < R.N + R.N$ and hence

$$0 \leq t < 2.N$$

This justifies that, why we return $t - N$ as the value for $T.R^{-1} \bmod N$ when $N \leq t < 2.N$. Since R is of the form 2^i for some $i > 1$, so the values for m and t in algorithm $Redc$ can be calculated easily and quickly using left shift operation.

Montgomery Residue: If $x \in \mathbb{Z}_N$, then Montgomery Residue of x is defined as $x' = (x.R) \bmod N$. Note that $0 \leq x' < N - 1$. It can also be proved that, Montgomery Residue is also a complete residue system, i.e., the mapping $(x.R) \bmod N$ is an one-one mapping from $\mathbb{Z}_N$ onto itself.

Now, consider that we want to compute $z = (x.y) \bmod N$ for $x, y \in \mathbb{Z}_N$. Then,

$$z' = (z.R) \bmod N$$
$$= (x.y)R \bmod N$$
$$= (x.R).(y.R).R^{-1} \bmod N$$
$$= (x'.y').R^{-1} \bmod N$$
$$= Redc(x'.y')$$

Now, since $z' = (z.R) \bmod N$, so

$$z = z'.R^{-1} \bmod N = Redc(z') = Redc(Redc(x'.y'))$$

This shows that, z can be computed by invoking $Redc$ algorithm twice successively and $Redc$ algorithm does not require any trial divison to be done since R is some power of 2. Any division by R can be easily implemented by using left shift operations. But, we need to compute $x' = (x.R) \bmod N$. Note that, $x' = (x.R) \bmod N = (x.R^2).R^{-1} \bmod N = Redc(x.R^2)$. So, we are also not required to divide by modulus N, even to compute x' and y'. But, we are still required to compute $R^2 \bmod N$ in order to compute $x' = Redc(x.R^2)$. But, since R is chosen before hand as a power of 2, computing $R^2 \bmod N$ is to be done only once and therefore does not add much to the whole computation.

Computing $z = x.y \bmod N$ using Montogomery Multiplication can therefore be summarized as follows.

1. Choose $R > N$ Where R is some power of 2 and also compute $R^2 \bmod N$. This step is required to be done only once for each N.
2. Compute $x' = Redc(x)$ and $y' = Redc(y)$
3. Compute $z = Redc(Redc(x'.y'))$

Let us now take an example to understand the whole procedure.

Example: Let, $N = 11$, $R = 16$. Then, $N^{-1} = -13$ and $R^{-1} = 9$. Let us take, $x = 6$, $y = 10$ and we are interested to find $z = (x.y) \bmod N = 5$ through this montgomery reduction process. We first compute, $R^2 \bmod N = 256 \bmod 11 = 3$ and then

$$x' = Redc(x.R^2) = Redc(18) = \frac{18 + (18.13 \bmod 16).11}{16} = 8,$$

and

$$y' = Redc(y.R^2) = Redc(30) = \frac{30 + (30.13 \bmod 16).11}{16} = 6.$$

We will first compute, $Redc(x'.y') = Redc(48)$. $Redc(48) = \frac{48+(48.13 \bmod 16).11}{16} = 3$, and therefore

$$z = Redc(3) = \frac{3 + (3.13 \bmod 16).11}{16} = 5.$$

And this proves the efficiency of Montgomery Reduction Algorithm.

3   Proposed Improvement

By properly choosing the value for R as power of 2, we can entirely eliminate the step of computing *Montgomery Residue*. In other words, in order to compute $z = (x.y) \bmod N$ for $x, y \in \mathbb{Z}_N$, we are not required to compute $x' = (x.R) \bmod N$ and $y' = (y.R) \bmod N$ as shown above in Step 2. In order to apply the Montgomery $Redc$ Algorithm efficiently, we are required to choose R as some power of 2. The same thing holds in the proposed improvement as well, but additionally we require $R(> N)$ to be such that $R^2 = 1 \bmod N$. Therefore, we need to prove the following first.

Theorem: For every odd N, there exists $R = 2^i$ (for some $i > 0$) such that $R > N$ and also $R^2 = 1 \, mod \, N$.

Proof: In number theory, Euler's theorem (also known as the Fermat–Euler theorem or Euler's totient theorem) states that if N and a are coprime positive integers, then

$$a^{\phi(N)} = 1 \, mod \, N,$$

where ϕ is the Euler's totient function. Since, N is odd therefore, $g.c.d(2, N) = 1$. Therefore, it follows that $2^{\phi(N)} = 1 \, mod \, N$.

By choosing $R = 2^{(\phi(N)/2)}$, we therefore see that $R^2 = 1 \, mod \, N$.

This completes the proof.

Note that, since $R^2 = 1 \, mod \, N$ so we have $R = R^{-1}$. Remember that, we want to compute $z = (x.y) \, mod \, N$.

$$z = (x.y) \, mod \, N$$
$$= (x.y).R^2 \, mod \, N$$
$$= (x.y.R^{-1}).R^{-1} \, mod \, N$$
$$= Redc(x.y.R^{-1})$$
$$= Redc(Redc(x.y))$$

Therefore, we see that the same formula and Algorithm applies for computing $z = (x.y) \, mod \, N$, but we are not required to compute x' and y'. Since, R has been chosen such that $R^2 = 1 \, mod \, N$, so Step 1 as stated above is also not required. This is a significant gain, since we have reduced the call to Redc algorithm for 4 to 2 and also we have eliminated the step where actual division by N was required to be done.

Let us now consider the same example as above with the exception that, for $N = 11$, we have now $R = 2^{(\phi(N)/2)} = 2^{10/2} = 32 = R^{-1}$. In this case, we have $N^{-1} = -93$. For $x = 6$, $y = 10$, we will first compute $Redc(x.y) = Redc(60)$. $Redc(60) = \frac{60 + (60.93 \, mod \, 32).11}{32} = 6$, and therefore

$$z = Redc(6) = \frac{6 + (6.93 \, mod \, 32).11}{32} = 5.$$

This justifies the proposed improvement over the Montgomery Multiplication Scheme.

4   Conclusion

Proposed improvement can be readily applied where modulo is required to be taken with respect to a prime number like Diffie-Hellman key exchange algorithm, Digital Signature Algorithm (DSA), ElGamal, etc. But, it is not readily applicable to RSA since the public modulus $N = p.q$ is a composite integer. The design of RSA does not allow us to make the $\phi(N)$ public, so the improvement can not be readily applied. However, since $\phi(N)$ is a private information, so the improvement can be applied while the cipher is to be decrypted using the private key. It is also to be noted that, in order to make RSA decryption faster most of the implementations use Chinese Remainder Theorem (RSA-CRT) [2] during decryption. In RSA-CRT, it is assumed that the factors of the public modulus N, i.e., the primes p and q are known in decryption side and modular exponentiations are done successively with respect to p and q. Therefore, the im- provement proposed in this paper can also be easily applied on the RSA-CRT method during decryption. In future, we plan to implement our proposed improvement in BigDigits [4] multi-precision montgomery implementation to quantify the extent of improvement.

Acknowledgment. We thank the referee of this paper for the helpful comments. It improved the presentation of the paper.

References

1. Montgomery, P.L.: Modular multiplication without trial division. Math. Comput. **44**(170), 519–521 (1985)
2. Quisquater, J.J., Couvreur, C.: Fast decipherment algorithm for RSA public-key cryptosystem. IEE Electron. Lett. **18**(21), 905907 (1982)
3. Rivest, R.L., Shamir, A., Adlemn, L.: A method for obtaining digital signatures and public-key cryptosystems. Commun. ACM **21**, 120–126 (1978)
4. BigDigits multiple-precision arithmetic source code. http://www.di-mgt.com.au/bigdigits.html

Faster Private Rating Update via Integer-Based Homomorphic Encryption

Pranav Verma[✉], Anish Mathuria, and Sourish Dasgupta

Dhirubhai Ambani Institute of Information and Communication Technology,
Gandhinagar, India
{pranav_verma,anish_mathuria,sourish_dasgupta}@daiict.ac.in

Abstract. In encryption-based privacy-preserving recommender systems (PPRS), the user sends encrypted ratings to the server. An encrypted rating vector can have thousands of ciphertexts, causing a communication overhead. In some encryption-based PPRS proposed in the literature, if a user wants to rate a single item, he/she is required to send the entire rating vector to hide which item was rated. A user's rating value and the item that is being rated both should remain private. This can be seen as a variant of the classical PIR-write problem. The goal is that each time a user wants to modify any data block, the communication should be minimal from the user.

In encryption-based PPRS, the ratings are required to be encrypted using homomorphic schemes so that the server can generate recommendations. Arjan proposed a private rating update protocol for the recommender system applications, whereas Lipmaa and Zhang gave a protocol for a more general database scenario. We propose a hybrid approach that combines the advantages of each protocol, yielding a more efficient protocol. Our approach has constant user-side computation, and it reduces the communication and computation overhead at the server-side compared to previous approaches.

1 Introduction

A recommendation system collects user preferences and suggests the new unseen but relevant items from the inventory. Many recommender systems collect sensitive information from their users, like financial or medical data. Such susceptible data requires utmost care and its security is very critical for the users of these applications. The users may not trust a recommender system and may need assurance that their data will be kept private. No one, even from the administrative team of the portal, maybe trusted with personal information. This type of setup is referred to as an untrusted server application. One solution to realize such an application is to use privacy-preserving recommender systems (PPRS) where the user's data is hidden from every other entity in the system, including the server storing the data.

© Springer Nature Switzerland AG 2021
S. Tripathy et al. (Eds.): ICISS 2021, LNCS 13146, pp. 218–236, 2021.
https://doi.org/10.1007/978-3-030-92571-0_15

There are two main approaches to achieving privacy in recommender systems: data obfuscation (or randomization) based [14, 22] and encryption based PPRS [11, 19]. The encryption-based PPRS uses homomorphic encryption schemes which allow computations to be performed directly over the encrypted data. Users encrypt their ratings using a homomorphic encryption scheme and then send the encrypted ratings to the server. The server can compute the recommendations from the encrypted ratings but cannot read the actual values of the ratings. The underlying encryption protocol requires a probabilistic encryption scheme; otherwise, ratings might become vulnerable to dictionary attacks as the message space in rating systems is very small.

An additional goal of PPRS is to hide the information regarding which items a user has rated. Since the server has access to the rating matrix and users rate very few items from the entire item set, the server may identify the specific items that a user has rated. The most straightforward approach is to have the user send the ratings for all the items in the item set to protect the user's privacy. It means that every time a user rates one (or few) item(s), he has to send the entire rating vector to the server so that the server cannot infer which ratings are modified by the user in the rating matrix. This approach has two significant drawbacks. Firstly, user communication overhead increases drastically for any practical recommender server with thousands of items in the item set. Secondly, each user has to keep track of their previously submitted ratings.

Goldreich and Ostrovsky [7] first proposed oblivious RAM (ORAM) to prevent software copyrights for organizations. It was later adapted in client-server models to protect user privacy while accessing the stored data from an external adversary and the non-trusted server. There have been many works in this domain focusing on reducing the communication costs and server storage [13, 17, 20, 21]. The major building blocks used in ORAM designs are probabilistic encryption schemes, hash tables, oblivious map-reduce, oblivious sorting, and randomized shuffle at the server. Probabilistic encryption ensures that the ciphertext changes every time the client touches the data block irrespective of values being updated or not. The other operations are needed to relocate the data blocks in the server's memory without mapping between the old and new locations. Some approaches use additional dummy data blocks to mask the actual data block relocations. Although the privacy goals of ORAM and PPRS are similar, ORAMs are not suitable for our purposes. Users may frequently update or access their rating vector, and the vector elements will be reshuffled whenever they do so. This will create inconsistency in recommendation generation.

Lipmaa and Zhang [12] proposed two PIR-write protocols based on binary decision diagrams and fully homomorphic encryption (FHE), respectively. The goal is to allow users to update any data stored at a remote server without revealing the location of the data and its value. The FHE-based solution is costly: it requires users to encrypt their ratings bit-by-bit. Arjan [10] was the first to propose a solution that reduces the user side costs using an integer-based partially homomorphic scheme. His approach relies on two non-colluding servers; this solution is costly in terms of the communication overhead at the servers.

Table 1. Comparison of protocols

Protocol	HE type	No. of encryptions per user	Inter-server comm.	Server storage per user
Lipmaa-Zhang	Fully HE	$\mathcal{O}(l + log n)$	nil	$\mathcal{O}(nl)$
Arjan	Partial HE	2	$\mathcal{O}(n)$	$\mathcal{O}(n)$
Proposed	Somewhat HE	2	$\mathcal{O}(log n)$	$\mathcal{O}(n)$

Our contribution. The features of our proposal are summarised below:

- The user performs a constant number of encryptions, namely two encryptions, to effect a rating update.
- The communication cost at the user-side is constant.
- The communication cost between the servers is significantly reduced as compared to Arjan [10].
- The number of costly operations at the servers i.e. encryption and decryption are reduced while increasing the number of less costly homomorphic arithmetic operations.

Table 1 summarises the main advantages of our work. In Lipmaa's protocol, the integer ratings are encrypted bit-by-bit, so the server has to store $\mathcal{O}(nl)$ ciphertexts, where l is the number of bits required to represent a rating and n is the total number of items. In Arjan's protocol, an entire encrypted rating vector is exchanged between the servers, so the communication cost is $\mathcal{O}(n)$. We reduce this cost to $\mathcal{O}(\log n)$ using a secure bit decomposition protocol [15].

In our proposed solution we only require a bounded number of arithmetic operations over the ciphertexts. We use a somewhat homomorphic scheme known as HE1N [4]. It is IND-CPA secure and also very efficient. As discussed in Sect. 5.4, HE1N scheme outperforms the Bresson's and Paillier's partial HE [1] used in [10] and [15], respectively.

The rest of the paper is organized as follows. In the next section, we discuss relevant previous work in the PIR-write domain. In Sect. 3 we describe the cryptographic building blocks we use in our protocol design. In Sect. 4 we describe our proposal and its privacy analysis. The cost analysis and experimental results are presented in Sect. 5. We conclude the paper in Sect. 6.

2   Related Works

2.1   Arjan's Protocol

The protocol uses an additive homomorphic encryption scheme by Bresson et al. [1] which offers double encryption that can be decrypted by either a master key or a local key. The protocol features three participants: user, dataserver, and keyserver. The keyserver has a public-private key pair, and the public key is shared with all the other parties. Every user uses this public key to encrypt ratings and send these encrypted ratings to the dataserver. Both the servers are assumed to be honest but curious. They do not deviate from the protocol but try to learn additional information from the data they have access to. Another assumption is that the servers are non-colluding. The keyserver does not have access to user data and the dataserver does not have access to the private key of the keyserver.

We sketch the steps for updating one rating in Table 2. For a detailed description, the reader is referred to [10].

The keyserver generates a public-private key pair (PK, SK) and publishes PK to the users. The dataserver has its own public-private key pair (PK^*, SK^*). Let r_i denote the rating assigned to item i. The notation $[r_i]_{PK}$ denotes r_i encrypted with public key PK. There are two sub-routine functions $CS(vec, a)$ that circular shifts the given vector vec with an offset a and $REP(vec, k, val)$ that replaces element at index k in vector vec with value val. The user sends a new rating value $[r']_{PK}$ and index $[i]_{PK}$ to the dataserver. The notation $\odot$ represents a homomorphic operation.

- The dataserver selects a random value $a \in_r \mathbb{Z}_N$ as offset to circular shift $(CS())$ the user's encrypted rating vector and adds a to index i as well. Then dataserver generates n random values b_i's to blind all encrypted ratings and the new rating $[r'_i]_{PK}$. The blinding values are also encrypted using PK and stored in a blinding vector as $[B]_{PK}$. The encrypted rating vector (blinded and circular shifted), blinded index $[i + a]_{PK}$, blinded new rating $[r'_i + b']_{PK}$, $[b']_{PK^*}$ and blinding vector encrypted element-wise with dataserver's public key $[B]_{PK^*}$ are sent to the keyserver.
- The keyserver uses the sub-routine $REP()$ that replaces $[r'_i + b']_{PK}$ at index k in $[S + B]_{PK}$ vector. The index k is calculated as $k = i + a - 1 (\mathrm{mod} n) + 1$ to make sure k belongs to the item set I. Keyserver also replaces blinding value b' in blinding vector $[B]_{PK}$. Then the keyserver selects n random values and masks the ratings and blinding vector received from the dataserver. Keyserver sends masked rating vector $[S' + B' + C]_{PK}$ and masked blinding vector $[B' + C]_{PK^*}$ to dataserver.
- The dataserver decrypts the blinding vector and subtracts it from the masked rating vector to get $[S']_{PK}$. Next, it uses the sub-routine $CS()$ with $-a$ offset to place the ratings at their original positions. Finally, the dataserver has the encrypted rating vector with a new rating $[r']_{PK}$ at location i.

In this protocol, a user sends only two ciphertexts and two servers perform the rest of the computations. The inter-server communication cost is $\mathcal{O}(n)$, where n is the number of items. For practical applications the value n can be very high (few thousand and more) which makes the rating update process slow and costly.

2.2   Lipmaa and Zhang's Protocol

In [12], the authors proposed two PIR writing protocols: a BDD-based protocol and a FHE-based protocol. The first protocol is based on DJ01 [3] and the

Table 2. Arjan's rating update protocol

Shared information: dataserver's public key PK and keyserver's public key PK^*

Information known to dataserver: $[R]_{PK}, [r']_{PK}, [i]_{PK}$

Dataserver	Keyserver
Circular shift the rating vector with offset a	
$a \in_r \mathbb{Z}_n$	
$[S]_{PK} = CS([R]_{PK}, a)$	
$[i+a]_{PK} = [i]_{PK} \odot [a]_{PK}$	
$\forall j \in I$, here I: set of items;	
$b_j, b' \in_r \mathbb{Z}_N$	
$[s_j + b_j]_{PK} = [s_j]_{PK} \odot [b_j]_{PK}$	
$[r'_i + b']_{PK} = [r'_i]_{PK} \odot [b']_{PK}$	
encrypt: $[b_j]_{PK^*}, [b']_{PK^*}$	

$$\xleftarrow{\quad [S+B]_{PK}, [r'_i+b']_{PK}, [i+a]_{PK}, [B]_{PK^*}, [b']_{PK^*} \quad}$$

	decrypt: $i+a$
	$k = i + a - 1 (\mathrm{mod}\, n) + 1$
	$[S'+B']_{PK} = REP([S+B]_{PK}, k, [r'_i + b']_{PK})$
	$[B']_{PK^*} = REP([B]_{PK^*}, k, [b']_{PK^*})$
	$\forall j \in I$;
	$c_j \in_r \mathbb{Z}_N$
	$[s'_j + b'_j + c_j]_{PK} = [s'_j + b'_j]_{PK} \odot [c_j]_{PK}$
	$[b'_j + c_j]_{PK^*} = [b'_j]_{PK^*} \odot [c_j]_{PK^*}$

$$\xleftarrow{\quad [S'+B'+C]_{PK}, [B'+C]_{PK^*} \quad}$$

decrypt: $B'+C$	
$\forall j \in I; [s'_j]_{PK} = [s'_j + b'_j + c_j]_{PK} \odot [-b'_j - c_j]_{PK}$	
$[R']_{PK} = CS([S']_{PK}, -a)$	

---

second protocol is based on Gentry's fully homomorphic encryption scheme [6]. In each of these schemes, the plaintext bits are encrypted bit by bit. Therefore, for a *l-bit* long file/data block the process has to be repeated l times. In our PPRS application since the ratings assigned to items are of integer form, these protocols turn out to be very expensive. In the FHE-based scheme, a client sends an index of the data block that he want to update along with the new value to be written. Both the index and the value are encrypted by the client. The server then iterates through all the data blocks in the database and the desired new value is replaced at given index without the server's knowledge of which index was updated.

The protocol is shown in Algorithm 1, here the core step is if i is known,

$$eq_i(x) = \begin{cases} 1, & \text{if } i = x, \\ 0, & \text{otherwise.} \end{cases}$$

Now server has to compute $eq_i(x)$ without learning the item index x. This is shown by the lemma below.

---

input   : **Common input:** Database size: n, $m \leftarrow \lceil log_2 n \rceil$, element length: l, FHE
algorithm: E
Client's input: Secret key: sk, $x = (x_0, \ldots, x_{m-1})$, $y \in \{0,1\}^l$
Server's input: Public key: pk, $c = (c_{00}, \ldots, c_{n-1,l-1})$ where $c_{i,j} = E_{pk}(f_{i,j})$
output: updated database: $c' = (c'_{00}, \ldots, c'_{n-1,l-1})$ which is private to server

1. Client sends: $E_{pk}(x_0), \ldots, E_{pk}(x_{m-1})$ and $E_{pk}(y_0), \ldots, E_{pk}(y_{l-1})$ to the server
2. The server does in parallel for $i \in \{0, \ldots, n-1\}$:
   - The server runs encrypted circuit $b_i \leftarrow E_{pk}(eq_i(x))$
   - For $0 \leq j \leq l$; the server computes and stores

$$c'_{i,j} \leftarrow (E_{pk}(y_i) - c_{i,j})b_i + c_{i,j}$$

Algorithm 1: Lipmaa-Zhang FHE based PIR-writing protocol

Lemma 1 [12]: Assume i is known and let $eq_i(x) = 1$ if $x = 1$ and 0 otherwise. Then a server who knows encryption of x_j ($E_{pk}(x_j)$), for $0 \leq j < m$, can homomorphically evaluate $E_{pk}(eq_i(x))$ by using a circuit of size $m-1$ and depth of $\lceil log_2 m \rceil$.

3 Preliminaries

As we discussed earlier in previous works, there is a high communication overhead either between keyserver and dataserver or between the user and the dataserver. Our goals are:

- To keep communication cost between the user and the dataserver constant.
- Reduce the communication overhead between keyserver and the dataserver

The first goal is achieved if a user sends two ciphertexts, namely the encrypted index and the encrypted new rating, to the dataserver. We utilize the HE1N somewhat homomorphic scheme [4] that encrypts the integer as one ciphertext, in contrast to other schemes suggested in [12] that encrypt a number in bits that results in more ciphertexts transfer. To achieve the second goal, we use Lemma 1 at the dataserver. However, this requires the dataserver to know the encrypted bit representation of the index. To this end, we use a secure bit decomposition protocol (SBD) between the dataserver and the keyserver [15]. The security of SBD implies that the keyserver does not learn the rating index to be updated. It only learns the bitwise encryption of the index.

3.1 HE1N Encryption Scheme

HE1N is part of the HE1 family of somewhat homomorphic encryption schemes. It supports a limited number of additions and multiplications over the ciphertexts. The core of this scheme is very similar to that of the DGHV scheme [18]. The HE1 scheme assumes there is sufficient entropy (randomness) in the message space, if this is not the case then the other variants of the scheme, like

HE1N etc. add external noise during encryption. The HE1 cryptosystems are symmetric-key schemes, but authors have shown that they can be modified to be used as a public-key scheme as well. Our target application does not have high entropy data, so we are using the HE1N scheme. In what follows, we will first describe the HE1N symmetric key scheme and then show how to convert it into a public key one.

Parameters. The security parameter λ, entropy ρ such that $\rho \gg \log \lambda$. Since ρ is very small in our case we have to add 'noise' as s a multiple (0 to κ) of an integer κ and now $\rho' = \rho + \log \lambda$. We compute $\eta = \lambda^2/\rho' - \lambda$ and $q \in_r [2^{\eta-1}, 2^\eta]$.

KeyGen. The secret key: (p, κ)

$$p \in_r [2^{\lambda-1}, 2^\lambda]$$
$$v = \rho' - \rho$$
$$\kappa \in_r [2^{v-1}, 2^v]$$
$$N = pq$$

Encryption. An integer message m is encrypted as:

$$r \in_r [1, q), s \in_r [0, \kappa)$$
$$c = (m + sk + rp) \bmod N$$

Decryption. To recover the message m from a ciphertext c:

$$m = (c \bmod p) \bmod \kappa$$

Conversion into Public Key Scheme: Following [18] we construct a public key version of HE1N as follows.

KeyGen. The secret key: (p, κ) as earlier, the public key x is generated as:

$$r \in_r [1, q), s \in_r [0, \kappa)$$
$$x_i = s_i \kappa + r_i p$$
$$x = \langle x_0, x_1, \ldots, x_\tau \rangle$$

Encryption. To encrypt a message m a subset A of public key x is used:

$$c = \left(m + \sum_{i \in A} x_i \right) \bmod N$$

The decryption process remains unchanged.

Input : **Common input:** Keyserver's public key pk, and modulus N
             Keyserver's input: private key: sk
             Dataserver's input: Encrypted $E_{pk}(x)$, $0 \leq x < 2^m$
Output: Dataserver learns: $\bar{x} = \langle E_{pk}(b_0), E_{pk}(b_1), \ldots, E_{pk}(b_{m-1}) \rangle$, and the
            keyserver learns nothing

1. $l = 2^{-1} \bmod N$
2. $T = E_{pk}(x)$
3. for $i = 0$ to $m - 1$ do:
    – $E_{pk}(x_i) \leftarrow Encrypted\_LSB(T,i)$
    – $Z \leftarrow T - E_{pk}(x_i) \bmod N$
    – $T = Z * l \bmod N$
4. end for
5. $\gamma \leftarrow SVR(E_{pk}(x), \langle E_{pk}(b_0), E_{pk}(b_1), \ldots, E_{pk}(b_{m-1}) \rangle)$
6. if $\gamma = 1$ then
      return
7. else
      go to step 2
8. end if

Algorithm 2: Secure bit decomposition protocol

3.2 Secure Bit Decomposition (SBD)

In the SBD protocol, there are two parties: Alice, who has a public key pk, and Bob who has a m bit integer x encrypted with pk. They both jointly run the SBD protocol and at the end Bob receives encrypted bits of $x = \langle E_{pk}(b_0), E_{pk}(b_1), \ldots, E_{pk}(b_{m-1}) \rangle$ whereas Alice learns nothing about x or its bits. We use the protocol proposed by Samanthula et al. [15], which is based on Paillier's additive homomorphic encryption scheme. The protocol is divided into two phases: Encrypted_LSB() computes the least significant bit of an encrypted integer input and SVR() verifies if the bits representation is correct for the corresponding integer (under encryption). Both these sub-routines cost Alice and Bob $\mathcal{O}(log n)$ communication. In our target application of PPRS, this communication overhead is smaller than that of Arjan's protocol as we will see in the next section. Algorithm 2 shows the working of the protocol between the dataserver and the keyserver with HE1N as the underlying homomorphic encryption scheme. The parameters in Algorithm 2 are chosen as shown in Sect. 3.1, the details of Encrypted_LSB() and SVR() are given in the Appendix A.

4 Proposed Protocol

Setup. The keyserver generates a pair of public-private keys (pk, sk) and shares pk with all users and the dataserver. Every user uses the same public key pk to encrypt their ratings. The user has a new rating value r' that he wishes to assign to an item located at index x, there are n items in the database, and $m = log_2(n)$ denotes the number of bits required to represent each index in binary. In the

---

Input : **Common input:** Rating vector size: n, $m \leftarrow \lceil \log_2 n \rceil$, y: index at
server's rating vector, public key: pk
   Client's input: Encrypted new rating: $E(r')$, Encrypted index: $E(x)$
   Dataserver's input: $c = (c_0, \ldots, c_{n-1})$ where $c_i = E_{pk}(r_i)$
   Keyserver's input: Secret key: sk
Output: Datasever has database: $c' = (c'_0, \ldots, c'_{n-1})$ where $D(E_{pk}(c'_x)) = r'$
 1. Client sends: $E_{pk}(r')$ and $E_{pk}(i)$ to the dataserver
 2. The dataserver and keyserver runs secure bit decomposition protocol:
   $SBD(pk, E_{pk}(x))$
   The dataserver receives: $\boldsymbol{x} = \langle E_{pk}(x_0), E_{pk}(x_1), \ldots, E_{pk}(x_{m-1}) \rangle$
 3. The dataserver in parallel computes for $i \in \{0, \ldots, n-1\}$:
   – Encrypt all bits of $y_i = \langle E_{pk}(y_{i,0}), E_{pk}(y_{i,1}) \ldots E_{pk}(y_{i,j}) \rangle$, $0 \le j \le m-1$:
     initialize $temp = 1$
   – for $j = 0$ to $m - 1$ do:
     – If $y_{i,j} == 0$:
       $temp = temp *_h E_{pk}(1 - x_j)$
     – Else:
       $temp = temp *_h E_{pk}(x_j)$
   – $R = temp *_h E_{pk}(r')$
   – $c'_i = c_i +_h R$

Algorithm 3: Proposed algorithm

Algorithm 3, the notations $*_h$ and $+_h$ denote homomorphic multiplication and addition, respectively. The notation $E_{pk}(m)$ represents homomorphic encryption of a message m using public key pk.

Problem Definition. The server has a rating matrix in the database where it stores the user ratings encrypted with pk. A rating vector $R = (E_{pk}(r_0), E_{pk}(r_1), \ldots, E_{pk}(r_{n-1}))$ has n ratings from the user, each rating is $l = |r_i|$ bits long. The private index x where user wants to update the rating r_x is known to the user only. After the protocol run the updated rating vector is $R' = (E_{pk}(r'_0), E_{pk}(r'_1), \ldots, E_{pk}(r'_{n-1}))$ where $E_{pk}(r_i)$ and $E_{pk}(r'_i)$ decrypt the same value when $i \ne x$.

Assumptions. We assume that the communication channel is secure. The two servers are assumed to be honest but curious. That is they will follow the protocol and will not alter any data, but they may try to perform some additional computations to learn more about the user data. It is assumed that the servers are non-colluding, that is they do not share any information other than what is defined in the protocol. It is assumed that the users are honest: they do not send out-of-range ratings and do not collude with either of the servers.

Description. The dataserver stores the encrypted user ratings as a vector. To update a rating the user first sends two ciphertexts to the dataserver: encrypted rating $(E_{pk}(r'))$ and encrypted index $(E_{pk}(x))$. The dataserver now

Table 3. Example of proposed algorithm

Index 0	Index 1	Index 2	Index 3
$temp = E(0) *_h E(0)$	$temp = E(0) *_h E(1)$	$temp = E(1) *_h E(0)$	$temp = E(1) *_h E(1)$
$= E(0)$	$= E(0)$	$= E(0)$	$= E(1)$
$R = temp *_h E(9)$	$R = temp *_h E(9)$	$R = temp *_h E(9)$	$R = temp *_h E(9)$
$c_0' = c_0 +_h = E(0)$	$c_1' = c_1 +_h R = E(0)$	$c_2' = C_2 +_h R = E(0)$	$c_3' = c_3 +_h R = E(9)$
Unchanged	Unchanged	Unchanged	Updated

needs to decompose $E_{pk}(x)$ into encrypted bits to update rating at index x. Now dataserver and keyserver execute the secure bit decomposition protocol between them. After executing the SBD protocol, the keyserver learns nothing about x, whereas the dataserver learns the encrypted bit representation of x as a vector $\boldsymbol{x} = \langle E_{pk}(x_0), E_{pk}(x_1), \ldots, E_{pk}(x_{m-1}) \rangle$.

Using $E_{pk}(r')$ and $\boldsymbol{x}$, the dataserver updates the rating stored at index x. The dataserver performs the following steps for all indexes i.e. m times:

– Dataserver converts each index into binary and encrypts each bit with the keyserver's public key. The dataserver can pre-compute compute these, as the pk is known. This step does not require interaction with keyserver or the user.
– Homomorphically subtract the received vector $\boldsymbol{x}$ from it, this is element-wise subtraction operation
– Homomorphically multiply all bits of the resultant vector obtained from the previous step
– Homomorphically multiply r' sent by the user
– Homomorphically add old rating with this value, the resultant value will be updated rating $(E_{pk}(r'))$ for this item.

Example: Suppose there are 4 items in the server's rating matrix all initialized with 0, and u_1 wants to assign $r_{1,3} = 9$. Here $*_h, +_h$ shows homomorphic multiplication, and addition respectively. The user computes two encryptions $(E_{pk}(9), E_{pk}(3))$ and sends them to the dataserver. Both servers run secure bit decomposition protocol together and dataserver receives encrypted bits as: $\langle E_{pk}(1), E_{pk}(1) \rangle$. Then the dataserver converts each index of the database into bits and performs operations as mentioned in step-3 of Algorithm 3. All these computations can be done in parallel by the server, as they are not dependent. Table 3 shows the calculations.

4.1 Privacy Analysis

The proposed approach is based on the HE1N homomorphic encryption scheme and secure bit decomposition protocol. Here we will describe our security parameter assumptions and how these building blocks are individually proven to be secure. Our modification does not compromise their properties.

Privacy Definition: As proposed in [12], we can define the privacy of a PIR-write protocol using the following game. The dataserver will act as a semi-honest probabilistic polynomial time adversary A. The user will be a challenger. Challenger generates a (pk, sk) pair with security parameter λ. The adversary knows pk and has a database encrypted with pk

- Challenge: Adversary randomly selects two index-value pairs $(x_0^*, r_0^*), (x_1^*, r_1^*)$, and sends them to challenger.
- The challenger picks $b_c \in \{0, 1\}$ and executes the PIR-write protocol with input as (x_b^*, r_b^*).
- Response: Adversary guesses the output $b_c^* \in \{0, 1\}$ for b_c
- The advantage for the adversary is

$$Adv_A(1^\lambda) := \left| Pr[b_c^* = b_c] - \frac{1}{2} \right|$$

A PIR-write protocol is client-private, if for all probabilistic polynomial time adversaries A, $Adv_A(1^\lambda)$ is a negligible function (in λ). In other words, if the server cannot differentiate between a random number and a ciphertext with a non-negligible probability, user data remains private.

HE1N Scheme. We chose HE1N over the HE1 scheme as the entropy ρ of plaintext in our application is very low, in fact for the experiments, we consider $\rho = 1$ as there are computations over encrypted bits. The HE1 scheme's security is based on a special partial approximate common divisor problem (PACDP).

Definition 1: The general approximate common divisor problem (GACDP) is to find the unknown p, given n inputs $x_i = pr_i + m_i$ for $i \in [1, n]$ where r_i, m_i are unknown integers such that $r_i << p$. If there is an additional input of the form $x_0 = pr_0$, then this problem is known as partial approximate common divisor problem (PACDP) [5].

If message m_i is τ bit long, the exhaustive search to find p in PACDP will require 2^τ gcd operations. The other fastest technique shown in [2] takes $2^{\tau/2}$ polynomial-time operations, which is the square root of the time required for exhaustive search. There is no algorithm available yet that can solve either PACDP or GACDP in polynomial time. The HE1 cryptosystem requires the entropy $\rho = \tau$ to be higher to prevent such attacks.

Definition 2: A semi-prime is a natural number that is a product of two primes.

Given a semi-prime n generated using primes p and q it is hard to find p and q from n in polynomial time. This is the well-known assumption about the computational hardness of factorization.

Definition 3: An encryption scheme is considered IND-CPA if an adversary cannot learn anything about the message m from its ciphertext c, the adversary's ability to guess the message is equal to a random guess [8]

The following two theorems prove that the HE1N scheme is as secure as the RSA cryptosystem and is IND-CPA under GACDP assumptions. For proofs of these theorems we refer the reader to [4].

Theorem 1. *The HE1 cryptosystem can be broken in polynomial time if and only if we can factorize a distinct semi-prime in polynomial time [4].*

Theorem 2. *HE1N satisfies IND-CPA under the assumption that GACDP is not polynomial-time solvable [4].*

In the public key version of the HE1N scheme, the public key is a vector of the form $x_i = s_i \kappa + r_i p$ where r_i, s_i are random numbers and κ, p are the secret keys. To encrypt a message, a subset-sum of the public key vector $\vec{x}$ is added with the message. The public key version also follows the encryption properties of the symmetric key HE1N and follows the theorems mentioned above. The question here is if the public key leaks some information about the secret keys κ and p, or leads to some new attacks. The encryption function in the public key scheme can be seen as an instance of a subset sum problem [16]. The subset problem is defined as follows. Given a set of n positive integers S and another positive integer Z, find a subset $s \subset S$ such that the sum of the elements of s results in Z. The subset sum problem is a well-known hard problem. The best known solution given by Graham and Joux [9] takes $\mathcal{O}(2^{.337n})$ time.

In our proposed algorithm, the user sends encrypted rating and index to the dataserver, which as per Theorem 2 cannot differentiate it from random noise. Thus, it satisfies our privacy definition. The dataserver does not learn anything from the user-submitted ciphertexts. Next, we will see if the joint execution of SBD by the keyserver and the dataserver leaks some information to either of the servers.

Secure Bit Decomposition. In our protocol, the encrypted user rating, and index are sent to the dataserver first, and then two servers communicate to convert the encrypted index into encrypted bits of the corresponding index. Assuming the encryption scheme is secure, the dataserver cannot break HE1N and learn about either value. Then the dataserver sends this encrypted index to the keyserver after masking it with a randomly chosen noise, so the keyserver cannot distinguish it from a random number even after decrypting the ciphertext. Now the keyserver sends $\alpha \in E(0), E(1)$ and the dataserver cannot differentiate between those two, so neither of the servers can learn anything about the encrypted index.

We modified the SBD protocol by replacing the Paillier cryptosystem with HE1N. We note that the user data in the original SBD protocol [15] is secure as long as the Paillier cryptosystem is semantically secure. Then we claim that the modified SBD is secure as long as the underlying HE1N is semantically secure. The HE1N is proven to be IND-CPA as mentioned in Theorem 2. This discussion shows that user data remains private under the given assumptions and appropriate selection of protocol parameters in our proposed algorithm.

5   Performance Evaluation

In this section, we analyze the efficiency of the proposed scheme with respect to Arjan's original proposal. We will only consider the costs incurred for each rating update; one-time computations are not considered for a cost comparison. For the sake of convenience, we assume each homomorphic arithmetic operation such as addition, subtraction, or multiplication has the same computational overhead. The results of the analysis are summarised in Table 4.

5.1   Communication Cost

In our scheme, the user performs two encryptions to execute a rating update: encryption of new rating and encryption of index, which is similar to what is required in Arjan's protocol as well. The communication cost between the two servers is reduced remarkably in the proposed scheme compared to Arjan's protocol. In [10], the dataserver first sends $3 + 2n$ ciphertexts to the keyserver and then keyserver sends $2n$ ciphertexts back to the dataserver. So a total of $3 + 4n$ ciphertexts are transferred between the servers to update a rating. In our proposed scheme, both servers communicate to execute the SBD protocol jointly. This requires $1 + 2 \log n$ ciphertexts to be transferred between the servers. So the proposed scheme reduces the communication cost from $\mathcal{O}(n)$ to $\mathcal{O}(\log n)$.

5.2   Computation Cost

Similar to Arjan's protocol, a constant number of encryptions are required at the user-side. In Bresson's additive HE scheme user performs two modular exponentiation operations to encrypt an integer, whereas HE1N only requires to perform one linear addition modulo operation, similarly the decryption process is also much simpler in HE1N comparatively.

Table 4 shows the computation cost comparison between the proposed and Arjan's protocol. In Arjan's protocol, the dataserver first masks all the ratings with noise and encrypts the noise values with the keyserver's public key, taking $2n$ encryptions and n homomorphic operations (HO). Then, the keyserver decrypts the offset (a), replaces the new rating and corresponding noise at location $a + i$, and again masks the ratings and noise vectors. This set of tasks requires the keyserver to perform 1 decryption, $2n$ encryption, and $2n$ HO. Finally, the dataserver removes all noises from the rating vector and performs a circular shift with negative offset to store the ratings at their original indices, the cost for this at dataserver is n decryption, n encryptions, and n HO. In our scheme, the dataserver in step-2 runs $SBD()$ protocol that internally calls $Enrypted\_LSB()$ and $SVR()$ sub-routines. The computation cost of the $Enrypted\_LSB()$ sub-routine at the dataserver is $n \log n$ HO while the keyserver has to perform $(1 + \log n)$ decryptions. The sub-routine $SVR()$ attracts the cost of $\log n$ HO and 1 decryption at the dataserver and keyserver, respectively. In step-3, the dataserver requires $n \log n$ HO while the keyserver computes nothing.

As we can observe from Table 4, in the proposed scheme the number of homomorphic operations at the keyserver is $\log n$ times more than in Arjan's protocol. We emphasize the fact that the cost of encryption and decryption operations is more as compared to homomorphic operations as shown in Table 5. We are reducing the computationally heavy operations and incurring more number of less expensive operations at the dataserver, this overall reduces the execution time. Similarly, at the keyserver in Arjan's protocol, the cost is $2n$ encryptions and $2n$ HO, which we are replacing with $(1 + \log n)$ decryptions. This reduces the cost overhead considerably from $\mathcal{O}(n)$ to $\mathcal{O}(\log n)$ at the keyserver.

5.3 Storage Cost

In Lipmaa's protocol, each rating is encrypted bit-by-bit, which requires $\mathcal{O}(nl)$ ciphertexts per user. The server storage cost is the same in the proposed work and Arjan's protocol, $\mathcal{O}(n)$ ciphertexts.

Table 4. Computation costs at servers, n: number of items, HO: homomorphic operations

	Dataserver			Keyserver		
	Enc	Dec	HO	Enc	Dec	HO
Arjan	$\mathcal{O}(n)$	$\mathcal{O}(n)$	$\mathcal{O}(n)$	$\mathcal{O}(n)$	$\mathcal{O}(1)$	$\mathcal{O}(n)$
Proposed	nil	nil	$\mathcal{O}(n \log n)$	nil	$\mathcal{O}(\log n)$	nil

Example: Assume $n = 50000$ items, then $m = \log n$ will be 16 bits. Now, if we assume that each ciphertext is 2048 bit or 256 byte long, then in the case of bit-by-bit encryption, we will need $50000 \times 6 \times 256$ bytes or about 74 MB storage for each user. On the other hand, if we encrypt the same ratings with an integer-based encryption scheme that produces 2048 bit long ciphertext, the server will require $1/6^{th}$ i.e., a little over 12 MB of storage for each user. This reduces the storage cost at the dataserver significantly since there are usually thousands of users on popular web applications.

5.4 Experimental Results

In this section, we experimentally demonstrate the speedup achieved by our proposal.

- We evaluate the time taken to encrypt one rating and one index using Bresson's encryption scheme and HE1N, respectively.
- We evaluate the computation time of the SBD protocol using Paillier and HE1N, respectively.
- We compare the execution time for encryption, decryption and homomorphic operations for Bresson's additive HE and HE1N somewhat HE schemes.

We implemented the encryption algorithm on a virtual machine with AMD Ryzen 7 processor and 10 GB RAM, Ubuntu-20.04 operating system, python-3.7 programming language, and Sagemath library. We use synthetic data as we are not generating recommendations or measuring accuracy. We took the Movie-lense dataset as a base with 58,000 movies (items) so we take this number in our implementation and measure computation time.

The parameters taken for different encryption schemes are shown in Table 6. In the HE1N scheme, since we have plaintexts in bits (less entropy), we take security parameters accordingly, whereas for Paillier and Bresson's cryptosystems, we have considered security parameter λ as 1024 bit. The results are shown in Table 7 and 8, all times are measured in milliseconds. Table 7 compares the time taken by a user to encrypt one rating of 3 bit and one index of 10 bit in length. Table 8 shows the comparison between two schemes for their respective time taken by servers to execute SBD protocol with varying length input (index size). In Table 5 the comparison of runtime for encryption, decryption, and homomorphic operation function on a 3 bit integer input is given that shows the encryption and decryption functions are costlier than HO.

Interestingly, though we have replaced the homomorphic encryption scheme from partial HE to somewhat HE in existing building blocks, this does not increase the computational costs. This advantage comes from the efficient design of the HE1N. The computation cost trade-off is at dataserver as shown in Table 4, but the homomorphic operation in HE1N is just the addition or multiplication of ciphertexts. It does not require exponentiations and is thus faster than Bresson's scheme.

Table 5. Computation time for different operations (in milliseconds)

Protocol	Encryption	Decryption	HO
Bresson's	65.560	35.430	3.623×10^{-3}
HE1N	0.105	0.674	3.576×10^{-4}

Table 6. Experimental parameters (in bits)

Parameter	Bresson's	Paillier	HE1N
λ	1024	1024	360
p	1024	1024	354
q	1024	1024	2056
Ciphertext modulus	N^2	N^2	N

Table 7. Computation time: user (in milliseconds)

Protocol	Time
Arjan (Bresson's)	129.867
Ours (HE1N)	0.1351

Table 8. Computation costs: SBD

Bit-length	SBD (Paillier)	SBD (HE1N)
5	6.147	5.172
10	7.872	5.582
15	8.545	6.894
20	11.687	7.397

6 Conclusion

In this work, we studied the private rating update problem in the privacy-preserving recommendation system, which essentially narrowed down to the secure data write problem. This problem has been studied for a long time and has much literature related to various solutions. Our goal was to find a solution that works on a target application of PPRS, where reducing the user-side computation and communication overhead was the primary aim. In this work, we gathered various cryptographic building blocks used in various previous approaches and adapted them to fit our goals, without compromising their security features. The outcome of our work is a protocol that uses HE1N homomorphic encryption scheme to protect user privacy and has minimal cost overhead. The theoretical and experimental results show that the proposed approach is better than the previous works of [12] and [10]. The security analysis shows that the user data is never revealed to any other party by design, even though the decryption keys are with one of the servers. The proposed scheme can be used in any FHE-based recommender system as an add-on. It is independent of the recommendation algorithm, thus the system's accuracy will not be affected. The comparative less communication overhead makes the protocol more scalable for real-time applications.

A Secure Bit Decomposition (SBD)

In SBD protocol there are two sub-protocols: Encrypted_LSB() and SVR(). In our proposed work, we have made some changes in these sub-protocols to make it work using the HE1N scheme. First, the Encrypted_LSB() routine takes two inputs: a ciphertext of an encrypted integer and an integer in plaintext, and returns the encrypted least significant bit of the encrypted integer passed to it. The two observations that this sub-protocol follows are:

Input   : **Dataserver's input:** Encrypted integer: T, and plain iteration
             number: i
             Keyserver's input: private key: sk
Output: Dataserver learns: Encrypted least significant bit of T as $E(x_i)$
  1. Dataserver:
     - $r \in_r \mathbb{Z}_\mathbb{N}$
     - $Y = E(r_i) + T$
     Send Y to keyserver
  2. Keyserver:
     - $y = D(Y)$
     - If y is even: $\alpha = E(0)$
     - Else: $\alpha = E(1)$
     - Send α to dataserver
  3. Dataserver:
     - If r is even: $E(x_i) = \alpha$
     - Else: $E(x_i) = \alpha(N-1) + 1 \mod N$
  4. Return $E(x_i)$

Algorithm 4: Secure bit decomposition sub-protocol: Encrypted_LSB()

Observation-I. For any given x, let $y = x + r \mod N$, where r is a random number in $\mathbb{Z}_n$. Here the relation between y and r depends on whether $x + r \mod N$ leads to an overflow or not. y is always greater than r if there is no overflow. Similarly, in the case of overflow y is always less than r.

Observation-II. For any given $y = x + r \mod N$, where N is odd, the following property regarding the least significant bit of x always hold:

$$x_0 = \begin{cases} \lambda_1 \oplus \lambda_2, & \text{if } r \text{ is even} \\ 1 - (\lambda_1 \oplus \lambda_2), & \text{otherwise} \end{cases}$$

Here λ_1 denotes whether an overflow occurs or not, and λ_2 denotes whether y is odd or not. That is $\lambda_1 = 1$ if $r > y$, and 0 otherwise. Similarly, $\lambda_2 = 1$ if y is odd and 0 otherwise, $\oplus$ denotes the XOR operation. It is noteworthy that N in the Paillier cryptosystem is always odd, this follows in the HE1N system as well.

The second half of the SBD protocol is to verify if the bit decomposition is correct or not from the step 5 to 8 in Algorithm 2. The sub-protocol: secure verification of result $(SVR())$ is used to perform this verification. Basically what the dataserver does here, it reconstructs the integer from the decomposed bits, masks it with some random noise, and send it to the keyserver for decryption. If the bit decomposition is correct, the keyserver will receive encryption of 0 otherwise some random encrypted number. The result is conveyed to the dataserver; if the decomposition is incorrect, the dataserver starts over from step 2 of Algorithm 2.

Input : **Dataserver's input:** $E(x), \langle E(x_0), E(x_1) \ldots, E(x_{m-1}) \rangle$
Output: Dataserver receives: $\gamma = 0$ if the decomposition was correct or 1
otherwise
1. Dataserver:
   - $U = \sum_{i=0}^{m-1} E(x_i) 2^i \mod N$
   - $V = U + E(x)(N - 1) \mod N$
   - $r' \in_r \mathbb{Z}_N$ and $W = V r' \mod N$
     Send W to keyserver
2. Keyserver:
   - If $D(W) = 0$: set $\gamma = 0$
   - Else: set $\gamma = 1$
     Send γ to dataserver

Algorithm 5: Secure bit decomposition sub-protocol: SVR()

References

1. Bresson, E., Catalano, D., Pointcheval, D.: A simple public-key cryptosystem with a double trapdoor decryption mechanism and its applications. In: Laih, C.-S. (ed.) ASIACRYPT 2003. LNCS, vol. 2894, pp. 37–54. Springer, Heidelberg (2003). https://doi.org/10.1007/978-3-540-40061-5_3

2. Chen, Y., Nguyen, P.Q.: Faster algorithms for approximate common divisors: breaking fully-homomorphic-encryption challenges over the integers. In: Pointcheval, D., Johansson, T. (eds.) EUROCRYPT 2012. LNCS, vol. 7237, pp. 502–519. Springer, Heidelberg (2012). https://doi.org/10.1007/978-3-642-29011-4_30

3. Damgård, I., Jurik, M.: A generalisation, a simplification and some applications of Paillier's probabilistic public-key system. In: Kim, K. (ed.) PKC 2001. LNCS, vol. 1992, pp. 119–136. Springer, Heidelberg (2001). https://doi.org/10.1007/3-540-44586-2_9

4. Dyer, J., Dyer, M., Xu, J.: Practical homomorphic encryption over the integers for secure computation in the cloud. Int. J. Inf. Secur. **18**(5), 549–579 (2019). https://doi.org/10.1007/s10207-019-00427-0

5. Galbraith, S.D., Gebregiyorgis, S.W., Murphy, S.: Algorithms for the approximate common divisor problem. LMS J. Comput. Math. **19**(A), 58–72 (2016)

6. Gentry, C., Boneh, D.: A Fully Homomorphic Encryption Scheme, vol. 20. Stanford University, Stanford (2009)

7. Goldreich, O., Ostrovsky, R.: Software protection and simulation on oblivious rams. J. ACM (JACM) **43**(3), 431–473 (1996)

8. Goldwasser, S., Micali, S.: Probabilistic encryption. J. Comput. Syst. Sci. **28**(2), 270–299 (1984)

9. Howgrave-Graham, N., Joux, A.: New generic algorithms for hard knapsacks. In: Gilbert, H. (ed.) EUROCRYPT 2010. LNCS, vol. 6110, pp. 235–256. Springer, Heidelberg (2010). https://doi.org/10.1007/978-3-642-13190-5_12

10. Jeckmans, A.J.P.: Cryptographically-Enhanced Privacy for Recommender Systems. University of Twente (2014)

11. Kim, J., Koo, D., Kim, Y., Yoon, H., Shin, J., Kim, S.: Efficient privacy-preserving matrix factorization for recommendation via fully homomorphic encryption. ACM Trans. Priv. Secur. (TOPS) **21**(4), 1–30 (2018)
12. Lipmaa, H., Zhang, B.: Two new efficient PIR-writing protocols. In: Zhou, J., Yung, M. (eds.) ACNS 2010. LNCS, vol. 6123, pp. 438–455. Springer, Heidelberg (2010). https://doi.org/10.1007/978-3-642-13708-2_26
13. Pinkas, B., Reinman, T.: Oblivious RAM revisited. In: Rabin, T. (ed.) CRYPTO 2010. LNCS, vol. 6223, pp. 502–519. Springer, Heidelberg (2010). https://doi.org/10.1007/978-3-642-14623-7_27
14. Polat, H., Du, W.: Privacy-preserving collaborative filtering using randomized perturbation techniques. In: Third IEEE International Conference on Data Mining, ICDM 2003, pp. 625–628. IEEE (2003)
15. Samanthula, B.K., Chun, H., Jiang, W.: An efficient and probabilistic secure bit-decomposition. In: Proceedings of the 8th ACM SIGSAC Symposium on Information, Computer and Communications Security, pp. 541–546 (2013)
16. Snook, M.: Integer-based fully homomorphic encryption. Rochester Institute of Technology (2011)
17. Stefanov, E., et al.: Path ORAM: an extremely simple oblivious ram protocol. In: Proceedings of the 2013 ACM SIGSAC Conference on Computer & Communications Security, pp. 299–310 (2013)
18. van Dijk, M., Gentry, C., Halevi, S., Vaikuntanathan, V.: Fully homomorphic encryption over the integers. In: Gilbert, H. (ed.) EUROCRYPT 2010. LNCS, vol. 6110, pp. 24–43. Springer, Heidelberg (2010). https://doi.org/10.1007/978-3-642-13190-5_2
19. Wang, J., Arriaga, A., Tang, Q., Ryan, P.Y.A.: CryptoRec: secure recommendations as a service. CoRR abs/1802.02432 (2018). arXiv:1802.02432
20. Williams, P., Sion, R.: Usable PIR. In: NDSS, pp. 139–152 (2008)
21. Williams, P., Sion, R., Carbunar, B.: Building castles out of mud: practical access pattern privacy and correctness on untrusted storage. In: Proceedings of the 15th ACM Conference on Computer and Communications Security, pp. 139–148 (2008)
22. Yakut, I., Polat, H.: Arbitrarily distributed data-based recommendations with privacy. Data Knowl. Eng. **72**, 239–256 (2012)

Author Index

Printed in the United States
by Baker & Taylor Publisher Services

Printed in the United States
by Baker & Taylor Publisher Services